A Certain Light

CYNTHIA BANHAM is a writer. She grew up in Sydney and worked there as a solicitor and, later, a journalist. Cynthia completed a Doctor of Philosophy and a Master in International Affairs at the Australian National University. In 2015 she was awarded a UQ Fellowship at the University of Queensland to research and teach in the School of Political Science and International Studies. Her first book, *Liberal Democracies and the Torture of Their Citizens*, based on her doctoral thesis, was published in 2017. She is currently a Visitor at the ANU's School of Regulation and Global Governance (RegNet).

She met her husband, Michael, while reporting for the *Sydney Morning Herald* in the Federal Parliamentary Press Gallery. Michael introduced her to Australian Rules football and she is now an ambassador for the Sydney Swans Football Club.

A Certain Light

A MEMOIR OF FAMILY, LOSS AND HOPE

Cynthia Banham

ALLEN&UNWIN
SYDNEY·MELBOURNE·AUCKLAND·LONDON

First published in 2018

Allen & Unwin
83 Alexander Street
Crows Nest NSW 2065
Australia
Phone: (61 2) 8425 0100
Email: info@allenandunwin.com
Web: www.allenandunwin.com

 A catalogue record for this book is available from the National Library of Australia

ISBN 978 1 76063 210 6

Extract on p. ix from *The Passion* by Jeanette Winterson (London: Vintage Books, 1987, 2001, p. 49) reprinted by permission of Peters Fraser & Dunlop (www.petersfraserdunlop.com) on behalf of Jeanette Winterson

Extract on p. 56 from 'Avevo' by Umberto Saba, from *Songbook: The Selected Poems of Umberto Saba* (trans G. Hochfield and L. Nathan, New Haven: Yale University Press, 2008, pp. 468–9)

Extract on p. 266 from 'Now That I Am in Madrid and Can Think' by Frank O'Hara, from D. Allen (ed.), *The Collected Poems of Frank O'Hara* (Berkeley: University of California Press, 1971, 1995, p. 356), reprinted by permission of Penguin Random House, New York

Text design by Sandy Cull
Set in 12.25/17 pt Fairfield LT Std by Bookhouse, Sydney
Printed and bound in Australia by Griffin Press

10 9 8 7 6 5 4 3 2 1

The paper in this book is FSC® certified. FSC® promotes environmentally responsible, socially beneficial and economically viable management of the world's forests.

I dedicate this book to my son

CONTENTS

Although wherever you are going is always in front of you, there is no such thing as straight ahead.

Jeanette Winterson, *The Passion*

A Letter to My Son

MY LITTLE CUB.

I started writing this book on your third birthday: 17 February 2015. It happened to be your first day of preschool (some birthday present!). You could already recite the alphabet and recognise the word 'book'.

Reading has, from your earliest days, been our special thing. One of your first favourites was *Who Sank the Boat?* Personally, I always liked *The Big Big Sea*, about the mother and child who go paddling in the sea by moonlight. Reading books together is special because it was one thing I could do for you as an infant, when there were so many other things I could not.

This book is of a very different kind, one to read when you are older. It tells a story that I tried to write many times before, but couldn't. For a long time, it was too painful to tell. It is also one I hadn't known how to tell. It had to be more than a story about surviving a plane crash, a random event without intrinsic meaning. Life is not defined by the bad things that happen to us. It certainly isn't for me.

You recently turned five. It is ten years since that awful day in 2007 and I have finished writing my story. Actually, this book is more a collection of stories. It comes after realising that I couldn't write about what happened to me without placing it in the context of our wider family history. If meaning was to be found, it was in the forces that shaped me, that caused me to never give up, to build a life every bit as rich as the one taken from me. For the last two and a half years, I chased these other stories of who came before and what happened to them. Some of them we chased together—you, me, your daddy, Nonni and Poppi—across Europe, through Italy, Austria and Germany.

Let me introduce you to some of the main characters.

There is your great-grandfather, Alfredo, born in Vicenza, Italy, in 1924, and his older sister, Amelia, a dancer, who—so relatives say—saved him from starvation in a German forced labour camp in the Second World War. Amelia, in an indirect way, inspired this book. I never knew her, but her story had me enthralled from the first moment I learnt about it. Alfredo, who encouraged my deep interest in our family's Italian heritage, died a month before my 21st birthday.

There is your grandmother, Loredana—you know her as Nonni—who emigrated with her family from Trieste, Italy, to Sydney, Australia, in 1957. Loredana missed out on all kinds of opportunities because of her parents' decision to leave Italy when she was nine.

I am my mother's eldest child. Unlike Mum, I had—and made much of—every opportunity. To my mother's enduring disappointment, I abandoned a promising career as a lawyer to go searching for a different someone, the person I wanted to be (I wanted to write). Unfortunately, almost as soon as I found this person, I lost her in a plane crash in a rice paddy field in Indonesia. I was 34.

The happy news is that your mamma was saved by love—powerful, multiple, sometimes challenging loves. Crawling out of that plane wreckage, I wanted to live because I loved my life,

I loved my family, I loved your daddy. I wasn't ready to let go of any of that yet.

You should know this about your daddy, Michael. Without your father's belief in us, if not for the promise he made while I was in a coma to dedicate his every moment to making a life for us as beautiful as the one that was lost, I wouldn't be here today.

Your father proposed to me for the second time in 2008 (you'll read about the first time in a later chapter). It was after another tedious nightly session massaging lanolin into my burns scars, in the bedroom of our boxy little home in Page, Canberra (we called the section where we lived 'Front Page' because it was one of the suburb's better streets). Your daddy unsheathed his replica Excalibur sword and walked into the room where I was lying in my bandages and burns garments.

'Marry me or run me through,' he declared.

Of course I agreed—and not because he had the point of a blade pressed to his ribs.

We married the following year on a hill in a vineyard in Murrumbateman, just outside Canberra, one Saturday afternoon in late March. We were surrounded by the bush, by the grey-green hues of the tall gum trees and the long, dry, waving grasses. A mob of kangaroos observed our nuptials from a distance.

I was determined to walk and your poppi held my arm as I stepped out of his white Jaguar onto the dirt path that led up to a small lawn, where a hundred of our family and friends waited. My voice trembled and broke as I repeated the part of the vow that goes 'whatever the future holds I will love you and stand by you as long as we both shall live'. Your daddy punched the air to loud cheers when we were declared husband and wife. A close friend's sister sang the Triffids' song, 'Bury Me Deep in Love'.

Afterwards, in a big corrugated-iron shed, among the wine barrels and long wooden tables, your father and I kicked off a night of bad karaoke with an ill-planned, out-of-tune rendition of the Bee Gees' 'To Love Somebody'. The evening was fuelled by sparkling shiraz—Black Knight—a gift from another special friend from our days in hospital in Perth.

We had a routine, your daddy and my family, in the burns unit. I am glad that you were not there to see it. My mother sat with me in the morning and Michael stayed in the evening.

The nights in hospital after your daddy had gone back to his serviced apartment were interminable, filled with dark thoughts. The dawn brought a new kind of agony when the dressings were peeled off my wounds and nurses showered me as I lay horizontal on a plastic-covered trolley because of my broken back. The nurses wrapped me again and I'd lie there, unable to sit up or use my arms, hooked up to oxygen, a catheter, a nasogastric tube, some-times antibiotics and a bag of blood, waiting for the clock to show 11 am, when I was allowed my first visitor of the day.

The only person I wanted was my mother. I craved her presence these mornings, when I felt utterly forsaken and crushed by life; I greeted her like a small child who can be comforted by nobody else. She'd enter my room bearing small nourishments: a cup of clear broth from a nearby Japanese takeaway or a juice, a magazine or newspaper, some cards and packages that had arrived overnight. Mum sat beside me, breaking my spell of desperation, and another day would begin.

Some of this will not make easy reading for you. But over these last two years I have learnt there is a cost when parents don't talk to their children about the past because it is too difficult, or to spare them. I have felt the regret of the second and third genera-tions who left it too late to ask for their parents' and grandparents' stories because they feared the burden of knowing their pain, or were just too busy with early adulthood. These stories shape who we are. They affect our relationships and knowing them, being aware of them, can help us to understand our parents and, ultimately, ourselves. It was this realisation that propelled me, in these pages, to explore my mother's story. Being the first child of a migrant undoubtedly influenced the person I am today.

One of the (many) frightening things about having a child is realising as they develop how much, as a parent, you can influence their outlook on life. Whether I want it to or not, my conduct and the way I relate to others affects your way of relating to the world. I see it so clearly now. If I'm anxious, raise my voice in anger, or if I'm calm, affectionate, respectful towards loved ones, you learn these behaviours are normal; they become your normal.

I think about my parents' influences on me. I inherited my sense of empathy from my father, John, your poppi, who always championed the marginalised and the underdog. I remember Dad chasing garbage trucks up our back lane at Christmas with six-packs of beer in his hands for the garbage men.

My need to prove myself over and again comes from my mother whom—no matter what I've achieved—I've struggled to please. My mother can be fierce. Fierce in her love. She will do absolutely anything for her children and grandchildren; her energy is bound-less, so too her capacity for self-sacrifice. She works and works and works—always for others, never for herself.

But Mum can be quick to judge and harsh in her judgements. She is like Stromboli, the island volcano off Sicily. You know the eruption is coming when Mum's green eyes turn steely grey. Certain eruptions are ingrained in my memory. Telling Mum, as she did the laundry, that I was leaving my job as a solicitor in a prestigious Sydney law firm to become a journalist, and her yelling at me that

I would fail, is one of them. My mother didn't think I was a failure or that I lacked the mettle to be a newspaper reporter. It's just that she has lived her life knowing she could have achieved so much more, been so much more, if only she'd been given the chance. She didn't want me to squander mine.

I view my upbringing, including my mother's demanding attitude and high expectations, as an important factor that contributed to my absolute determination after the crash to keep going, to pile on the challenges and meet every one. Like flying in planes again, undergoing IVF, doing a PhD, applying for postdoctoral fellowships, building a third career.

Sometimes, I worry about the residual traumas that I am passing on to you. Trauma, it is said, can haunt later generations, can be 'remembered' by those who did not live it or know it in their own bodies. This transgenerational reach of trauma can result in confusion and a sense of responsibility on the part of affected children. It can manifest in a desire to repair and in a consciousness that their own, the child's, existence may be a kind of compensation for the parent's unutterable loss.[1]

Is this true? Will you, my son, grow up with 'memories' of your mother's suffering, feeling that you are somehow my compensation? Will you feel responsible for me, or—worse—resentful? How can I stop myself transmitting my trauma to you and prevent such a sad inheritance?

When you were three, you refused to look at my legs, what remains of them. You covered them with my long, soft, jersey skirt if they were inadvertently exposed. You refused to hold my scarred and disfigured left hand, with its half fingers. Already he knows I'm different, I despaired.

'Why don't you want to hold my hand?' I asked you.

'Because it's bumpy.'

When you were four, you kissed my 'bumpy' grafted skin. Rather than being repelled by it, you wanted to make it better for me.

At five, I carefully wash your precious little toes when you have your bath and, yes, I do think of my losses as I feel the smooth bridges of your feet underneath my fingertips. When I notice the pale brown birthmark on one of your ankles, I remember that I had a similar mark on one of mine.

Right now I am your world, I am all you want, I am all you know. But I am damaged. I don't feel whole. I couldn't walk you to sleep when we brought you home from hospital; others had to do that. I couldn't breastfeed you beyond the first few weeks because of the burns on my left breast. I couldn't lay you down in your bassinet; my wheelchair was too low. I couldn't place you in your pram and go for a walk to the local park as I watched other mothers do. I couldn't grab your hand and take you down to the beach like the mother in *The Big Big Sea*.

I am in so many ways broken. When you were a toddler, I wondered how you would feel about me when you got older, when you became more aware of my limitations and compared your mamma to the more 'normal', able mothers of your friends.

'Mummy, I wish you could walk,' is something you have said to me at night in your bed as we waited together for you to fall asleep.

'I wish you had your legs back, Mum,' is another.

There was a day in the summer just before you turned four. We were at the coast, the beaches swarmed with families, with parents playing in the sand and running in the waves with their children. Your daddy took you to the beach while I waited back at the house and when you got back you saw I was upset.

'Why are you crying, Mummy?' you asked.

'I'm crying because I can't run with you and Daddy on the sand and in the waves,' I said, then immediately regretted it.

To distract you I told you a story, a beautiful story, of how your daddy and I used to go trekking through the rainforest at Wilsons Promontory in Victoria, how we camped out at night, setting up our two-man tent near the beach. One night, after going to the self-composting toilet at the Little Waterloo Bay campsite, we returned to the tent to find a possum munching through our only loaf of bread. We called the possum Trevor and watched him finish the loaf.

'Why did Trevor eat your bread, Mummy?' you asked.

'Because he was hungry,' I said.

This explanation was enough for you in that moment, and my earlier tears were forgotten.

Sometimes I get out the few photographs I have from when I was heavily pregnant. I have hardly any; these photos were taken the day I was admitted to hospital for a planned caesarean. You love looking at my pregnant tummy, and I take a special delight in showing the pictures to you. But I wonder sometimes at my motives. Do the photos make me feel more legitimate, like a real mother, because I have proof of my protruding belly? Because, deep down, with all the things I couldn't do for you after you were born, very often I don't feel like a legitimate mother at all.

Six weeks after the crash, lying in the burns unit, I asked the surgeon, Dr Fiona Wood, if I would be able to have children. The burns went right up to my inner thighs; I lost almost all the flesh on my left buttock; a huge chunk of tissue was gone from my abdomen on the left side; my periods had stopped. She said yes, she could see no reason why not.

Four years later, we were on our second cycle of IVF when I got pregnant with you. I was 38. I had weaned myself off the drugs for the maddening phantom pain I (still) experience from my missing limbs, which would have been dangerous for a developing foetus. The IVF process was so emotionally and physically draining that

I didn't think I could do another. Then a blood test came back positive: I was having a baby. I took the call from the clinic while sitting in my office at the Australian National University. In disbelief I called your daddy to tell him. He came and picked me up. Walking to the car, we couldn't stop smiling at each other.

We kept you secret for many months, only telling our families and the closest of our friends. I was afraid that if I allowed myself to believe I was pregnant, something would go wrong. Having a baby was something that happened to other, 'normal' people—not someone like me. I feared the pity if something bad happened but, also, I didn't want to make the news as the plane crash survivor who lost her legs then had a baby. Sitting in a wheelchair, wearing loose-fitting clothes, working long hours on a PhD from home—an intense, solitary experience anyway—it was not difficult to hide my growing girth. I rang a few interstate friends the week before I was due to tell them I was about to give birth. So successful were we in keeping the pregnancy secret, I worried that people would not believe I had carried you myself.

As you formed, my tummy expanded like a giant skin-covered balloon, the grafts on my abdomen stretching without complications. I'd lie in bed at night feeling you move inside me and began to accept that you were real. To help me believe, a Scottish midwife encouraged me to put up pictures of your ultrasound scans on the bookshelves in my study. You had beautiful plump lips even in the womb. It was three weeks before your arrival when I finally hired a painter to paint your room green. (Green was the colour I painted my room as soon as my parents would let me.) On one of the walls your daddy and I put up a huge decal tree full of birds and forest creatures.

We found out you'd be arriving by caesarean section 38 weeks into the pregnancy, when our doctor informed us that the burns on my belly were stopping you from engaging. Two days later I was wheeled into the operating theatre with your daddy and the most magnificent team of senior obstetricians, anaesthetists and midwives the Canberra Hospital could assemble. I heard your cries before I saw you—white and bloody and luminous—as the doctors lifted you above my head. Your daddy choked up and a midwife laid you down on my chest and you curled around my face so that I couldn't speak and she pulled a blanket over you. I was happier than I had been at any time in my life.

We took you home a week later. You gave us your first smile on our third wedding anniversary. You called your first toy, a woolly lion from my sister, 'Hergal'. Your first word was 'dada', for your daddy, and an expression that sounded like 'good to go' soon followed. You called me 'baba'. You showed an early appreciation for your father's music (Belinda Carlisle and Roxette) and screamed when you heard mine (the Smiths). Like me, you detested breakfast cereal of any kind and were able to multi-task (at eight months you could turn the page of your book, *That's Not My Puppy*, with one hand while touching the dog with the hairy coat with the other). You loved pureed pumpkin more than anything until one day I let you eat too much and you fell ill and never ate it again. You crawled for the first time at eleven months on the carpeted floor of my prosthetist's consulting room. You developed a special smile reserved only for your parents that was as broad as your face and it said, 'I love you and I want you to love me too.'

A great year, 2012—your birth year—was topped off when our football team, the Sydney Swans, won the premiership, though only your daddy and I were at the Melbourne Cricket Ground that day. You watched the grand final on TV with your paternal grandparents, Sonny and Lol, who are (gulp) Collingwood supporters. Football has a special place in our family, as you are learning.

Sometimes when I look at you, I feel as if my heart cannot contain the love that's in there. It hurts to love someone this much.

'Sit on me,' you'd say when you first learnt to talk, by which you meant you wanted to sit on my wheelchair, on me, and even though it was thirty degrees outside and my right leg was throbbing with an infection, I pulled you onto my lap.

I am acutely aware of how precious you are, that I have no more important a purpose now as your mother than to love you.

Six months after you were born I tried to put on paper the kind of mother I want to be, the example I want to set for you. I want you to learn tolerance and empathy, and to always treat others as you'd like to be treated yourself. I want you to feel that you can tell me anything, be anything, without fearing my response. I want you to understand that no situation defines you, that you are defined by who you are inside, that the power to lead a happy and full life resides within you. I want you to be surrounded by love, as I have been. I never want to be a burden on you.

This book is for you, my son. It is my attempt, fragmented and belated, to authenticate the stories of five generations of our family, to unpack some of the myths we have told each other for 70 years, and to place my own story in the context of that history. I didn't find all the information I sought about our family. I wish I had asked more questions when I had the chance; that my mother had asked more questions of her father; that I had interviewed my mother's parents when they were still alive; that my grandparents had kept more records for me to discover after they were gone. I wish I had turned on a dictaphone and recorded my reflections on what was happening to me while I lay in the burns unit in Perth, as one doctor suggested I do.

Sometimes you have to wait for the pain to subside—it never disappears completely—before you can begin to tell your story.

But sometimes you wait so long the questions become unaskable, the answers you seek unknowable.

While certain historical family secrets have eluded me, in searching I discovered truths of a more abstract kind. In the end, it was the process of researching and writing the stories gathered here that enabled me to make sense out of a personal tragedy that, by itself, made none. I found a place for myself among my family's stories, an unexpected solace in the continuum of time.

I hope this book answers some of your questions.

Just know, my precious boy, that you are loved.

Your mamma
March 2017

1

The Boxes

I

I LAY ON MY BACK ON THE HOSPITAL BED, under a dark blue, speckled blanket, as a male orderly steered me towards the familiar swinging doors. Another operating theatre. Another surgical removal of a piece of me.

Although this time it was only a minor part—a bone spur from the end of my right tibia that was preventing me from walking on prostheses—it would be taken while I was unconscious, with no control over what was being done to me, over how much of my leg bone would ultimately be taken. The thought of losing more of myself this way was, in this moment, overwhelming.

A young woman doctor directed Michael where to wait, so the medical staff could find him when I was out of recovery.

'Follow this red line,' she said, pointing to the floor.

Michael smiled at me. I could see he was reluctant to go; he didn't leave until I was out of sight.

In the operating theatre, the anaesthetist searched for a compliant vein. He was experienced, but the first effort failed. I don't have many places for a cannula to go; the only accessible veins are in my right arm.

Outside was the Canberra winter. It was minus five when we arrived at hospital earlier that morning. In the operating room the air was hot. I heard the beeping of the monitoring machines that, to me, always signal personal peril. The room was filled with doctors and nurses. I could hear some of them discussing antibiotics.

'Just one gram?'

'Well, she's only small.'

With no lower limbs, I suppose I was.

The vascular surgeon must have seen my tears, though I tried to be discreet, and he reassured me. 'Think of this as happy surgery,' the surgeon said. 'This is not sad surgery like the first time, this is happy surgery to fix a problem.'

I forced a smile, appreciating his compassion.

With two cannulas inserted into my hand I was wheeled around so that my bed lay alongside the operating table. The lights were bright. I stared at the clock in front of me: 11.55 am. The room was buzzing with the voices of people I could not see. Someone, a nurse maybe, was sticking plugs all over my body, reaching down my hospital gown. A young doctor put a rolled-up towel under my head. The big operating theatre lights loomed overhead, waiting to be pulled down into place when the cutting started. I was to lie on my stomach for this surgery and would have to be turned over, but, before any of that happened, I lost consciousness.

One minute I was trying to answer questions about my career—'Yes, I was a journalist, but I'm not anymore,' I told the anaesthetist—the next I was opening my eyes, on my back again. Two hours had passed.

'She's awake!' the anaesthetist called, startling me in my newly conscious state.

I struggled to remember where I was, to shake myself out of a dream which, though vivid, had already vanished. Why was my throat so sore? A breathing tube had been inserted down it, the anaesthetist told me.

Later, I asked Michael about his reluctance to leave me that morning. 'Why did you look so sad when they wheeled me away to theatre?'

'Because in Perth, when they wheeled you away, I never knew whether the doctors would come back and tell us "Sorry—we did everything we could for her", and you would be gone.'

It was June 2015. Eight years had passed since my legs were amputated to save my life after a plane crash in Indonesia. My career as a journalist officially ended in 2012, the year my son was born. I finished a five-year PhD thesis on human rights and the 'war on terror' in October 2014.

Then, my life substantially rebuilt, I opened the boxes.

II

How to describe the boxes? There are two kinds; a set of boxes for each set of difficult memories.

First, there are the boxes from the crash. They'd been stored in the garage for over seven years. They held all the documents from my time in the Royal Perth Hospital Burns Unit, where I spent nearly three months, and the rehabilitation hospital, another three months. Cards, emails, letters, notebooks, newspaper clippings, phone messages, photographs that covered a wall of my hospital room, CDs, small gifts, books of poetry, religious icons, postcards, children's artwork. All the well-wishes and thoughtful sentiments people sent me during that period. Among them was a bright red lipstick; an olive-green shawl that somebody, a stranger, knitted for me; a painting of a beach scene from Stradbroke Island.

For years I was conscious these kindnesses were there waiting for me to engage with them but, for now, they were safely contained in their cardboard vault, out of sight. I felt guilty that I had not properly read them. Their authors had been moved to write to me, to knit, to paint. How could I not read their missives, reply to them, thank them?

In the burns unit I could not bring myself to read them, though my family did. During those (almost) six months in Perth, I could not read at all. It wasn't just that I couldn't physically hold a book for the wounds and splints and bandages. A nurse brought me a special book stand. It didn't help. I love books but I couldn't make it past the first sentence, no matter the subject. It was as the French writer, Charlotte Delbo, wrote about her discouragement with books after her own wartime trauma: I could see through the words. I had 'lost the faculty of dreaming' and books could offer me no escape, no solace.[1]

Nor could I write. Indeed, much of the time I could barely speak—certainly not about what had happened, what was happening, to me. I couldn't speak to friends or colleagues, nor let them visit. Some understood that, some did not. I could be with no one apart from Michael and my immediate family: those people who would love me no matter what they saw, no matter what I told them, how grim, how desperate. Those who demanded nothing of me except that I live. I could be anything, I could be nothing. To them, I would still be Cynthia. My world closed in for that terrible time of suffering and loss. It would open up again when I was ready, and not before.

When that period ended, those months in hospital, I returned home to Canberra by train, on the Indian Pacific (via Sydney)—I could not conceive of flying again at that point—and the boxes came with me. But, still, I could not open them. Every time I did

I was overcome by terrible sadness, an overwhelming grief. They were so full of hurt that, had I read their contents, the pain would have paralysed me. And I wanted to live.

There was another smaller box that had also been awaiting my attention. Its contents were nowhere near as confronting, but just as brimming with meaning. It was the box containing my Italian grandparents' papers that I salvaged after Nonna, my mother's mother, died in 2009. A precious collection, it included Nonno's papers from the Second World War, when he was held as a prisoner of war by the Germans.

I had not examined the box's contents since claiming them from my grandparents' house. But in there, I knew, was my grandfather's POW tag. I first saw it when I was studying history in the middle years of high school. We were learning about the world wars. This prompted Mum to tell me her father had been interned in a Nazi concentration camp (as she called it). Nonno retrieved the metal tag from its place in his cupboard to show me one Saturday afternoon following lunch. I remember his pale blue eyes filling with tears. When Nonna died, having survived her husband by sixteen years, the tag was the one thing I wanted to find and keep.

There were links between the two sets of boxes, though it took me years to see them. The boxes contained my family's stories, ones infused with trauma and survival, stories that were untold.

Nonno's story, as I knew it at that point, was this. Alfredo, aged nineteen, was bound for war in 1943, following the armistice in which Italy changed sides and joined the Allies, when his train was captured by German soldiers. He was taken prisoner and sent to various POW camps in Austria and/or Germany, where his captors starved him. His sister Amelia, older by seven years, was a wild-spirited young woman, a dancer. Somehow, she managed to get food to her younger brother in the camps and, by doing so, helped keep him alive. In 1945, Alfredo was liberated by the Russians and repatriated to Italy. Two years after the war ended, my mother was born. Amelia departed Italy for America in 1951. Nine years later, she died in the United States in troubled circumstances.

I had carried the bones of this story around with me since I was fourteen, when Nonno showed me his tag. I learnt about the intriguing role of Amelia on a visit back to Trieste many years later, in 2001 (I was 29 by then). I was a little like the wilful, freedom-loving Amelia, relatives told me, and I was happy to believe them. Amelia had chased adventure and refused to settle down. I suppose they saw a likeness in my restlessness, determination to see the world, and independence. When I returned home, my mother told me about Amelia's diary. Mum had read it as a teenager following her aunt's death. She told me it contained disturbing details of Amelia's life in America, including the physical abuse she endured there. Nobody knew where the diary was now.

Amelia's life had an allure and romance about it. She was a figure who was only distantly connected to my life, yet her story gripped me in a way that I still find hard to explain. Knowing more of it today, I doubt I was anything like Amelia: a woman who took huge risks and defied the social norms and conventions of her day. She was an outlier, unlike anyone else in our family.

I resolved, after that 2001 trip, to write a book about Amelia, my grandfather's resourceful sister, his brave protector during the war, whose life ended violently and too soon. However, things— career, travel, love—meant I kept putting it off.

Then 2007 happened.

I was foreign affairs and defence reporter for the *Sydney Morning Herald*, and that March I travelled to Indonesia with the foreign affairs minister. En route from Jakarta to Yogyakarta, where I was meant to meet the minister and fly back to Australia in the government VIP jet, I was in a plane crash. I survived (one of 119 people to do so). Twenty-one others, including five Australians who were travelling with me as a part of the same group meeting up with the foreign minister later that morning, did not.

Now I had another story, one publishers clamoured for. From almost the moment I woke from a week-long induced coma, everyone—publishers, agents, colleagues, doctors, friends, strangers—asked me: was I going to write a book about it?

I couldn't do it. A book about the plane crash seemed utterly pointless to me. What would it be? A voyeur's account for those people who, as one publisher put it, 'have always wondered what it would be like to be in a plane crash'?

I refused to let this completely random event define who I was. Most of all, I was not going to write a book that caused me further pain at a time when every part of me, every exertion, every thought, every effort I could muster, was being channelled into rebuilding a life worth surviving such an event. If I wrote a book, it would have to come much later. It would have to be something else.

The American memoirist Eileen Simpson was an orphan who lost her mother as an infant and then her father aged seven. She only mourned the loss of her parents after the death of her second husband, when she was in her fifties. In writing her memoir, the publisher wanted her to begin with this moment: this explosion of the feeling of being an orphan that followed her husband's passing. Simpson couldn't do it. Anxiety gripped her, and she realised she wanted to put the material about herself at the end of the book, 'because I didn't want to examine what had happened'. So instead she decided to 'back into the book'.

'I would start by doing some research on how orphans have been treated historically,' she wrote. 'That would be easier than writing about my own childhood because it was more objective.'[2]

I think, unwittingly at first, this is what I was doing too: backing into my book. I could not face the trauma of the set of boxes about the crash without immersing myself in the other box, in Nonno's wartime story of survival.

That I had Nonno's story to tell at all was thanks to a salvage mission I had undertaken some years before.

III

How do you visit your grandparents' house for the last time, the house where you spent every Saturday of your childhood, knowing they are both gone forever?

It was a childhood of Saturdays spent eating my grandmother's lunches of spaghetti, schnitzel and radicchio salad; of listening to my mother and her sister conversing across the table with their parents in the Trieste dialect; of learning, gradually, to drink coffee, which Nonna made in a small pot on the stove, disguising its bitterness with lots of milk and sugar.

Every weekend we'd take the number 492 or 494 bus to my grandparents' house in Campsie, in Sydney's south-west, us four children and Mum. It was a winding, interminable trip through the back streets of Five Dock, Ashfield and Burwood, that was always worse on the return journey with a full stomach.

I passed through the rickety front gate of the Fletcher Street house for the final time in late 2010. Nonna had died in Concord Hospital the previous year; her funeral was on my birthday. The house had been sold. Now its contents were being packed up, picked through for memories and keepsakes her children and grandchildren couldn't yet let go of, the remainder donated to the Salvation Army, or just thrown away. My sister took a rolling pin and Nonno's double set of red-and-green, tartan-patterned Triestine playing cards. I took a pair of chipped ceramic cats and Nonno's heavy, battered Italian dictionary. Mum took the old Parkinson-Rinnai gas heater that reminds me, when I see it now, of cold Saturday afternoons in winter playing with my younger cousins in our grandparents' living room, as we waited for word that it was time to go home.

The Campsie house was the only one my grandparents ever owned. Alfredo and Anna arrived in Australia with their daughters, Loredana and Marina, aged nine and six, in 1957. They lived with other Italian families in terraces in Paddington and Newtown before purchasing their house in Campsie in 1961. For a deposit they used compensation money Nonna received after losing a fingertip in a work accident in a tobacco factory in Waterloo. (The remaining nail grew back curved over the top of the shortened finger, a jarring sight.) My grandparents couldn't afford the loan repayments on their high-interest solicitor's loan at first, so Nonna's sister and her family rented a room in the two-bedroom semi-detached house. Loredana and Marina slept in a fibro annexe connected to the house. During inclement weather, the sound of rain pounding the tin roof of the annexe was unbearable. When my mother was fifteen, she left school and got a job that helped pay off her parents' mortgage.

I pushed my wheelchair up the cement path to the front door of the red-brick house. It was neatly lined with white gardenias and Shasta daisies when Nonna was alive, but was now unkempt. Nonna hadn't lived in the house for the twelve months before she died. Fiercely independent, or unwilling to let go of the home she had spent 50 years in and that was filled with memories of her family, my grandmother refused invitations to move into a 'granny flat' at the back of my parents' house. Then she had a stroke, the first of two, and went into a nursing home operated by the Little Sisters of the Poor, in the street parallel to my parents'. Nonna tried to run away from the Little Sisters, but only ever made it as far as my parents' house.

I must have offered little consolation to Nonna in the final years of her life. Preoccupied with my own injuries, I had no reserves of comfort for anybody else, and our talks were brief and strained. I spoke with her only once during my hospitalisation. I was at the rehabilitation hospital by then, and we talked over the mobile phone. I was lying in my hospital bed; I don't remember if she spoke in English or Italian.

'I knew you would be okay, Cinzia, because it was you,' she told me.

I remember Nonna's last thoughtful Christmas gift to me—a hamper. She would have seen the baskets of seasonal goods in the shops and noted they were a popular gift. But this was one she put together herself. The basket was filled with such an odd collection of items it makes me smile to recall it: among them was a green oven mitt with a picture of a parrot and a bottle of Cougar Bourbon.

After the strokes, Nonna had trouble finding words and forming sentences. I remember one visit to my parents' house. Nonna, who was there for the day, sat on a chair in the sunroom. Her silvery-blue hair was styled with rollers into large curls, as always. She tried to smile at me but her eyes were sad and she didn't make a lot of sense. I didn't speak Italian with her as I'd done in previous years and which she always appreciated; it required more effort of me than I felt able to muster that day. Nonna died a few months later.

Before the plane crash, I'd intended to bring Nonna to Canberra on the train and have her stay the weekend with me, in my spare room. I'd purchased (with the barest minimum of a deposit) a small flat in Campbell, a suburb close to the Australian War Memorial on the northern edge of Lake Burley Griffin. Nonna had bought me my first (brand-new) washing machine as a gift for the new apartment. Sitting together at my worn, extendable dining table, reclaimed from the scrap heap after my last share house dispersed, I planned to turn on a tape recorder and interview her about her life, about Nonno, about Amelia's role in his survival during the war. The trip never transpired, the interview was never conducted.

I recall a time in late 2003 when I took a day off work to accompany Nonna on an excursion with her local church group to a lavender farm in the Southern Highlands of New South Wales. We boarded the bus with other elderly parishioners outside St Mel's in Campsie, the Catholic church where my parents were married. Nonna and I were ambling around the farm, navigating the paths and smelling the fragrant flowers, marvelling at the different varieties of English lavender, the many shades of blue and purple and pink, when I got a call from my office, the Canberra bureau of the *Herald*. The prime minister had announced a cabinet reshuffle, and one of 'my' ministers, the minister for immigration, was moving into the attorney-general's portfolio. Ridiculously, I thought this was an important story and one that had to be written by myself. I abandoned Nonna, her group and the flowers. I found our bus, and spent the rest of the day filing my story about the ministerial portfolio change over my mobile phone to copytakers in the newspaper's head office in Sydney. The foolish self-importance of it all: it was the one and only occasion I spent with Nonna like this, and I couldn't give her the whole day.

I peered over the low wire fence of my grandparents' house to the adjoining semi as I approached the porch. Next door was a rental property, whose occupants were constantly changing. It was never well cared for. On the other side of my grandparents' place sat a small block of red-brick home units. Their own house was modest but comfortable. Canterbury Hospital was at one end of their street; an Italian restaurant and the bus stop were at the other. We had walked its length so many times with heavy shopping bags: the fruit and vegetables were cheaper in Campsie. We always took the bus to my grandparents' so my father could have the family car for the Saturday lawn-mowing jobs that paid for his flying lessons. (Dad was passionate about flying; our Sundays were spent lying on picnic rugs in the dry, dusty paddocks of Hoxton Park in western Sydney, staring up at the clouds while Dad flew Cessna 150s with instructors from the NSW Police Aero Club.)

The suburb of Campsie has been home to a shifting tide of migrant groups: English, Scottish and Irish before 1945; Greek, Italian and Lebanese after the Second World War; and, since the 1980s, Vietnamese and Korean. The changing streetscape of the main shopping strip, Beamish Street, has reflected this over the decades in the language of its signage, the types of food shops and restaurants, and the faces of the shoppers. My mother bought fruit and vegetables from a Lebanese fruiterer and crusty bread rolls from the Vietnamese baker. Nonna always seemed at ease among the mixed ethnicities, haggling shopkeepers and Turkish bazaar-like atmosphere of the Campsie shopping experience. To my bemusement, no matter the person's background, if they were from somewhere in Asia she always called them 'cinesi', Chinese.

My grandparents kept separate bedrooms. First on the left as you entered their house was Nonno's room, and Nonna's was behind it. It was here, in a cupboard behind the door of the second bedroom, that Alfredo's old war artefacts, if they were still in the house, would be found. Neither my mother nor my aunt had come across them yet. I had driven with Michael from Canberra to Campsie to search the cupboard myself, refusing to believe the relics might already be gone.

The house's rooms were in varying stages of emptiness. A few pictures hung on the walls in the lounge room, but there were painful absences. The noisy cuckoo clock was no longer there, nor the framed portraits of my mother and her sister as teenagers. In the cosy kitchen, the swirly black-and-red linoleum had been replaced in recent years with floating timber floorboards. The chair on which Nonno's cap sat for years after his passing was still there, pushed against the wall behind his old place at the dining table where we once played the card game Remi together. (When I lost at Remi, Nonna would tell me 'unlucky in cards, lucky in love', which seemed poor consolation at the time.) A menagerie of noisy birds once shared the sunroom at the back of the house with the washing machine—breeding budgerigars, yellow and orange canaries, the odd galah or convalescing pigeon, and an old cockatoo, Koki. Nonno took Koki out of his cage sometimes so he could sit with his clipped wings on a wooden perch in the garden for a few hours. The sunroom floor was always littered with a light sprinkling of bird seed. Now, the room stood quiet, bare apart from a couple of old armchairs.

I didn't venture down the cracked concrete steps outside that led into the backyard—I couldn't anyway in the wheelchair. But I was glad not to have to see what remained of my grandparents' once-bountiful, busy yard: Nonno's perfectly manicured lawn; his abundant beds of tomatoes and radicchio; the grapevines that grew above the old wooden swing; the loquat tree with its downy, yellow fruit that occupied us for hours over many summers; the big rusty bathtub in which my grandfather washed his much-loved German shepherd, Tommy.

I glanced around the house quickly, not letting myself reflect too deeply on the permanence of the loss of these two people who had played such a central role in the first twenty years of my life. I was here to find some papers. I'd immerse myself in their lives and legacies when I had the time, the space, to think.

At first it seemed like the papers spilling from the cupboard in Nonna's room would reveal nothing more than old bank passbooks and electricity bills. I knew exactly what I was looking for, although it had been more than two decades. Standing in the kitchen doorway that day, Nonno had pulled his POW tag from a small pink packet. The tag was made of metal and, in my teenage imagination, I saw traces of blood on it, though it was probably rust. We talked a little about his experiences, about the constant hunger, how he was lucky to eat potato peels scavenged from the garbage. The tag was put away and no one ever asked him about it again. Mentally, I was preparing myself for the possibility that the identity tag was gone, that it had been thrown away by Nonna or my mother or aunt in the course of packing up the house.

Then, suddenly, there it was: the dark pink Commonwealth Savings Bank of Australia pouch, and inside it the engraved metal tag, prisoner number 111547. The tag was four centimetres wide, six centimetres long, with three punched holes and a piece of gold-coloured elastic threaded through one of them. It felt as though the tag had been waiting for me to find it, and I held it to myself, closing my eyes to let the moment register. Had I not come that day to personally locate Alfredo's tag, it almost certainly would have been discarded with the other unclaimed remnants of my grandparents' lives.

I gathered up the rest of the documents that were with the POW tag, not pausing to see what they contained. The finality of that visit, knowing I would never see my grandparents' house again, was too heavy to contemplate. I left the house quickly, got into the car with Michael and drove away.

When I arrived home, I put the tag and the other papers into a blue-and-white-striped cardboard box, and stored it away in an old cupboard in a spare room.

For the next five years I occasionally peered into the box. There were school reports from the 1930s, military papers, copies of a

Alfredo's POW tag

marriage certificate, immigration papers, mortgage documents, house renovation plans, black-and-white photographs, newspaper cuttings, recipes, sympathy cards from Nonno's funeral. Traces of a life, two lives, now reduced to a box.

I left the documents unscrutinised, their German and Italian untranslated, knowing I would come back to them someday.

IV

I have never found it easy to revisit my past.

I don't know that I liked being a child: getting told what to do, how to think, being so dependent on others. I remember shocking a teacher in year eleven at my Catholic high school in a discussion about abortion. He was a crotchety man with a beard who taught us chemistry as well as religion (though not at the same time), and threw chalk at the unfortunate girls who snoozed like tired birds, perched on elevated stools behind the high desks of the science labs. One religion class, I put up my hand and declared women should have the right to choose for themselves. Such heresy! (Yet I was awarded the religion prize in my final year, my mortification alleviated only by the fact that I also won the prize for English.)

I was impatient to be an adult, to be my own person, to be self-sufficient.

I kept a diary in primary school. I started out writing entries in a journal and, when the pages ran out, I wrote on individual pieces of different-coloured floral paper that were held together with bobby pins. I faithfully documented the most banal events of daily life, from what I ate for breakfast to quarrels with siblings and the care of our many pets. Then, in year six, I was bullied at school for twelve months—tormented and taunted, emotionally and occasionally physically, by the eight other girls in my all-girl class.

At the time, there seemed no escape other than to see the year out and start afresh in a bigger high school with different people.

Reading the diaries afterwards, even knowing they existed, with their sad record of the emotional pain of my eleven-year-old self, was too much to bear. One day I took the diaries outside and sat down on the cement path in our backyard.

'I'm going to burn these,' I told my sister. 'I don't want to read them ever again.'

I lit a match and burnt every last piece of paper. If I could not read about those awful things that had happened, I thought, they couldn't hurt me.

For years after the bullying, I believed the problem was me.

I attended a Catholic school in Sydney's inner-western suburbs run by the Presentation Sisters. They wore pale brown tunics and simple habits that covered their hair, and lived in a convent next door to the school. A rickety wire gate linked the bare playground—with its solitary tree and cracked bitumen surface—to the sisters' house.

The headmistress called me into her office one day towards the end of year six. She had short grey wiry hair, glasses and a heaving bosom. Her face wore an almost permanent scowl and she grimaced rather than smiled. I stood before her desk as she told me I had to repeat year six and remain at the school for another year. I was the youngest in the class. It was my age, she implied, that had caused me to be singled out by the other girls.

Without hesitation, I refused. There was no way I was going to spend an extra day in that school beyond what I absolutely had to.

I look back at this little girl in her maroon-chequered uniform standing up to that large, intimidating principal and see the emergence of a formidable spirit. My primary school left me permanently uneasy around large groups of females and temporarily set me back in my mathematics education. But it instilled in me a resilience and determination, and an enduring belief in the power of individuals to change their destiny, no matter their situation.

The suspicion, planted by the primary school experience, that I was the cause of my own bullying gnawed away at me, however, throughout high school. It undermined my confidence every year, even as I was voted class captain. It was only when I started an arts/law degree at Macquarie University at age seventeen, and found a group of like-minded, bookish, slightly eccentric male and female friends, that I began to believe I was capable of nurturing deep friendships after all. It had taken me a long time to find kindred spirits; it took even longer to find a vocation that satisfied me and to finally feel comfortable with myself.

Nevertheless, deep inside my psyche, doubts about my self-worth lingered. This goes some way towards explaining why I experienced the 2007 plane crash as a kind of failure, something I must have brought upon myself. That it happened meant, at some level, I had failed as a journalist and—more importantly—as a human being. This feeling is connected to the inevitable questions that follow such an event. Why me? Why was I singled out? (Such thoughts are, of course, nonsense. You might as easily ask, 'Why not me?') Having read so much about the experiences of my grandfather and people in his situation, I know that such feelings are not uncommon among survivors of trauma. A loss of agency, a crushing of personality, a deep sense of shame no matter how irrational affects many survivors.[3]

While I do not compare my trauma to that endured by survivors of the brutalities of the world wars, I identify with some of the feelings they experienced, including a loss of identity and dignity. The crash stripped me of both, and restoring them has been a gradual process—is still a work in progress. I have felt, and will always feel, the heavy isolation that deep suffering imposes on the individual. One becomes painfully detached, as if trapped in a cage: life goes on outside the cage, you can still see it, hear it, but you can never again be a part of it—not in the way you once were.

I have gone through things nobody around me could ever begin to understand. Losing both legs and with this the career, the interactions, the independence and freedom I had before was, is, a profoundly alienating experience.

I experience episodes of phantom pain that can last a whole night and day. Anguished, tormented, I sit alone in my dark study when the rest of the house is asleep—the pain peaks at 2 or 3 am—and press my legs into the cushion of the wheelchair, begging my damaged nerves to relent. The vibrations inside my legs feel like drilling jackhammers or firing electric currents. The shocks come at regular intervals with a ten- or twenty-second pause in between.

At other times the pain is like a sharp blade slicing through the length of my limbs, over and over. I told this to a GP once, not expecting him to understand what I was talking about.

He looked it up on his computer. 'Lancinating,' he said of the slicing sensation. 'It's called lancinating pain.'

I found myself oddly satisfied to finally have a word for something that had seemed impossible to communicate, and therefore share, before.

The skin grafts on my legs are extremely fragile; I lost so much flesh from beneath the skin. If I accidentally tear the skin, and it doesn't take much, I can't wear prostheses. This sometimes means weeks of not walking. My body no longer regulates heat properly and I quickly overheat wearing prosthetic limbs in warmer and more humid temperatures. Yet I don't feel heat or cold through my burnt skin. I have accidentally poured boiling water from a saucepan on my leg and not felt a thing—just stared, panicked but mesmerised, as the pink skin shrivelled and blistered before my eyes.

Having an injury so few others have, certainly nobody I ever knew, propelled me into a loneliness I've not emerged from. The only way I could separate the crash from feelings of shame and failure was by telling myself the event was without deeper meaning and there was nothing to be gained by thinking or talking about the crash.

I tried to block it, to banish thoughts of it from my mind.

V

There was another reason to block out the event. I am afraid of remembering.

Memory is fluid, malleable, untrustworthy. I have memories from that day that have subsided with time, some that have become distorted so as to be plain wrong. Others, memories I should have, are not there at all. Will they come back? I wonder.

My colleague, Mark Forbes, who was my newspaper's Jakarta correspondent and the first to locate me, in a Yogyakarta hospital, wrote in a dispatch the day of the crash that I told him, 'I saw them burning alive.' But I don't remember this. I don't know if I did see passengers burning, and have forgotten it. I told my sister I heard screaming. I don't remember this either. I cannot visualise the scene I must have witnessed around me after the plane crashed, upon realising I was on fire—I cannot see it, cannot hear it, cannot smell it.

Liz O'Neill, the public affairs official from the Department of Foreign Affairs and Trade, sat next to me, on my right side, on the plane, and Morgan Mellish, the *Australian Financial Review* journalist, was across the aisle on my left. We shared coffee and juice together that morning before the flight and they died next to me in their seats. When I think about them I can still feel them sitting next to me, sleepily anticipating the busy day ahead. It's like they occupy those places on either side of me permanently now. But did I see them, or anybody else, after the crash? Did I see what was happening around me? Or did the smoke prevent me? Has my mind suppressed images that one day I will be able to see?

In 2012 I tried to write down what I remembered of the crash. I wrote that I was left lying on my back on a stretcher in a corridor in a Yogyakarta hospital where I begged passers-by for water. Then I went back and read an earlier attempt I'd made in 2008 to write about the same experience and was startled to find that I recalled being left lying on *my front* on the stretcher in the hospital corridor, in a more undignified manner. I asked Michael about it.

'Did this happen to me, was I actually lying face down?'

'Yes, don't you remember that episode in the rehab gym?'

I remembered the episode. A physiotherapist at the rehabilitation hospital in Perth asked me to do an exercise that required me to lie face down on a plinth. It was the first time since the crash that I had been asked to lie on my front. I did it, and was immediately overcome with panic. My breathing became rapid, I started sobbing uncontrollably. Michael and the physiotherapist quickly sat me up and grabbed some screens to give me privacy. It took a long time for me to calm down and resume the rehab. The feeling of lying on my stomach had brought on all kinds of traumatic memories and feelings of that morning when I was abandoned on a stretcher, lying face down in a congested corridor. But, by 2012, my memory had wiped that disturbing detail.

Sometimes, I have flashes—small details that my mind retrieves without warning. These episodes are always unsettling.

Like my watch. Recently, I was reading an article about the horrific injuries suffered by the Japanese victims of the Hiroshima atomic bomb, and how the burns had made patterns on their skin of the clothes they were wearing at the time. Suddenly I remembered the watch I was wearing the day of the crash. It was metallic, the brand was Fossil. I last saw its metal band dangling unhinged from my arm, blackened and charred; the clasp was broken. The watch must have protected me from the fire, for one of the only unscarred pieces of skin on my left arm—still pink like a newborn's and hairless, but flat and smooth—is a patch the size of a twenty-cent piece on the top of my wrist, where the watch face would have been.

Another flash, a few days after the watch. We were in the car, driving to Sydney, Michael and I, when suddenly an image came into my head. I was lying on a bed in the hospital in Yogyakarta.

One of the Indonesian nurses had a big pair of scissors and was cutting off the burnt and soiled clothes I had been wearing on the plane. In ten years, Michael had never heard me mention this detail before.

I am most afraid of dreaming details of the crash.

I have recurring dreams about flying in aeroplanes where the plane is out of control, but, mercifully, in my dreams I am always spared. We land safely. Will my dreams always end this way?

In 2011, I was pregnant and dreamt the baby was delivered while I was unconscious and it was decided for me that the child would be named after one of the passengers who died in the crash.

After Malaysia Airlines Flight 17 crashed over the Ukraine in 2014, I read a news article about a reporter who picked through the personal belongings of the victims among the debris. It upset me and made me wonder what happened to my own luggage I had with me that day, and whether there were remnants left. Had people sifted through them too? I had always assumed my phone, wallet, passport, keys and laptop were completely destroyed in the fire. Perhaps they weren't.

That night I dreamt I visited a large hangar in Indonesia where all the belongings of the dead and injured passengers from my flight were stored. My things were there, laid out on high metal shelves, in this hangar of my dream-making, after all this time.

VI

These are the reasons I could not, for so long, look in the boxes. This is why I could not, for so long, write about what happened to me. This is why I could not, still cannot, speak of it. It was self-preservation.

I told a psychologist at the rehabilitation hospital in Perth something of what had happened to me in Indonesia.

'I have never met anyone who has experienced so much trauma,' she said later.

In the years since, I have revisited traumatic events when absolutely necessary, in order to overcome some psychological barrier that threatened to stop me functioning (because I had to fly to Perth for more surgery, for instance, or because I had to go to hospital to have a caesarean section). I knew, however, that had I spent any more time than this with my memories of the crash, I would not have had the mental capacity, the strength, to do the things I had fought so hard to stay alive for.

Countless people, including my father, urged me to read the Douglas Bader biography, *Reach for the Sky*. Bader lost both legs when he crashed his Bulldog aeroplane doing aerobatics in 1930 and went on to become the Royal Air Force's most celebrated Second World War fighter pilot. The entreaties to read the book were well-meaning. Bader's bravery and resilience (he survived nearly three years as a prisoner of war of the Germans, without legs) were no doubt inspirational, but for years I refused to read it.

Finally, in the autumn of 2015, I decided I was ready, and picked up the book.

There is a moment in it where Bader, who'd just met a ten-year-old boy who lost both legs after spilling burning petrol all over himself, speaks to the child's father.

'The boy just doesn't realise how serious it is yet,' the father tells Bader worriedly.

Bader responds, '[T]hat's the one thing he must *never* realise. You've got to make him feel this is another game he's got to learn, not something that will cripple him. Once you frighten him with it he's beaten.'[4]

It wasn't denial that stopped me revisiting the event before now. It was survival.

The first time I spoke to Paul Roos, who was then coach of the Sydney Swans AFL team, I was being wheeled from the burns unit to have an MRI scan. (The Swans learnt of my situation after they were contacted by a friend of Michael's who knew I was a supporter of the club.) Roosy had rung a few days earlier, but I had been too down to take the call. I started to tell him that I had been a marathon runner, that I used to run every day, that I couldn't imagine a life without running.

'Focus on what you can do and not on what you can't,' Roosy told me.

I did.

I refused to dwell on what had happened, on what I had lost. I focused all my energy on making the life I still had worthwhile. What could I do to make that a happy life? This was the only question I was interested in. I had to silence the past in order to keep going. I had to live in the present and the future and open myself to what was still possible.

I declined requests for interviews about the crash from other journalists and documentary filmmakers. If somebody (friend, colleague, stranger) asked me about the crash, I had an instant physical and emotional response: I froze. I still freeze at the unexpected interrogation, even after writing this. My mind and body just shut down.

Soon after returning home to Canberra, I told a friend I didn't want to think or talk about the crash.

'So, when *do* you think you will be able to confront what happened to you?' the person asked.

I could only stare in disbelief.

An editor I'd never met emailed me after I arrived home from hospital and asked: 'I am really curious, what do you think was going through the pilot's head when he crashed the plane?'

Feeling sick in my stomach, appalled at the invasive, ghoulish question, I replied that it was too upsetting for me to talk about.

A friend of a colleague I met for the first time, years after the crash, asked breathlessly, after the briefest of introductions: 'I hear you were in a plane crash. Was it life-changing?'

I had to fight the urge to get straight back into the car and drive away.

The awful impotence that is associated with trauma also explains why I guarded my story so fiercely. Trauma divests you of control over yourself, your life, your destiny as you imagined it until that point. I lost so many things in the plane crash, one thing I would not let it take was my story and the telling of it. I grew very protective of the story of my trauma.

My story was unknowable, except through me.

VII

Seven years had passed when, in the lead up to Christmas 2014, I tentatively opened the crash boxes.

I asked Michael to bring them in from the garage and, not knowing what sort of response I would have this time, I opened the first one.

Something magical happened. I kept reading; I couldn't stop. Days flowed into nights. I found myself smiling. There were tears, but they were often happy ones. I even laughed. A torrent of positive emotions—love, fondness, affection—flowed from those boxes. I was stunned by the generosity and strength of feeling that lifted from the pages of the cards, letters and emails, and by their eloquence.

'With the morning's first light I thought of you, and this afternoon you were on my mind,' wrote Audrey, a stranger.

'We're all joyous that you made it, as only you could, and only you can. And these are just the thoughts of someone who's never met you,' wrote Suzanne.

Written on a hospital napkin was a note from the father of one of the passengers who had died on the plane with me. 'Chin up love,' he'd scrawled in blue pen. Next to his name was a picture of a heart with an arrow through it.

The love was like a physical force, a warmth that wrapped itself around me. I can feel it even as I write these words. I found such genuine affection in those boxes: so many people—friends, colleagues, contacts, people from my past and absolute strangers— cared about me, were willing me to survive, to keep fighting, to recover, to get back to living.

'Anonymous' wrote to me about losing a close family member in an accident when he or she was twenty: 'I would do anything in the world to have this person back in my life . . . his soul and his laughs . . . if I am sharing this with you now [it] is because it is always important to remember that one heart is more important than 2 legs or 2 arms.'

The governor-general wrote to me about how as company commander in Vietnam he had several soldiers lose both their legs to the top of the thigh through anti-personnel mines. His soldiers, with their new legs, 'took it upon themselves to meet subsequent casualty aircraft returning from Vietnam to show those badly wounded that all was not lost'.

Among the senders were people from almost every episode of my life: high-school friends and teachers, classmates and lecturers from my university days, former flatmates, rowers from my rowing days, travellers I'd met overseas, family friends. Some told me things they'd never shared before.

An old friend of my mother wrote that when she asked my father (an Australian of English ancestry) after my birth what he thought of the name my mother had given me, he said he preferred the Italian version ('Cinzia'), while in his heavy Italian accent my grandfather told her he would have preferred 'Sharon'.

A friend from my law student days, a man of very few words, wrote in a letter: 'While watching you row in a regatta at Penrith . . . your dad said something. At the time you hated your job. (I think you were the lift controller at David Jones?) He said something along the lines of, "you could do things you hated", that you just did it. Even though other people couldn't, he said you were strong. I don't think he really knew.'

Another friend of ours from Macquarie University was a man to whom words came much more easily, but perhaps not these: 'I call them "my Cynthia moments". Every single day without fail I think of you. These moments are part of my day, part of my routine . . . I have always been proud of you. I've always admired you. It was like that before any of this tragedy—not because of it . . . Cynthia changed her career with courage I haven't been able to muster. She set out to see the world, make her mark on it, engage in adventure through Africa and South America—she triumphed over her adversity because that is who she is, it is a manifestation of what it means to be Cynthia.'

There were lawyers from the two Sydney firms I had worked at, friends and colleagues from my newspaper and the wider journalism fraternity, contacts I had made reporting (refugee advocates, diplomats, war veterans, members of the defence force hierarchy, politicians and their staffers). There were people who had experienced major burns, limb amputations and spinal injuries and their families, religious people, flight attendants. It was a profound well of human kindness.

A lawyer I'd worked with at my last law firm job, but hadn't spoken to since the day I left, wrote: 'I will always remember our "neighbourly" chats at Allens, where you impressed me with your determination to follow your heart, to pursue your dreams, to embark on a career in writing for a different audience and cause. You told me you loved to write. I suspect your excellent advice on exclusions/limitations of liability . . . (endorsed not only by your employers but also a leading SC) may have been a turning point, convincing you that your talents were better suited to conveying a different message, irrespective of the rewarding career had you stayed. I remember asking you what you wanted to achieve, and you saying that you wanted to work in foreign affairs, or be a foreign correspondent. I think you're almost there.'

There was the business card of Ron Walker, the chairman of Fairfax, the company that owned my newspaper. (Ron stood out among all the newspaper bosses in never stopping, in ten years, to look out for me.) It simply said: 'Dearest Cynthia—we love you very much—Ron Walker.'

One of the most moving messages was a letter from a woman from the company's payroll, whose surname I do not know, whom I have never met and could not track down when I tried. She knitted the green shawl. She described herself as 'one of those obsessive women, who does not leave the house without knitting in my bag'.

'I just love the whole process—flipping through pattern books, choosing colours and yarns, the anticipation of a journey as the first stitch is cast on.'

Uncertainties had initially held her back, she told me.

'Will you feel your privacy has been invaded, perhaps green is not your colour, maybe you hate handmade things or, worse, lace.'

But then: 'This wrap was a particular challenge, particularly the crisscross ends. They were unpicked and knitted, then unpicked and reknitted again, while I slowly tore my hair out. But in the end I got there, and this wrap is the most beautiful piece of knitting I've ever done. I'm not in the habit of knitting for complete strangers, but your story motivated and moved me to pick up pins and cast on.'

It is perhaps unfortunate that I did not permit myself to engage with and absorb all this positive feeling long before now. But the fact is, I couldn't.

In the box was a letter from the artist who painted the Stradbroke Island landscape.

'What has happened to you has moved me and my family greatly,' he wrote. His eleven-year-old daughter had chosen the painting from among others in his studio because it was 'happy'.

In February 2015, after finding the artist's letter in the crash boxes, I decided to contact him. I sent him an email, apologising for how long it had taken me to get in touch. I tried to explain my tardiness, and told him how much his painting had meant to me (and Michael) at the time.

'We would look at it and promise ourselves that one day, when I got out, we would get a beach shack with a view like the one you painted. It was a part of our dreaming and our promises to each other about how we would rebuild our lives,' I wrote.

The artist did not write back for many months, and I told myself I'd obviously left it too late. Then, in May, an email arrived. He invited us to attend his latest exhibition in Sydney. Michael and I drove to the gallery in Kings Cross one Saturday afternoon.

'I sent you the painting because I was told your hospital room had no windows,' he said.

'Michael and I would look at the painting at night and it would transport us out of whatever terrible moment we were in,' I said.

We embraced. That I was there in the gallery, in my wheelchair, was another sign that I was finally beginning to heal.

VIII

Opening the boxes wasn't hard only for me.

Michael was Canberra bureau chief of the *Herald Sun* in 2007. We had been together since late 2003 and, after a tumultuous few years, including a number of torrid break-ups, I moved into Michael's house in February 2007, the month before the plane crash. Ours was the only serious relationship I'd had and I knew from its earliest days I wanted no other.

On the day of the plane crash Michael was at his head office in Melbourne, preparing to interview the prime minister, John Howard, that afternoon. He was jotting down ideas for his interview and a newspaper column into a Spirax notebook when news of the crash reached him. The same notebook became the place where he recorded everything that happened next—phone calls, conversations, messages—as he frantically tried to find me and establish whether I was alive.

Michael's notes were written in his perfect shorthand, learnt with great proficiency as a newspaper cadet when he was hired straight out of high school at eighteen. It was totally indecipherable by me. I couldn't understand a word and, for seven years, that didn't bother me. As I was going through the crash boxes, however, I knew the time had come to ask Michael to translate his shorthand notes into English. His was the only comprehensive record I had of what happened to me in the hours, days, weeks after the crash, since I had written nothing myself.

I underestimated the effect transcribing this material would have on Michael. I thought of the crash as my own personal tragedy and assumed that when I was ready to confront the details of it, my husband and family would be too. Michael resisted the transcriptions for weeks.

'We'll just do half an hour a night,' I suggested.

He kept putting me off. I begged, pleaded, demanded, argued. Finally, Michael gave in.

We started the task of transcription: Michael reading slowly, me typing impatiently. I soon saw the latent grief resurfacing as I forced him to revisit this period in our lives. There were surprises in Michael's notes, things that happened while I was in the coma—beautiful moments—that he had never told me about before. But there were also moments of intense pain.

On Friday, 9 March, two days after the crash, Michael transcribed a text message from his phone. It was left late that night by a friend of his from the press gallery in Canberra. She was at a bowling club some of us frequented at the end of the week for beers and karaoke. My signature song (I felt I should have one since karaoke was one of Michael's favourite pastimes) was the Motels' 'Total Control'.

Michael read out the phone message to me: 'Hope this does not wake you. We are at karaoke. Tony [the karaoke host] grabbed me and asked me about Cynthia. He asked me to sing "Total Control" for Cynthia so I just did. I had tears in my eyes. Fuck, Harvs, we are missing Cynthia and you.'

Michael cried as he read it out, and so did I, for how much hurt it caused him to remember this time.

IX

There was an email I kept from that period, one of the very few I wrote from Perth.

It was, in hindsight, a wretched plea to the people who inhabited my old world, the one I'd been snatched from, to treat me the same way, think of me the same way, as they had before the crash.

I wrote it in July, from the rehabilitation hospital, to a friend in Canberra, on the BlackBerry that Ron Walker insisted be organised for me (though he called it a 'Blueberry'). I had, that day, worn the back brace for my spinal fracture for the last time, and I was allowed to start walking again. My new legs were about to be cast in plaster.

'They'll be shorter than I was but it's just a start,' I told Andrew, forcing myself to sound positive.

I mentioned my hair was falling out; a delayed reaction to trauma, I was told by nurses.

Then this: 'I miss you too, miss my old life, it's a new one now . . . no legs and an all-over body burn to grapple with . . . Anyway, I hope it doesn't affect friendships or work when I get back—I am still me with the same sense of humour.'

Even as I wrote it, I don't think I believed it, though I desperately wanted to, and I wanted others to as well. My world had ruptured; I wasn't 'still me'.

The letters and cards in the boxes were written about an attractive, popular young woman in her early thirties who loved her friends, her colleagues, her job, her career, who—as my old lawyer colleague said—was on the cusp of becoming a foreign correspondent. She was athletic, adventurous, an intrepid traveller to exotic places. She read fashion magazines as well as newspapers and international relations textbooks, wore pencil skirts to work and fitted jeans to the pub, loved high heels as much as hiking boots. She was vivacious, she made people laugh, she had the world at her feet. She had feet.

That was the person colleagues wrote about, who was depicted in the extensive media coverage of the crash. That was the person the kind strangers thought they were writing to. The truth was that person did not make it out of the plane crash. She was not the woman who pulled herself with a broken back and burnt legs and arms from the wreckage begging to be saved.

For a long time, it was unbearable for me to read about that other person, to remember her, to celebrate her as those in the boxes did. Many of the correspondents in the boxes wrote about her as if she was coming back—as if she were going to, any week now, return to her desk, to her job and glamorous identity as a foreign affairs reporter, and carry on just as she had been doing so spiritedly before. Lying in hospital in Perth, I was coming to terms with the reality that she was forever gone.

For similar reasons, it was sometimes easier for me to deal with new friends and acquaintances, people who had not known me before the crash. It was too painful to see the heartbreak in the eyes of old friends who kept remembering and comparing me to how I was. I was certain I heard one of them, out of deep concern for me, offer to help end my life if it became too much to bear. Today I don't know if the words really were spoken, or if I only imagined them. Another friend of many years silenced me when I tried to talk about how my closeness to death had affected me. She did not let me say that, sometimes, I felt that I also died with those other passengers on the plane.

I realised that while the world and the people around me remained unchanged, I was different now. I understood life differently. My injuries changed the way I related to the world and the way the world related to me. Even language was no longer the same for me. Common expressions I hadn't thought twice about using myself before—'no leg to stand on', 'pull the other leg'—could unsettle me now. I learnt early on to hide my feelings, though. I didn't want to become awkward for people to be around.

It took seven years to mourn that person who existed before the crash, to the point where I could read what others had written about her without feeling like my insides were being ripped apart. Now, I can read about that Cynthia with affection. What a girl! What fun she must have had.

Along the way, I created a new me, someone I could present to the world, someone the people who knew me before would not have to feel so sorry for.

X

Meanwhile, there was the other box. As I processed my feelings about the contents of the crash boxes, I began looking more closely through my grandparents' papers.

My grandparents' box was a receptacle of secrets that, each time I opened it, offered up tantalising new details of their early lives. But the revelations were always frustratingly incomplete, leading to more questions. I'd discover a new fact about Nonno's wartime experiences—the location of a work camp, for instance— so I researched it further. The trail would go cold. I returned to the box again and again, reopening envelopes I'd already searched, hoping to find something I had missed.

As I pieced together the story of my grandfather's internment, I longed to stumble on a clue that would to lead me to Amelia and her time during the war.

I sent off documents to Italian and German friends and colleagues to be translated. I wrote emails and letters to museums and historians and various official archives throughout Australia, Italy and Germany. Some were helpful; others were not. I contacted the International Tracing Service in Bad Arolsen, Germany, the archive for documents relating to the victims of Nazism. They found no records of my grandfather. I wrote to the Italian Ministry of Defence, to the historical offices of the Italian navy, to Italy's embassy and its consulate in Australia, to German companies. I read accounts of Italian POWs that I could find in English and my mother translated the ones written in Italian. I wrote to the different foundations and agencies in Germany dedicated to POWs. I hired researchers: an Italian academic to help me locate documents from official archives in Trieste; a librarian in America to look for remnants of Amelia's life there; a German PhD student to search for information about POWs held in Germany. I dispatched friends to photograph camps, factories, work sites, graves. I contacted the Italian Society of Authors and Publishers and scoured eBay in a futile quest to locate old cast lists of productions in Italy that Amelia may have danced in as a young woman. I emailed churches, opera companies and local chapters of the Red Cross in the United States. I engaged an Italian tutor from Turin who helped me with translations and research in Canberra, while her daughter scoured libraries and archives in Europe, Naples, Rome and the United Nations High Commissioner for Refugees (UNHCR) headquarters in Geneva. Later, I hired professional genealogical researchers in Germany and the United States.

Some of the revelations my investigations produced were disquieting, particularly for my mother. It became apparent how minimal her knowledge was of her father's experiences as a POW— how little he had told her; how little she had asked him. My mother was defensive when I questioned her about this.

'By the time I was old enough to be interested I had four children and I never had anyone to look after them,' she said.

I wondered if it was my mother's lack of curiosity or time that meant she didn't ask more questions, or something else: an unspoken understanding that this was a subject her father did not wish to speak about with his daughters. In place of his own fuller narrative about his POW experiences, Alfredo's family clung to fragments—vague, sometimes contradictory and, it seemed to me, slightly mythical stories—which my intrusions were disturbing. I was throwing small pebbles into a still but deep ocean rock pool, which started to lose its clarity.

One of my first discoveries was a card in my grandparents' papers with the word 'ALKETT' in large capital letters on one side. Below it was my grandfather's name, the number 680332, and some German writing, which translated means: 'This card entitles the holder to pass through the main gate. It must be shown to supervisors, gatekeepers and firemen. The card is non-transferable.'

There was a large red 'I' in the background (which at first I mistook for a 'J', but my grandfather was Catholic, not Jewish), and the number 189 stamped across the face of the card. At the bottom was written: 'ALKETT ALTMÄRKISCHES KETTENWERK GmbH BERLIN-BORSIGWALDE'. On the other side of the pass was a photograph of my grandfather, looking young and dreadfully sad. The photograph was stamped, and below it was an Italian translation of the German words on the front of the pass.

I looked up the name, Alkett, on the internet. It was, according to a Wikipedia entry, a 'major manufacturer of armored vehicles for the Wehrmacht during World War II'. The main factory was located in Berlin, in the neighbourhood of Borsigwalde. Between 3000 and 4000 employees worked at the Alkett plants, including forced labourers—among them Italian POWs. Soviet troops occupied the Alkett plants on 23 April 1945. Documents from among my nonno's papers told me he was liberated from internment the following day.

Was Nonno a forced labourer?

From here some pieces of Alfredo's story began falling into place. The Italian armistice was signed by Italy's new Badoglio

Alfredo's Alkett pass

government on 8 September 1943, following the arrest of Benito Mussolini six weeks earlier. German troops in Italy immediately began rounding up Italian soldiers and deporting them to transit, labour and concentration camps in Germany and elsewhere.

Alfredo, according to his military papers, was captured by the German armed forces on 9 September 1943. Adolf Hitler issued an order on 20 September 1943 that Italian prisoners of war were to be known as Italian Military Internees (IMIs), denying them international law protections normally afforded to POWs.

Suddenly I understood: my grandfather was an IMI—a Second World War classification I had not heard of before—and was forced by the Nazis to work in a tank factory.

My mother had no idea her father had been a forced labourer, and at first it seemed she didn't want to believe me. It was as though I was lessening the legacy of her father's trauma. As a forced labourer,

Alfredo suffered grave indignities to his mind and body, physical and psychological traumas. He would have seen fellow prisoners die and believed he would die too. But the image my mother had in her head was shaped by watching documentaries about Nazi concentration camps. The idea of her father as a forced labourer did not fit with this narrative.

I showed my mother the photographs a German friend took for me of Alkett as it looks today: a factory on a suburban Berlin street with red bricks and white window frames, a tall arch and a big metal gate.

'I think this is where Nonno was a forced labourer.'

'It looks nothing like the picture I had in my mind.'

'What picture did you have in your mind?'

'I pictured Auschwitz.'

I realised how fragile my mother's memories of her father were as my investigations began to destabilise them.

There were other documents from the war. There was some kind of passport of the Deutsches Reich, pink in colour, issued to Alfredo in August 1944. I later discovered that it was a provisional alien's passport, the Third Reich's temporary pass for foreigners given to POWs and forced labourers deported to Germany. Most of the pages were blank, but there was that same sad photo of young Alfredo again, stamped with the Nazi Party symbol: the eagle standing over the swastika. It looked as though it had been folded in half—perhaps to fit into a pocket.

There was also a handwritten postcard, written in Italian on the official POW stationery, dated January 1944 and addressed to his eldest sister, Assunta, in Trieste. He asked her to send 'bread, chocolate, cigarettes not above 5 kg'. Did his family send him bread from Italy? Was he allowed to receive chocolate in the Nazi-run camp? I had so many questions, the barest minimum of documents, and nobody to ask.

Among the military records were a small number of items that hinted at my grandparents' inner lives.

There was, for example, a clipping from 1937: a newsletter item about Alfredo, who received an award when he was thirteen for rescuing a drowning child. Alfredo was pictured wearing his Balilla uniform, the outfit of the Fascist youth organisation to which all children in Italy at that time had to belong. His eagle-badged cap sat slightly lower over his right eye; a scarf was draped around his shoulders. The paper was old and crumbling, held together with three pieces of sticky tape.

There were also poems. One was titled 'La Mia Prigionia' ('My Imprisonment'). It was about a young prisoner of war who dreamt about going home to his mother. The poem was written in faded pencil on a piece of ancient-looking yellowed paper with what looked like a burn mark on one edge. There was also a typed version, with smudged 'm's and 'n's and white-out in a couple of places.

Who was the author? I wondered. And why had Alfredo's wife, my nonna, kept it all those years?

XI

There was, to my great disappointment, little about Amelia among my grandparents' documents. The sum total was a few photographs and a holy card.

The pictures were stunning, professional shots (no one in Amelia's family owned a camera at that time). In one, Amelia's head was turned. Her features in profile were angular, her chin pronounced, her dark hair long and wavy.

Another photograph was especially beguiling: Amelia in full vaudeville-style theatrical make-up. Her face was heavily painted. Her eyebrows were razor sharp and pointed outwards in two diagonal straight lines from the bridge of her nose. Her eyelashes were thick and long and separated so that it looked as though they may have been painted carefully on to the photograph afterwards. Her lips were like the smiling joker's in a pack of cards, slathered with thick, shiny lipstick. On the back of the photograph was the name and address of a professional photography shop, Diana Foto, near the Trevi Fountain in Rome. The photo was undated. (At the address today, I discovered, there is a cafe called Planet Pizza. With my researcher's assistance, I tried to find out more about the photography shop, but we were frustrated by a typically obstructive Italian bureaucracy. The relevant archives in Rome were moving office, the archivists couldn't say when they would reopen and, in any case, they'd need the name of the original shop owner, which I didn't have.)

The holy card was laminated, with Mary's image on the front. On the back was Amelia's name, the date of her death and a prayer that began, 'We have loved her during her life'. Jesus' mother, Mary, featured prominently in all my family's stories, I discovered. She was the human link to God—more accessible, when God could seem so indifferent, so unmoved.

There was a time when my grandparents would have had many old letters from Amelia. My aunt, Marina, remembers how her parents spoke in hushed tones whenever one arrived from America. Amelia was a 'closed subject'.

'I used to see these letters being passed around that dining table, but they waited for me to be out of the room or busy somewhere before they discussed them.'

My aunt told me her mother probably threw away Amelia's letters in the last big clean-out she did before suffering the strokes, when she divided up the family photos between her daughters and discarded old documents she thought would be of no interest to anyone. I received this information with helpless regret. Had I asked my grandmother's permission to read these letters, what might I have found in them? What insights had they contained into Amelia and her history with her brother?

I did find documentary records from Amelia's life elsewhere. Her death notice was online and I was also able to track down where she was buried. I asked a couple of Canadian friends working in the United States to visit the cemetery. Her grave was unmarked. My friends emailed photos of the site, and told me she was 'buried at the edge next to the fence and near a small tree'.

I discovered a picture of Amelia's last address listed in the death notice on a real estate website: a century-old red-and-grey wooden American Foursquare-style house, two storeys high with an 'unfinished basement' and a triangular roof and porch.

Freelance researchers located entries for Amelia in the city directories where she lived: her different residences, the names of the boarders she lived with, some of her employers. I learnt that in 1951 she worked in the alteration department of a men's clothing store. There was a gap after that. Her next listed employer was a hospital, in 1956, where she was a waitress in the cafeteria. She worked for a time at a small bridal shop, and her last job was as a seamstress at a tweed shop. I looked up the various employers. The bridal shop was now a hair salon specialising in African-American weaves, cuts and braids. The different shop proprietors were all deceased; one died as recently as 2014.

Subsequently, professional genealogical researchers obtained Amelia's official papers: her American citizenship documents, her probate file, and deed index references showing she owned property in the United States. Much later, they retrieved Amelia's 'Alien

File', the collection of documents the US government keeps on all non-citizens.

One of the first documents the researchers sent was a copy of Amelia's death certificate. Mum had told me that in America, Amelia had been physically assaulted, repeatedly, by a man she was associated with. He had beaten her breasts.

According to the death certificate, Amelia's direct cause of death was brain and lung cancer. The cancer originated in her right breast, which was removed in an operation, possibly a month before she died.

Amelia was 42 when she died—the age I was when I finally started to research her life.

XII

I soon found a possible answer to one of my questions: why my grandfather had not spoken more about his experiences.

I came across a book, *Hitler's Slaves*, published in 2010, about forced labourers in the Second World War. Despite the volumes that had been written about the Holocaust, this was the first book to attempt to comprehensively tell the stories of Hitler's slave labourers, men and women from 27 different countries, of different religious and ethnic backgrounds.

'For decades the history of forced labour has . . . been relatively neglected by research historians,' the authors wrote.[5]

While for many years concentration camp survivors were given an official platform of commemoration and remembrance, this was not the case for forced labourers. Their experiences were viewed as less important than those of other prisoners, even something to be ashamed of. Forced labourers were offered no assistance for dealing with their painful pasts, and kept silent about their stories.

Recognition did not come for the forced labourers of Nazi Germany until the late 1980s. The German government set up a fund (into which some businesses contributed) that, from 2001, belatedly began making modest compensation payments to some of the forced labourers who were victims of National Socialism.

By the time researchers began to systematically collect the individual stories of the forced labourers themselves, in 2005 (2005!), many had already died. Of those still alive, most agreed to provide their testimonies. The survivors said they had felt excluded from history. They told researchers they had never shared their experiences or documents or photos from their time as forced labourers with their children or grandchildren.

'You cannot speak it out. And you are not able to forget,' one person said.[6]

In Italy, the silencing of forced labourers took a slightly different form. Hundreds of thousands of Italian soldiers were taken prisoner by the Germans and sent to internment and work camps in Germany and Poland. But nobody in post-war Italy wanted to hear the stories of members of Italy's armed forces that so ingloriously disbanded in 1943. Political leaders and the Italian public preferred to focus on the anti-Fascist partisan resistance, who fought the German occupiers. The IMIs were forgotten.

Was this how my grandfather felt about his imprisonment? That his experiences were not worthy of remembering, that they were something to be ashamed of? Did he think he was somehow to blame for what happened to him, that it was his fault that he had been forced into working for the German war effort? Is this why he never told his daughters what happened to him in Germany? The more I uncovered of Alfredo's story, the more I wanted to know.

It is a common tale, the grandchildren of survivors of the horrors of the Second World War (the third generation) becoming interested in their grandparents' stories in a way their own children (the second generation) didn't. It is different for the grandchildren, of course. The grandchildren have greater emotional distance than their parents had; it is both easier for them to hear the stories of their grandparents as it is for their grandparents to tell them. For the second generation of survivors of wartime atrocities, their parents' pain could be impenetrable and frightening.

I wondered, if Alfredo were alive today, what would he be telling me? Which parts of his story would he share, which would he not disclose? My mother's sister visited Dachau, the German concentration camp, on a trip to Europe when she was 21. When she got home she asked her father about his POW experiences. He spoke about the hunger and the cold, but nothing more. According to my mother, her father never spoke to her about what Amelia did for him while he was interned. Amelia's role was something my mother only learnt from relatives in Italy, through me. Why did he never speak of it? Did he think his daughters would not be interested? Was it too painful? Had his nieces and nephews inflated her role over time?

I missed my chance to ask my grandfather about what happened to him in the Second World War and I failed to ask my grandmother about her husband's experiences after he was gone. It grieved me that Alfredo's story, and that of his sister who risked so much to help him, was unknowable to me.

XIII

In early 2015, I began planning a trip to Europe.

My parents were already travelling to Italy later that year; they were taking a cruise that began in Istanbul and ended in Rome. Michael, our son and I would meet up with them in Trieste.

I had never been to my mother's birthplace with her before (though I'd been many times on my own). This was my chance to see Trieste through her eyes, to talk to Nonno's remaining relatives with her and to involve her in my research, which was, after all, about her father. We would visit a museum for IMIs in Padua. Then, from Trieste, I would go on to Austria and Germany with Michael and our son.

It was a huge undertaking: it meant flying to Europe for the first time since the crash, and navigating cobblestoned streets in old cities in a wheelchair. But there was no time to waste. All Alfredo's siblings in Trieste had died, but they had children, my mother's cousins, some of whom were old enough to remember Amelia.

It was in the early stages of planning this trip that a light turned on in my head. Literally, as if someone had flicked a switch, I suddenly saw there was one glaring omission from the stories I was pursuing. My mother's. How could I have overlooked this?

I had just hosted a lunch for my family at our house. I was thinking about the book, about new research from the United States that I had received about Amelia. The festivities had barely wrapped up when I argued with my mother over her disapproval of something or other that I had done. There were tears and anger on both sides and off she stormed, returning home to Sydney early.

I spent the next couple of days trying to understand why we argued.

'Why do I always quarrel with Mum?' I asked my younger sister.

'Because you've always needed her approval, I've never understood it,' Juliette replied, implying she knew better than to seek it and also that, unlike me, she didn't need it in the first place.

While I told Mum things, good and bad—knowing the repercussions, I showed her all my school grades, for example—my sister learnt to withhold information that could get her into trouble. She kept the poor marks to herself.

Finally, it hit me. My mother's high demands and expectations. My desperate need to please her, the sense that no matter how hard I tried, I never could. The memories of her disapproval that still lingered, decades on. Like the afternoon, early in high school, when I came home with the news that for the first and only time I had failed a maths test, and she yelled at me in front of her friend. (I went on to take 4 Unit Mathematics, the highest level, for the Higher School Certificate.) Of course, some of this—my mother's reactions, my responses—could be traced back to Mum's challenges as a migrant child.

Wrenched from her home, her relatives, her language, her city, deposited in Australia, a hostile place for southern Europeans in the 1950s, Mum was forced to go to work from the age of fifteen to help pay off her parents' mortgage. These were experiences I had never probed her about. I knew Mum's childhood memories of Australia were incredibly painful for her. I gathered there was a link between them and her sensitivities around her Italian heritage. But I was also aware that if I knew more about her hurt, it would become my hurt. A typical second-generation response: until now, I had wanted to spare myself.

Suddenly, I saw that I had to ask Mum for her story too. My mother was the link between my grandfather and me. In a way, my mother's immigrant experiences had broken something in her, as her father's POW experiences had done for him, as mine had broken me. We each of us had rebuilt ourselves, kept going in the face of the brokenness, but were never the same for it. I had left it too late to know Alfredo's story from his own telling. I now had an opportunity to try to understand my mother's story, as I processed my own.

There was a common theme among these lives that I was trying to decode: Alfredo's, my mother's, Amelia's and my own. Our lives were all interrupted by events and experiences outside our control, in ways that meant we could no longer have the futures we desired and felt destined for.

I was the custodian of my family's shared life. I was the documenter of our interrupted lives.

2

Trieste

I

TRIESTE IS A PLACE I HAVE CARRIED IN MY heart, certainly since I first saw it at nineteen, but probably much longer than that.

My mother says when I returned from that first trip, in 1991, I told her arriving in Trieste had felt strangely like coming home. It made no sense to her then, and still doesn't today. I think my nonno understood or, at least, it made him happy to know I felt that way. Something awoke in me then—or was given form. Trieste was no longer a place that only existed through other people's stories.

Trieste sits in the upper far-right corner of Italy on the Adriatic coast, a former imperial Austro-Hungarian seaport, today a city at the edge of the Italian nation. Pressed up against the Slovenian border, it remains unsure of its own identity, yet it is a huge part of my own.

Jan Morris, the Welsh writer who was stationed in Trieste as a young soldier (then called James) at the end of the Second World War, described the city as 'half-real, half-imagined'.[1]

We look for meaning where we want to find it, and the Trieste of my imagination is full of deeper truths.

II

We sat in a lounge at Sydney Airport, Michael, our son and I, and watched through the window as the Emirates A380 taxied to the gate.

It was mid-October 2015. My parents were already in Europe. They'd been in Turkey; a deadly bombing occurred in Ankara the day their cruise ship left Istanbul. We were all due to arrive in Italy the same day. My parents would disembark in Rome and fly to Trieste, while we were to fly to Venice from Dubai and drive the final 160 kilometres.

Reading emails at the airport I learnt that a local historian in Klagenfurt, Austria, whom I'd arranged to meet there, had located the site where Italian POWs were forced to work in the Second World War. I also received a reply, finally, from the Nazi Forced Labour Documentation Centre in Berlin, confirming it would be open on the dates of our visit.

Away from Canberra, and the intensity of my first postdoctoral year in academia, I felt my head shift into a more reflective space. I reached up to my neck and clasped Nonna's heavy gold medallion with the religious image of the Virgin Mary on one side, and the inscription *Alfredo a Anna* [Alfredo to Anna] *I VI 1953*, marking their sixth wedding anniversary, on the other. The memory of my grandparents was so strong in me at that moment.

I'd already passed through security in my wheelchair, where I explained to the female guard as she started patting me down that my legs were metal.

'What happened to you?'

'Plane crash.'

'Oooooh. A big plane?'

'Yes. Indonesia.'

'I remember that one.'

The pat-down awaiting me in Dubai was worse. I was ushered by a female security guard into a white, windowless room, while Michael waited with our son outside. She closed the door and I stared fixedly at a crumpled paper napkin on the floor as her hands felt my prostheses.

'What's this?' she demanded.

I pulled up my trouser leg to show her my C-Leg—the prosthetic limb with a computerised knee that I wear in place of my left leg. Her face was expressionless; I kept mine the same. She exited the room abruptly, shutting me inside, where it was warm, sticky and airless. I waited alone, wondering what was going to happen next. Did the guard consider my metal legs to be some kind of threat?

Finally, after what may have been fifteen minutes—there was no clock in the room—the unsmiling woman came back and signalled to me that I could go.

I used to love airports. During my law school days, I'd sometimes drive out to Sydney Airport with a friend and we'd sit in one of the coffee lounges watching the people and planes coming and going, daydreaming about our next overseas trips (India and Peru were always high on my list).

My first excursions to Sydney Airport as a child were to see my grandparents off when they left for visits back to Italy. They were emotional farewells, but us grandchildren were consoled by thoughts of the gifts they'd bring back.

I channelled these positive feelings as I sat watching the A380, so that I didn't have to think about getting on an aircraft.

The following afternoon, after a night in Dubai without my wheelchair (which the airline wrongly checked through to Italy), I finally spotted Venice through the aeroplane window. I could see the white sails of the boats against the blue sea. I smiled and scribbled in my notebook: 'Trieste is in me and it is not me. It feels foreign, Italy. My ambivalence is like Trieste's ambivalence, the belonging but not quite belonging.'

I looked out the window again. I saw the strange land formations in the now-indigo sea, the half-submerged islands, the sandbanks, the cupola of the Basilica di San Marco, a passing flock of white birds. I breathed deeply, held on tight to my son, who was sleeping, and we landed.

My wheelchair and our car were thankfully waiting at Venice Airport. Outside, I breathed in the exhaust fumes and thick cigarette smoke and rejoiced at being back on Italian soil after so long. We headed north on the autostrada. Spotting my parents' plane from Rome flying overhead, we decided to surprise them, and picked them up at Trieste's airport on our way into the city.

III

Approaching Trieste from the south by car, you follow a road that winds along the shimmering, expansive waters of the Gulf of Trieste. You enter Trieste through a rocky arch, cut out of the limestone that forms part of a steep plateau above the city. In the autumn, the rock is covered with the crimson leaves of the sumac bush that is typical of the Carso (in German, the Karst) region that Trieste shares with Slovenia.

Umberto Saba, the Trieste-born poet, described the city's aspect simply and sorrowfully in his poem, 'Avevo' (I Had):

Avevo una città bella tra i monti / rocciosi e il mare luminoso.
I had a beautiful city between the stony / hills and the radiant sea.[2]

Trieste's history is rich with literary luminaries, and their personal stories reflect the city's turbulent political past. Saba, whose mother was Jewish, had an antique bookshop in Trieste that he was forced to give up under the Fascist anti-Jewish laws of the 1930s. In this particular poem he was deeply bitter and aggrieved at the losses he suffered under the Fascists and Nazis.

On the way into Trieste, you pass Castello di Miramare, the city's white, fairytale-like castle. It was built in the 1850s, when Trieste was under Austrian rule, for Archduke Ferdinand Maximilian, who never lived to enjoy it (he was executed in Mexico aged 34 and his wife, Charlotte, went mad). The castle, designed in the Romantic European architectural style, rests enchantingly on a rocky promontory staring out to sea, like a wedding cake decoration without its cake. From 1943 to 1945, when Trieste was occupied by Nazi Germany, the castle was used as a residence for officers. After the war, it served as headquarters for the Allied administrators, who stayed until 1954. Today it's a museum.

The Irish writer James Joyce lived for many years as a young man in Trieste, arriving in 1904. He mentioned Miramare in a letter to his partner, Nora Barnacle, on a trip back to his native Dublin, and pondered how he would feel when he saw the castle again, situated among the trees and quays of Trieste. James looked upon the Adriatic city with 'eyes of longing'. He felt nearer to his 'soul's peace' in Trieste, and was dismayed by the city's deterioration under the Italians, who annexed the city in 1918.[3]

Joyce departed Trieste for good in 1920, but his presence is immortalised in a bronze statue on a pedestrian bridge over the Canal Grande, which flows from the sea into the city up to the steps of the blue-domed St Spyridon, a Serbian Orthodox church.

We arrived at our hotel on the Corso Camillo Benso Conte di Cavour, a short distance from the Canal Grande, and I was momentarily dismayed by its nondescript modern exterior. I had chosen it over the more historic hotels rich with character on the Piazza dell'Unita, Trieste's spectacular central square that fronts the Adriatic, because it was accessible. It had a special-purpose lift that opened directly onto the street and had to be unlocked by a receptionist at the front desk each time we needed to use it.

It was almost sunset and I wanted to show Michael the piazza before it got dark, so we left a tired child with my parents and headed out with the wheelchair.

Bumping and jolting along the broken pavement, I peered down the side streets at the centuries-old white stone buildings. None was more than five or six storeys high, some were greyed with pollution and rundown, but they were charming all the same with their large, ornate, wooden doors.

I felt a swirl of conflicting emotions.

I was so grateful to be here—to be well enough to travel to Trieste again, to be finally sharing this with Michael, to be experiencing the city with my mother. Yet I was restricted by the wheelchair. I would not spend leisurely afternoons exploring these cobblestoned back streets on foot, as I had done many times before. I would not experience those unscripted moments of foreign travel that happen when you can walk uneven surfaces, hilly streets and ancient stony stairways unthinkingly, without the worry of a C-Leg coming loose from perspiration and causing skin grafts to blister and break down.

Trieste was sparkling.

A cruise ship, the *Costa Mediterranea*, was docked in front of the Piazza dell'Unita, its decks illuminated by cabin lights. The sky was cloudy, the sun had almost gone, and there was a smattering of people in the piazza on this mild night. The streetlamps were lit. The town hall, with its big clock, was ablaze, facing directly out to the sea. Miramare was visible in the distance along the coast towards the west.

I took Michael for a meal at Rudy's, a pub behind our hotel, for some typical Trieste fare. We ate thick slices of *prosciutto crudo*, *jota* (bean and pork soup), *patate in tecia* (potatoes with bacon and onion), and more-familiar schnitzel. Michael was underwhelmed by the traditional dishes, which seemed more Austrian than Italian to him—but that's Trieste. The Trieste-born writer Scipio Slataper, who died fighting the Austrians in the First World War as a volunteer in the Italian army, described the city as one without cultural traditions, 'a point where cultures meet'.[4]

I was eager for Michael—who always needs time to embrace new ideas—to love Trieste instantly. I'd been anticipating this moment, our first meal together in this city of my mother and grandparents, from our earliest days together. Yet Michael just wanted to sleep.

We left Rudy's, Michael pushing my wheelchair. On the way back to our hotel we passed through Piazza Vittorio Veneto. Its huge fountain—three tritons holding up a giant shell on their backs—was softly illuminated in the lightly falling rain.

IV

My first trip to Trieste, in the early 1990s, was sponsored by an association for Italian immigrants, Giuliani nel Mondo.

My grandfather learnt of the trip in the Italian language newspaper, *La Fiamma*, and he and my grandmother paid for the flight. I went as part of a group of 30 young adults, the majority of them South Americans, whose parents had emigrated from the northeast Italian region of Friuli Venezia Giulia. For a month, I visited Trieste's monuments, listened to lectures in Italian, and got to know my mother's extended family. The trip ended with a magical tour through Venice, Florence and Rome.

The last time I was in Trieste was September 2001.

I was there for a fortnight, staying with relatives. During that time I took a short train trip into Slovenia, and spent a night on my own in the capital, Ljubljana. On 11 September, I was at the house of my mother's cousin, Giuliana, whose daughter, Vera, is the same age as me. Vera lived with me while we both worked in London in the mid-1990s. It was early afternoon when someone turned on the television and we watched the hijacked airliners fly into the twin towers of the World Trade Center in New York. It was disconcerting to be so far from home that day, having to listen to the coverage of the unfolding horror in a language that wasn't my own.

I had my first experience of a foreign hospital during that trip.

On a break from my job reporting legal affairs in the press gallery in Canberra (a previously quiet round that was about to become swamped by national security issues), I decided to get a nose stud. Something discreet, elegant yet bohemian was what I had in mind. A relative worked in a jewellery shop and arranged the piercing: a chunky, plastic-encased diamante. My nose quickly became infected.

I couldn't get the stud out of my nose, and when my nostril became alarmingly inflamed and painful, Vera took me to hospital for a medical extraction. At the Ospedale Maggiore, a team of four or five doctors and nurses surrounded me on a table and one of them began pulling the object from my nose with what looked like a set of pliers.

'*Oh mio Dio,*' I heard one nurse mutter. 'Oh my God.'

'*Che grande buco!*' another gasped. 'What a big hole!'

The stud, when it was finally pulled free, was the size of a wisdom tooth. I left hospital with a big plaster covering the giant crater on the side of my nose, feeling sore and ridiculous.

Having spent my twenties coming and going from Trieste, I thought I knew the city's character well. But Trieste is elusive, difficult to know, and my capacity to penetrate its veneer was limited by my level of proficiency in Italian, which is conversational but not completely fluent (Mum refused to speak to us in Italian when we were children).

The city's complex character was reinforced for me when I read Saba's poetry with my Italian tutor, a university lecturer in Italian language and literature.

Saba's poems are deceptively simple: he works in tone, not images, it is said. Beneath apparently clear language lie complex meanings that draw on autobiographical material from Saba's life. In his poem 'Trieste', Saba writes of Trieste having '*una scontrosa / grazia*'. How to translate this, how to understand what Saba is conveying about the city? *Scontrosa* can mean moody or sullen, while *grazia* means grace. 'Trieste has a rude charm' is one scholarly translation.[5]

A city that, the poet hinted, is at once familiar, yet strange. Would the city about which Saba wrote ever make itself known to me? Had it already?

Researching Trieste's history, I was surprised to discover that the city's Italianness is much more tenuous than I had once believed. An Italian identity has at different times, for different reasons, been forced onto Trieste.

My earliest consciousness of Trieste as a place was through the colourful souvenir tea towels with which I dried dishes in my grandparents' kitchen as a child. On these tea towels, which you can purchase in *tabaccherie* along the Canal Grande, Trieste is always depicted through the puffing, cartoonish face of la Bora, the powerful wind that blows from the north-east in cold, unpredictable gusts during winter. It is so fierce that some of Trieste's footpaths have handrails made of chains for pedestrians to grip to stop them from falling over.

La Bora is also invoked as a metaphor for the way the city has been buffeted throughout its history, claimed variously by Austria, Germany, Italy and Yugoslavia as rightfully their own.[6]

Italy's claim to Trieste dates to 177 BC, when the city was established as a Roman colony. Yet Trieste had more than five centuries of Austrian guardianship from 1382, after it sought the protection of the Habsburg monarchy from a voracious Venetian Republic. The city prospered under the Austrians, who gave it free port privileges from the early eighteenth century. It was an important commercial centre of European trade, a bustling cosmopolitan city that attracted business people of diverse nationalities, ethnicities and religions.

Following Italian unification in 1861, Trieste loomed large in the appeals of the irredentists, who argued for the restoration of Italian-speaking districts to Italy. For them, the city was a natural part of the Italian national corpus, its 'unredeemed bride'. Italy received its wish, acquiring Trieste under the post-First World War international peace negotiations, as payoff for joining the Triple Alliance and the war against Germany and Austria–Hungary in 1915.[7]

Once attained, however, Trieste was, if not a trophy wife, then one whose place in the Italian family was largely symbolic. The economic reality was that Italy did not need another point of access for ships on the Adriatic. It did not invest in Trieste's commercial future, rendering its place as a port city obsolete.

Before 1918, Trieste was an 'orgy of colours', a 'mixture of smells', a 'confusion of languages and dialects', as ships arrived from the

Italian coasts and the Orient, carrying a flourishing trade and exotic merchandise.[8]

This was before my grandparents' time, before the traumas and upheaval of the twentieth century.

V

Yearning and regret: thinking of Trieste's place in my mother's family's story conjures these emotions. They are feelings not unique to our family. Nostalgia is an emotion that permeates the whole city.

I see my grandmother, Anna, as an old woman, sitting on a public bench somewhere along Trieste's expansive waterfront, looking out towards the Adriatic Sea. She is wiping tears from her eyes because in a day she will be leaving Trieste, once again, for Australia, and she knows this is probably the last time she will see her city. It's a powerful image stored solidly in my memory, yet I don't know where it comes from, why I have it, nor who gave it to me.

Among the papers I rescued after Nonna died were the words to a song that she knew as 'Cantier San Marco', the name of a shipyard in Trieste. Written in the Trieste dialect, the song tells the story of how, under the Italians, an internationally oriented commercial port was reduced to an Italian border city, and how this betrayal affected the city's inhabitants.

My mother did not know the song when I asked her to translate it for me.

Trieste is 'like a lover undressed by all'. The tone is fatalistic and sardonic, as in the following translated passage:

They are taking everything away and are stopping the cranes
Even San Marco has gone on his way

They are promising us that many ferries here will be built
But so big that maybe we won't even see them.

Somehow, this song survived my grandmother's purges of documents over the decades. It speaks of a complex history and geopolitics that, for my mother's family, was very personal. It was Anna, tired of living with her in-laws, who pushed her husband to emigrate in 1957. The impetus for leaving, though, ultimately had as much to do with national politics as family dynamics. Their resultant exile from their much-loved city was one from which the family never psychologically recovered.

VI

The next day, Sunday, our first full day in Trieste, we headed up to the Carso with Vera and her family.

On the way, we made a detour to Servola, a small working-class suburb on the eastern side of Trieste that is dominated by the local steelworks. This was where my mother grew up. Mum's house, La Casa Rossa, the Red House, still stands, neglected and in a state of protracted decay. Nearby, up the hill, is San Lorenzo, the Catholic church where she made her first communion, and her primary school, Ezio De Marchi (named for a teacher and irredentist who died fighting in the First World War).

I had visited most of these places before, but never with Mum, and I thought this time would be different, that I would get to see a new dimension of the city and of her.

La Casa Rossa is actually a small apartment block of three storeys. The building's colour was more faded salmon than red, apart from the ground floor, which looked as though it were repainted more recently and was a deeper maroon. The paint of the upper floors was peeling—it had not been touched since she was a child, Mum said. There were five long windows across the middle floor, five tiny windows on the top floor where Mum lived with her grandparents, parents and sister, and the remains of an *osteria* or tavern on the ground floor. The building's timber window frames were warped and rotting, the glass was broken, the blue shutters were faded and the plaster around the windows was cracked. The walls were covered with ivy and the ground outside the building consisted of perilously mossy and broken concrete.

Some of the restaurant tables were visible inside the abandoned *osteria*, and an old faded blue-and-white menu, its edges curled and gnawed by insects, still sat inside a glass case behind over-grown vines at the entrance to the building. (It was in the *osteria* that my mother saw her first black-and-white television, which drew crowds to La Casa Rossa; everyone wanted to watch *Lascia*

The menu outside La Casa Rossa

o raddoppia—*Leave It or Double It*—a popular Italian game show that first aired in the mid-1950s.)

There was an old external staircase leading up to a blue door on the second floor, where Mum used to play as a child. I took photos of her and her grandson sitting together on the steps. Around the back of the block was an old cherry tree, a child's swing and washing lines with drying clothes.

La Casa Rossa had a certain 'rude charm' about it, and was so rundown as to look uninhabitable, though it was very much lived in. An old woman peered out of a top-corner window, the window of my great-grandparents' former two-bedroom apartment, and regarded us suspiciously. My mother and her cousin, Giuliana, got talking to another, friendlier tenant, a young Croatian woman called Samia, who was with her two-year-old daughter. The suspicious old woman, Samia said, was a southern Italian, as if that explained her behaviour. Vera told me later that Samia was so friendly because she was Croatian; a native Triestina would never stop to chat to strangers.

Samia also told us that La Casa Rossa was for sale for 100,000 euros, by the same family who owned it when Mum lived there. My father wanted to make an offer but Mum wasn't interested.

My mother pointed out where the vegetable garden used to be, where the pigs were kept, where her family would go to sit in the heat of the summer under an ivy-covered pergola at the front of the small complex. She showed us the steelworks where her father worked, directly across the road from La Casa Rossa, and the nearby grocery store, subsidised by his employer, where they bought their bread and salami.

Back in the car, we passed the plumbing shop where Mum's father completed his apprenticeship, and the cemetery of Sant'Anna, where her grandparents were buried.

'Do you want to go inside?' I asked, as we sat in our hire car outside the walls of Sant'Anna.

'There's nobody there now,' Mum said. 'Your nonna went back to look for her parents once and their graves had been removed.'

I asked my mother how she felt seeing all this—her house, the church where her grandmother took her for mass every Sunday, the cemetery—for the first time with one of her children, with me?

'I feel nothing.'

I didn't know whether to believe her. I believed her when she said, later, that she feels like a foreigner in Trieste and a foreigner in Australia. It's an ambivalence that reflects the displacement of her migration. But I suspect her lack of emotional attachment to Trieste is a feature of the fortress-like defences she has erected around her, the way she protects herself from feeling the full extent of her loss.

In any case, because my mother wouldn't let herself feel anything, my experience of visiting these places together wasn't all that different to my previous visits without her. I still sensed the deep but uncertain attachment I had to Trieste, but beyond that, I struggled to feel more.

VII

We drove up into the hills close to the border, where all the signage is in both Italian and Slovenian.

I wanted Michael to experience lunch at a traditional Triestine *osmiza*, the bucolic farms in the Carso where the owners produce and sell their own products: wines, eggs, salami, prosciutto, cheeses, pickled peppers, bread. You know a farm is open for business when you see a dried tree branch hanging out the front of the premises.

In the car, Mum started talking about the *foibe*, and told a story I'd not heard before. The *foibe* are very deep natural pits in the Carso region. Towards the end of the Second World War, they were used by the Yugoslav partisans to dispose of their political enemies: thousands of Italians are said to have been thrown to their deaths into these pits. Some of the corpses were eventually retrieved, but many were not. According to my mother, two of her aunts (my nonna's sisters) were keen rock climbers in their youth, and on their expeditions in the Carso came across dead bodies.

The *foibe* episode is a highly contentious one among historians on either side of the Italian–Slovenian border, who continue to dispute its details. The sensitivities surrounding it are typical of the unresolved historical enmities that exist in the region. The Italians accuse the Communist Yugoslavs of barbarism during their 40-day occupation of Trieste after the defeat of the Nazis in 1945. The Yugoslavs accuse the Italians of racism, of perpetuating stereotypes of the uncivilised Balkans, and of failing to come to terms with Italy's Fascist legacy, when ethnic Slavs in Italian-controlled territories were subject to persecution.[9]

My nonna recalled this period—the six weeks in May and June 1945 when Josip Tito's army took control of Trieste—with terror. Tito's forces moved to dismantle the Italian Fascist administration. Suspected Fascists, including individuals who were denounced by members of the populace, were subject to arrest and summary execution or deportation by the Yugoslav partisans.

'When the partisans were there you could point out to them, "Oh, that one there did this and this during the war", even if it was a lie, and they'd take them away and shoot them,' my grandmother told my mother.

Nonna's mother, my great-grandmother, Natalina, was from Bologna and dark-haired (unlike the typical fairer Triestine), with strikingly round, almost black, heavily lidded eyes. Natalina was standing in a line waiting for food rations one day during this period, when a woman she knew with poor eyesight pointed her out by mistake to nearby partisans.

'They were in lines waiting for food and these partisans came,' Nonna said, 'and they took her mother until her mother screamed, "It's not me, it's not me", and this woman went up close and recognised her and said, "Sorry, I made a mistake."'

The Italian–Slavic animosity lived on in my family through my grandparents' sensitivity over their surname. As a child, I was aware of my mother's family's touchiness about the spelling of their name. It was spelt with a 'gh' at the end—not with a 'ch', which would indicate a Slavic background. Nonno in particular became upset when people got it wrong. I assumed these feelings were founded in pride in our Italian heritage, clueless about the underlying cultural and political baggage.

Yugoslavia's rule over Trieste was brief. The Allies arrived in the city close on the heels of the Yugoslavs and quickly reached an agreement. The disputed Italian territories of the upper Adriatic were divided into two zones: Zone A (including Trieste) would be administered by the Allies, while Zone B (most of the Istrian peninsula plus Fiume, now Rijeka) would remain under Yugoslav control. Tensions between Italy and Yugoslavia remained high and, in 1947, the nascent United Nations Security Council established the Free Territory of Trieste, formalising the two zones, a situation that continued until 1954. Throughout the intervening period, in the early Cold War years, Tito maintained Yugoslavia's claim to Trieste, while the Americans viewed keeping Trieste under Italian control as important strategically for containing the Communist threat.

By 1954, Trieste's international significance had waned. Following years of delicate international diplomatic negotiations, Trieste was reassigned to Italy, ending nine years of Allied military governance. Yugoslavia's sovereignty over the Istrian peninsula (and Fiume) became permanent.

Meanwhile, the shifting Italian–Yugoslav border (which changed eight times between 1918 and 1954) forced the movement of hundreds of thousands of ethnic Italians and Slavs into and out of newly created borderlands, with a substantial number eventually leaving Europe altogether.[10] My grandfather's sister, Amelia, I would learn, became entangled in the scramble of the post-war exodus of Italian refugees.

Back at the *osmiza* with Vera and her family, we recalled our memories of my nonno, who loved long lunches in the Carso.

Alfredo was a generous and outgoing man, who was at his most content eating, drinking and (in his earlier years) singing in the company of friends and family. My father said it was heartbreaking for Alfredo to leave a country where he was happy and accepted and had many good friends for one where he felt ostracised as a 'new Australian' and a 'wog'.

'It was very painful for him.'

I recalled the obvious joy Nonno took in treating his eight grandchildren to a special feast on our birthdays. We eagerly anticipated these occasions when Nonno dispatched my grandmother to Beamish Street to buy wads of finely sliced *prosciutto crudo* from the delicatessen and some more typically 'Australian' fare: buckets of takeaway Kentucky Fried Chicken, a luxury of sorts back in the early 1980s.

I also remembered thinking, as a child, how lonely and isolated my Italian grandparents seemed in their little house in Campsie— as if we were all they had.

Vera described Alfredo's first visit back to Trieste in 1983. She was twelve. He spent that trip sitting with old friends playing cards and drinking wine in a small seafood restaurant in Servola, and chain-smoking with his sister Rosina (Vera's nonna) in her tiny apartment, talking about Australia and his grandchildren. My nonno was surprised, Vera said, at how much the city had changed. He disliked the traffic; there were so many more cars in Trieste than before. It troubled him how even the language was no longer the same. The Triestini spoke more Italian and less of the local dialect than when he left 26 years earlier.

'Maybe he thought Trieste had stopped,' Vera said.

Time can stop at the point of rupture for those who reluctantly leave home and country. The displaced migrant's memories can ossify like bone while, a world away, the city of their birth continues to change and renew. Though Trieste was not as he remembered it, Alfredo never felt like he belonged in Australia. He would have loved to return to Italy permanently, but by the time he could afford to, his daughters had grown up and were settled in Australia. He would never leave without them. (Early on, my grandfather tried to orchestrate a return: he encouraged his eldest daughter, at nineteen, to travel to Italy in the secret hope that she would meet an Italian man and remain in Italy, so he could then return home too. His plan didn't work. By then my mother, oblivious to her father's motivations, had met my father, who was waiting at home in a most agitated state.)

A couple of days after the *osmiza* lunch, I learnt something about my grandfather that neither I nor my mother had known. Alfredo had wanted his ashes to be interred after his death in Trieste, not in Australia. It never happened. His remains sit in a small box beside those of his wife in the crypt at the Catholic church attached to my old primary school in Sydney. It's a place where I don't feel comfortable either.

Even in death, my nonno was displaced.

VIII

That evening, we had dinner with more of my mother's cousins: Gloria and Anna.

I was looking for new pieces of Nonno's story—anything to shed further light on his wartime experience and the role his sister, Amelia, played in helping him to survive his internment. We went to Anna's small rented apartment in Servola, up two flights of stairs with no lift, and ordered pizzas from the local pizzeria. We ate them with a bottle of white wine.

Gloria and Anna are daughters of Alfredo's siblings, Silvio and Assunta. Alfredo, born in 1924, was the youngest of seven children of Amedeo and Anna-Maria. Two of their children, boys, died in infancy, leaving Silvio, the eldest son, and, in descending order of age, Assunta, Rosina, Amelia and Alfredo. All but Amelia, born in 1917, had their own children, and all apart from one of these cousins of my mother were alive and living in Trieste when we visited.

My ambitions that night were modest. I never thought, for instance, that I would discover the location of Amelia's long-lost diary, the one that Mum had read after her aunt's death. But I hoped that if I sat in a room with my mother and her cousins, both of whom I'd spent time with before, and a tape recorder, I might dislodge some deeply buried memories.

I was unprepared for what unfolded instead: a frustrating night of contradictory memories, of stories reluctantly given, of the questioning of my motives, all delivered in rapid dialect. When I asked questions about Amelia I sensed a bristling in the room that mystified me. I was used to press secretaries regarding me suspiciously; the constant mistrust was, for me, the most unpleasant part of being a journalist. But to experience such wariness from my own family—born, I understand, out of a protectiveness of Amelia's memory—made me uncomfortable.

The cousins spoke over each other, finishing the other's memories so that I couldn't distinguish whose they were. Meanwhile, an overtired three-year-old whined on my lap, my father muttered interview tips in my ear, and my pleas to my mother to translate and slow the conversation down went ignored.

'Ze un cazin con tutta questa roba qua,' quipped Gloria's husband, who was sympathetic to my situation, in dialect. 'It's like a house of prostitutes here.'

Much of what I heard that night I already knew.

My mother's cousins, unlike my mother, were aware that Alfredo had been forced to work in an armaments factory but were adamant that he was a prisoner of war outside Klagenfurt, in Austria. They knew nothing of Berlin. (While Berlin appears in Alfredo's military papers, Klagenfurt does not, and I've never found any official documents to verify he was there.)

They told me Alfredo was captured in Pola, which was part of Italy before the Second World War; today it's a city in Croatia called Pula. (According to his documents, Nonno enlisted at the Italian naval base in Pola on 21 August 1943 and was captured by the Germans eighteen days later.)

Anna said Alfredo was brought back to Trieste and kept in the silos next to the railway for eight days. (A Trieste historian confirmed soldiers were detained in the railway station silos; he told me 30,000 Italian soldiers were disarmed, arrested and interned by 100 German soldiers in Pola.)

According to my mother's cousins, Amelia went to work for the Germans—they insisted it was in Klagenfurt—after Alfredo's family learnt that he was not receiving the parcels of food and clothes they were sending. She resolved to deliver them to her brother herself.

'Your grandfather never spoke of any of this,' said Anna, who was nevertheless a fount of family folklore, in dialect.

There was discussion of Alfredo's brother's career in the Fascist Italian Royal Navy. Someone mentioned that one of his sisters in Trieste gave temporary shelter to a young German soldier trying to evade the partisans after the Second World War ended. I was reminded of Italy's ambivalent wartime allegiances. Moral uncertainties must have confronted inhabitants of this northern, formerly Austrian, city that had once embraced Fascism and, after Mussolini's ousting, was absorbed into Greater Germany by the Nazis, while the country's south was under the Allies.

My pizza went uneaten as I balanced my notebook and a sleeping child on my lap on an old sofa. Eight of us were squeezed into the cramped room which was dominated by a large table, now covered with a tablecloth, pizza boxes, glasses and two tape recorders. A large dresser stood opposite me, filled with statues, pictures and glasses. Anna's husband, Pino, had been an avid painter. In his youth, according to my mother, Pino was a great dancer, but a devastating motorcycle accident meant he spent most of his adult life unable to walk or communicate properly. He could paint though. On my first trip to Italy, Pino, who was always friendly and smiling—I can still see his crooked, toothy smile—gave me one of his paintings, of Miramare. He has since passed away. At the far end of the room in the apartment was a doorway that led into the smallest of kitchens; next to the sofa, a window faced onto the narrow, hilly street. One of Anna's sons poked his head around the doorway, greeted us and promptly left.

I felt the awkwardness of my mission. I hadn't seen my relatives in fifteen years but tonight, over a few quick pizzas, I was attempting to prise sensitive information from them about events that occurred more than half a century ago. I pressed for more details about Amelia, and here I did pick up new threads about her life. I noted them down, intending to follow them up when I got home.

Amelia, I was told, was a wanderer who refused to settle down. Her relatives linked her *'anima senza pace'*, 'soul without peace', to the meningitis she contracted and recovered from as a child, a disease that claimed the life of an older brother, Armando, who died aged three (another brother died in infancy too, though nobody can remember his name). Could surviving a fatal illness as a girl have shaped Amelia's outlook on life in such a dramatic way?

Amelia was a dancer, a member of the *corpo di ballo* (corps de ballet), and performed in musical revues in theatres around Italy, from Trieste to Turin, Genoa, Rome and Naples. Anna told us Amelia belonged to a ballet company associated with Carlo Dapporto, a famous Italian comedian and star of the stage and later the screen (he appeared in some 35 films). Amelia danced in Rome with another young woman from Trieste, Augusta, who later became Dapporto's wife. Amelia then moved to Naples, where she had a wealthy suitor, Vincenzo. 'Uncle Vincenzino', as my mother called him, was in love with Amelia and wanted to marry her, but her sights were firmly fixed on America. (My mother told me Vincenzo was a senior executive of an international lift company, 'a wonderful older man who treated Amelia's family like his own even after she left Italy'. Mum visited him when she returned to Italy in 1966, her first visit back since her family's migration to Australia. Vincenzo remained single and, even then, 'still adored' Amelia.)

Amelia, Mum's cousins said, left Naples in 1951 for the United States on dubious immigration papers. In America, she became entangled with a Sicilian-born man with Mafia connections, who discovered the truth behind her emigration and threatened to expose her if she ever tried to leave him.

I was still digesting this information when there came an even more startling revelation. I asked about Amelia's diary, the diary that was meant to no longer exist, and the cousins began talking about it as if somebody in the family still had it, as if everybody had read it.

I was dumbstruck. My mother stopped translating completely. My father kept muttering something about going out and buying a photocopier. The room suddenly felt very hot. I looked over at Michael—it was as though a set of leaked cabinet papers had just been dangled in front of us. There was a suggestion that the diary was with another relative, the wife of Gloria's recently deceased brother, Alessandro, in Udine, outside Trieste. But the cousins insisted it was '*brutto*', terrible, full of suffering, that they wouldn't read it if you paid them, and why did I want to read it anyway, when there was nothing in there about Alfredo?

My mind raced: I would be one week in Trieste; I didn't know where the diary was, exactly, and it seemed that my relatives didn't want me to read it anyway. I was desperate to read it—I had been imagining Amelia's story for fifteen years—but it was unlikely I would locate the diary in the limited time we had. I was elated and despondent at the same time.

IX

The next day, Monday, Mum and I caught a taxi to La Risiera di San Sabba. While we visited the former rice-husking factory, Michael and our son toured Miramare with my father.

La Risiera was built in the late nineteenth century. In October 1943, the Nazis converted it into a barracks, prison and deportation and extermination camp for Italian and Slav partisans, political prisoners and Jews. It was Italy's only Second World War concentration camp equipped with cremating ovens. An estimated 3000 to 5000 people were murdered there, many of them members of the resistance. While Jews were held and executed at La Risiera, most were transported on to camps in Poland and Germany, with some 22 transports leaving Trieste for Auschwitz between October 1943 and November 1944. Trieste's 5000-strong Jewish population was previously well assimilated and influential in economic circles—a legacy of the tolerant approach the Habsburgs adopted towards Jews in Trieste from the eighteenth century (which wasn't the case in other parts of the empire). While the persecution of the Jews started under the Fascists in 1938, it escalated under the Nazis and no more than 500 Triestine Jews remained after the war.[11]

It was raining when the taxi dropped us outside the front entrance of La Risiera. I was surprised by how close we were to where my mother's family lived. The old rice factory was located in a busy, built-up industrial area. I remembered my mother telling me that Nonna said they could smell the bodies burning at La Risiera.

My grandmother mentioned other things from that time. Like the distinctive, rock-crunching sound of the German soldiers' jackboots.

'She used to hear them marching in the street, and if you ever heard them you would try to hide because they were so fearful of them,' Mum told me.

There was also the sudden disappearance of Nonna's best friend, a Jewish girl, whom she never heard from again. Both my grandparents lost a number of Jewish friends in that period of German occupation.

'They all knew that they ended up down at La Risiera.'

'Did they realise what was happening to the prisoners at La Risiera?'

'They knew, yes, they knew. They knew because apparently they could smell it.'

'What did they smell?'

'There was smoke and they could smell burning. I don't know what it smells like when humans are burnt to death.'

I think about Nonna's best friend, who would have been a teenager, a young woman of nineteen or so like herself. I wonder what she looked like, what her name was, about the other members of her family.

I found a photo in my grandparents' papers of Nonna from that time with another girl. Anna, my grandmother, was smiling, her face pressed against the face of the other girl, whose chin rested on Anna's shoulder. I don't know who the girl was and my mother can't tell me. The photo was dated 31 August 1944.

You enter La Risiera through a long, narrow passage wedged between two very high concrete walls. At the end of the walkway, which is paved with large rectangular stones, there is an archway. Above the archway is an ochre-coloured building of three more storeys, with three pairs of long windows stacked one above the other. On the other side is a large courtyard. Marked out on the ground of the courtyard is an imprint of the crematorium, which was built by the Germans and destroyed by them when they left in 1945. The ovens were a dozen metres from the cells where the prisoners were kept. The Nazis played German marching music while they carried out killings at night. The sounds of trucks, radios and barking dogs muffled the screams of the victims. Meanwhile, outside the walls of La Risiera, the rest of Trieste remained silent, its inhabitants waiting for the arrival of the Allies, hoping they would reach the city before the Yugoslavs did.

La Risiera was made a national monument in 1965. Historians have criticised the memorialisation of what the German Nazis did there for failing to adequately account for the complicity of Italian Fascists.[12]

La Risiera today (the outline of the oven is visible on the wall)

I sat in one of La Risiera's rooms, the memorial space which contains exhibits, and watched a short documentary film about the persecution of Jews in the war. In vain I searched the photographs and video footage of crowds and street scenes in Trieste for Anna's young face. I tried to imagine what it must have been like to live in the city in those anxious, troubled years.

X

Mum and I returned to the hotel and waited in the lobby for the others to arrive.

We sat together at a small table and I ordered a coffee. It was a rare, quiet moment, not only because the week was crammed with activities, but because Mum and I never did this, just the two of us. I took a deep breath, and readied myself to ask my mother a question that had been weighing on my mind for some time.

Back in Australia, I had been talking to my siblings, separately, about March 2007, about the devastating week when I was in the coma. I was trying to piece together, from my family's fractured memories, the sequence of events, when and how the agonising decisions were taken to amputate the different parts of me. All these conversations with my sister and brothers were difficult ones. There were tears as they recalled this time; deep, painful sighs; distant stares; long silences. It was as though the recalling of those days transported their very beings back to the actual happenings, which were more than memories stored in the mind, but rather still-existing moments to which my siblings could phys-ically return.

These conversations were conducted over weeks and months, over the telephone and in person. From them, I knew that, of my family members, only Mum didn't want the doctors to take my legs. Knowing this only vaguely troubled me. Who was I to judge how a mother, bewildered and completely unprepared for what was happening to her daughter, would feel in a situation of such anguish? At the same time, I know how much I wanted to live. I did not agree with Mum's position, but I wanted to understand it better. I was curious, not judgemental.

I had been holding off asking my mother for her memories of these decisions, her particular version. There was never going to be a right time, but I thought an opportunity might offer itself on this trip. Though we were in a public place, in the reception area of the Hotel NH Trieste, it had been a morning of sombre reflec-tion, and I saw my moment now.

My question for my mother was this: I wanted to know whether she still believed the doctors should have left my limbs intact, knowing that I would have certainly died, knowing what my life looked like now with a family of my own, a new career. Understanding that, after everything, after all that rebuilding and reassembling of my world, we were here together in Trieste—Trieste!—the five of us.

'Surely, Mum, you can see now that the decision to take my legs and let me live was the right one?'

'When I look at your son, I think the right decision was made. But when I look at you and everything you go through all the time, I keep thinking, "If that was me, what decision would I take?" I would take the decision don't amputate, just let me survive if I am meant to survive. I couldn't see myself living without arms and legs.'

A part of me couldn't believe my mother would think this, after eight years of having me, her daughter, present in the world, still living a full and rich life. Though I wanted her to say otherwise, I was not surprised. My mother loves me. But she views the world in binaries, in black and white; there is little space for grey, for the unconventional or imperfect, in her thinking.

XI

Later that afternoon I went with Vera to the recently opened Museo della Guerra per la Pace, the Museum of War for Peace.

I was hoping to find information about the Italian POWs in the Second World War, but the museum's collection mostly related to the First World War. We asked the museum curators where in Trieste we might go to learn about the Italian Military Internees (IMIs). They looked at us blankly, unable to help.

I wondered aloud how it was that this group of men, the IMIs of whom there were 600,000, could remain so forgotten?

'History is about the big moment,' Vera observed, in her typically sharp but understated way.

XII

We were invited for dinner that night—for *sugo* (sauce) and polenta—to the home of Gloria and her husband, Armando, up in the heights of Trieste.

The apartment was not large, but had the luxury of an old-fashioned lift and a balcony that opened onto views of the city and the sea beyond. Michael and I were greeted as we entered the building with that typical, strangely welcoming, Trieste apartment smell: a mix of stale cigarettes, a hint of mould and aromatic Italian cooking.

I'd been there before. Gloria and Armando, who have no children of their own, took me skiing to Tarvisio, on the frontier between Italy, Austria and Slovenia, when I was nineteen. On the way home we stopped at a pizzeria where the chef made me my first *capricciosa* pizza. The pizza caused much mirth: it was in the shape of a heart. Armando called me *tesoro*, treasure, and gave me pieces of jewellery—pretty bracelets, hooped gold earrings. Gloria had a habit of raiding her wardrobe every time I visited to give me cast-offs I might find useful: a one-piece grey-and-red ski suit on that first visit, on this occasion a warmer-looking jumper than the one I had brought with me. Gloria is an extrovert: her voice is deep and throaty, she is quick to laugh and make friends. She taught my mother to rollerskate when she was a child in Trieste. Mum says her older cousin was 'the life of the party when she was young'.

Gloria and Armando are enthusiastic, generous and, sometimes, overwhelming people.

The evening lacked the chaos of the one in Anna's apartment. Because Mum wasn't there, my relatives were forced to slow down, to repeat themselves, and they had to speak in Italian, not dialect. A couple of unexpected things happened.

I had just sunk back into a sofa in the living room (also the dining room), when Gloria produced a photo album containing an extensive collection of photographs of Amelia. They included the only images I had ever seen of her in her ballet costumes. I stared in amazement and disbelief as Amelia the dancer, whom I had heard so much about but never seen, materialised before me: thin, smiling, glamorous, delicate, lovely. There were about twenty photographs in total, from different stages of her life. Amelia was a chameleon, her appearance changing according to the setting.

I focused on the four theatrical pictures. Amelia in a short tutu and shiny high-heeled dancing shoes, her arms thin and graceful, with painted fingernails and a cigarette held casually in one dainty hand. Amelia in a long flouncy skirt, the sides of which she held out like a fan, with a sequinned top displaying her flat midriff and a flower in her dark curly hair. Amelia and another dancer with big flowers on their folk dancing skirts and lacy petticoats underneath, puffy sleeves, and big bows in their hair.

I was surprised by the amount of skin on display for that time: the 1930s and early 1940s. I understood more once I began researching *teatro di varietà*, the kind of escapist spectaculars Amelia performed in, and saw pictures of the choruses of women in skimpy bikinis and grass skirts. Amelia's costumes were, by comparison, modest.

The last photograph of Amelia looked like a modelling shot. She was heavily made up with dark lips and eyebrows and rouge

Amelia in ballet costume

on her cheeks. She wore a long strapless satin dress, embroidered with sparkling birds. Underneath the image was written '"Novel Film" Palazzo lo Grattacielo—Genova'. I subsequently learnt that the Teatro Grattacielo (*grattacielo* means skyscraper in Italian) was a major theatre in Genova that hosted jazz, vaudeville and opera stars. It was home to the city's temporary opera house while the permanent one was rebuilt after extensive damage in the Second World War. (At the time Amelia was dancing, Teatro Grattacielo was the location of a wartime mystery involving the Trio Lescano, three popular Italian sisters and singers who also performed with the comedian, Dapporto. The sisters, of Dutch–Jewish origin, alleged they were arrested and imprisoned by Fascist police after a concert at the Teatro Grattacielo in 1943 on charges they were spies and were communicating with the enemy through the lyrics of their songs. Their account was never verified.)

I took photos of the images of Amelia with my smartphone. I was slightly baffled as to why Gloria had so many photos of her aunt. Gloria mentioned how people thought she bore a resemblance to Amelia, and I realised that I wasn't the only woman in our family to have felt a personal connection to Amelia's story.

There were other photographs of interest. The next day Michael and I were going to Pula, in Croatia, where Alfredo enlisted and was possibly captured. Gloria showed us photographs of her father, Nonno's brother Silvio, in military parades in the ruins of the ancient Roman amphitheatre in Pula.

We left the photographs and moved to the table. Midway through dinner, the telephone rang. It was Gloria's niece, Romana, who I hadn't seen in two decades.

'Are you going to come and see us while you are here?' Romana asked me.

Romana and her family lived on a farm in Cividale, an hour from Trieste. She and her siblings were born in Rhodesia (now Zimbabwe). Her father—my mother's cousin Alessandro—lived there from his late teens, before returning to Italy with his family when the political situation in Zimbabwe deteriorated.

Cividale is a picturesque, ancient city, settled in 50 BC by Julius Caesar. It has medieval buildings, a spectacular fifteenth century bridge, the Ponte del Diavolo (the Devil's Bridge), and is surrounded by terraced hills and vineyards. Cividale is also 15 kilometres east of Udine.

I told Romana we did not have much time, but would be changing trains in Udine that Friday on our way to Klagenfurt. She offered to pick us up from our hotel in Trieste, take us to lunch at her sister's house, and drive us to the train station in Udine afterwards.

I liked Romana. We had instantly warmed to each other when we first met, twenty years ago. Alessandro had been fond of his uncle, Alfredo, my nonno. I agreed to the change of plans immediately, excited at the prospect of seeing her again, of renewing our friendship, and showing Michael her beautiful town. There was also every chance Amelia's diary was in a stack of papers at Romana's mother's house, in nearby Udine.

XIII

The drive to Pula from Trieste takes an hour and a half.

The route passes briefly through Slovenia on the way to Croatia. Michael and I changed euros into kune at a little scenic hilltop roadside bar overlooking the Adriatic. Not long after, we arrived at what looked at first to be an unremarkable commercial city on the coast—until we located the Roman ruins. Well-preserved, the first-century amphitheatre is positioned in the city centre on the incline of a small hill that descends towards the nearby sea. Its outer three-storey walls reach 33 metres in height and dominate the urban landscape.

I stood with my walking sticks in the middle of the arena on a sunny but cool day. The sky behind the gleaming limestone blocks of the open-air stadium was a brilliant blue. A worker was trimming the carefully manicured grass that grew inside the ruins. The presence of a wheelchair-accessible toilet was surprising but encouragingly inclusive. Noticing the signage, I felt the world reopen itself just a little more to me.

I read up on Pula's history in the bookshop underneath the 2000-year-old structure. The Austrians relocated their navy from Venice to Pola, as it was then known, in the mid-nineteenth century amid concerns over Italy's unification struggles. The city, which

The author in the Roman amphitheatre in Pula

had grown to meet the needs of the empire's military forces, lost much of its purpose under the Italians after the First World War, and became little more than an administrative centre.

In the 1930s, as Mussolini's forces invaded Abyssinia (Ethiopia today), and as Hitler steered Germany towards certain war, the Roman ruins in Pola were used by the Italians for staging military ceremonies. I had seen some of these grand parades in Gloria's photos of her father: thousands of Italian navy and army personnel standing to attention in rows in the centre of the amphitheatre as they were inspected by senior commanders. The Germans occupied Pola in 1943, and it was heavily bombed.

My grandfather's time in Pola was short, less than three weeks. From what relatives say, he wasn't marching in military parades but digging trenches for the Germans before his capture.

Michael and I ate lunch at a seafood restaurant at the nearby marina, looking back to the ancient Roman edifice on the shore. It was not peak tourist season and we ate alone, the only patrons:

a platter of whitebait, sardines and scampi. The water was emerald green and full of large fish and I listened to the creaking of the boats on their moorings.

Alfredo's experiences here more than 70 years ago were lost to me now.

XIV

We made it back to Trieste in time to join our son and my parents for afternoon coffees and beers at our new favourite cafe: the nineteenth-century Viennese coffeehouse Caffé degli Specchi (Cafe of Mirrors) on Piazza Dell'Unità.

Trieste's old cafes are known as much for the famous writers who drank at them over a century ago as they are for the superior quality of their coffee today (Illy coffee comes from Trieste). James Joyce and his good friend, the pioneering Trieste-born novelist Italo Svevo, frequented Caffé degli Specchi in the early twentieth century. Almost fifty years later, the entire building was used as headquarters for the Allies from 1947 until their withdrawal.

Today, the interior of the cafe is warm and recalls another time, with its timber-panelled bar, Greek columns, dramatic red drapes, frescos on the ceiling and portraits on the walls.

We had taken to sitting every afternoon, the five of us, on the comfortable lounges out the front of the cafe in our big jackets. Looking out towards the mid-eighteenth-century Fountain of Four Continents, we watched the passing parade of Triestini and their little pampered dogs (dogs being a far more common sight in Trieste than children) as the sun went down. Breathing in the sea air, I shared my latest research findings and heard about my boy's adventures that day.

Trieste had changed in the fifteen years since I was last there. There were fewer horns, fewer motorcycles, fewer sirens and less disorder than I remembered. Sometimes, from my lounge chair in the square, I'd count the wheelchairs; one day I saw six pass by. I felt reassured that, although this was an old city, people in a situation like mine were able to make a life there.

These afternoons were, in many ways, the most special times from that week in Trieste: sitting in the beautiful piazza overlooking the sea in Mum's city with her and Dad, Michael and our child. Though my mother said she felt nothing the day of our visit to La Casa Rossa, at Caffé degli Specchi I heard her suggest otherwise.

'I can't believe I am here, in Trieste, with my grandson,' she said.

The sun had almost set. We made our way home to the hotel, taking the back streets, walking and wheeling past the shops and the buskers. We crossed over the bridge on the Canal Grande, bidding good evening to Joyce. I felt the melancholy of finding oneself in a moment so unexpectedly precious and transient that one begins mourning its passing before it has even finished.

XV

On Wednesday, we took the ferry from Trieste to Muggia, a small Italian town to the south-east of Trieste.

It was my chance to talk to Gigi, another of my mother's cousins (the son of Alfredo's eldest sister, Assunta). Gigi was a plumber like Alfredo. Though relatives say they shared similar personality traits, Gigi is more of a raconteur than I recall Nonno ever being. His conversation is punctuated by jokes and he loves to talk—in dialect, at a million miles an hour. During my 2001 visit, Gigi took me to Grotta Gigante, a giant network of caves on the Italian side of the Carso. He told stories about my grandfather, and it was from those conversations on the drive to the caves that the idea to write a book about Alfredo and Amelia first lodged in my mind.

This time, I sat with Gigi on the breezy boat ride across the Gulf of Trieste and tried to make sense of his memories of Alfredo's internment. Gigi was four years old in 1943. Like his sister, Anna, he knew nothing of any POW camp in Berlin, only Klagenfurt.

According to Gigi, the Germans brought Alfredo back to Trieste from Pola by truck. As our ferry wove past the more industrial areas of the coast towards Servola, Gigi pointed out a building where he said Nonno was kept prisoner for a few days after his capture in Pola. From the street below, Alfredo's mother talked to her nineteen-year-old-son who was imprisoned on the fourth floor, and brought him food and other small comforts. After a few days, the Germans took Alfredo and the other Italian prisoners to Klagenfurt by crowded train.

Gigi told me a fresh detail about Nonno's wartime experiences. There was an Italian *capo* (a prisoner assigned by the German guards to oversee other prisoners) from Barcola, who was lenient with Alfredo because he recognised from his accent that they came from the same part of Italy (Barcola is a beach neighbourhood of Trieste). When Alfredo became very sick with fever, the *capo* from Barcola excused him from having to work. However, the rest of the prisoners detested the *capo*, who was cruel to everybody else. After their camp was liberated by the Russians in 1945, the other prisoners took a pair of scissors and cut out the *capo*'s heart. (Another of Mum's cousins corroborated part of the *capo* story; the guards were bad people, she told me, but the *capo* from Barcola was less bad.)

I thought Muggia would be a nice place for lunch, as it's a pretty town with obvious Venetian influences. When we arrived, the main square was almost empty of people. Gloria and her husband joined us and, at a table at Pane Vino e San Daniele, I pressed Gigi for more information about Alfredo and Amelia.

When Alfredo's family learnt that he was sick and starving in the POW camp, Gigi said, Amelia volunteered to work for German officers.

'What work?' I asked.

'Secretarial work,' he replied with a shrug.

Gigi told me Alfredo would have died, if not for Amelia.

He told me his first memory of Amelia was when he was seven, shortly after the war. She lived for a time at La Casa Rossa with her parents. She was beautiful, Gigi said. She brought caramels for the children, and taught his sister Anna to make belts out of lolly wrappers. Amelia travelled around a lot; he remembered she worked as a dancer in Naples.

Gigi also had further information about Amelia's emigration to America. The details, as always, were sketchy, and I overlooked their significance at first. According to Gigi, Amelia put herself in a displaced persons camp, saying she had been married in Istria and was a refugee, in order to get accepted into the United States. She met a 'financier' at the camp who helped her prepare her documents to emigrate. Once in America, Amelia feared she would be exposed. She somehow became involved with the shadowy man with Mafia connections, and worked at his restaurant. Gigi said the man beat her, and worse.

I did some research when I returned home. US immigration policies became very restrictive after the First World War, but after the Second World War, under the Displaced Persons Act 1948, America allowed in 400,000 refugees over four years. Two thousand of them were from the Venezia Giulia area, which had been ceded to Yugoslavia.[13]

Could Amelia have been among them?

I looked up displaced persons camps in Italy and saw that after the war one operated at Bagnoli, near Naples, until 1951. It was run by the International Refugee Organization (an intergovernmental organisation founded in 1946 to deal with the massive refugee problem created by the war). Was Amelia at Bagnoli?

I soon realised that, while I had applied to the International Tracing Service for documents about Alfredo (without success), I had not done the same for Amelia. The ITS was set up in 1948 to trace millions of deported and displaced persons from the Second World War. Among its huge repository of archives are individual documents from the early post-war years from the Allies and their relief organisations, including files on displaced persons who registered for support with the IRO.

If Amelia had emigrated from Italy as a displaced person after the war, chances were the ITS had a file on her. I fired off a fresh email inquiry to Bad Arolsen in Germany about Amelia.

At that lunch at Muggia, Gloria had a surprise for me. She pulled from her bag the album containing the photographs of Amelia I had seen at her apartment, and gave it to me. Her entire collection, without explanation, was mine to take back to Australia.

I studied the photographs properly when I returned home. They were from different stages of Amelia's life. There was the teenage Amelia, her face plump and girlish, her wavy hair pushed back behind her ears, which were adorned with large pearl earrings. In another, an older but still youthful Amelia sat on a stone bench, a purse in her lap. She looked disdainfully at the unknown, smiling young man with slicked-back hair who had his hand on her shoulder, and one leg up, knee bent, on the bench beside her. One of Amelia's many admiring suitors?

Then there were the post-war photos, when Amelia's features had noticeably hardened. Amelia was 27 in 1945, when the war finished. But in a photograph taken that year, she looked a good decade older.

I stared at this, the most arresting of the photos. Amelia looked directly into the camera, her head on a slight tilt. Her face, once soft, had become severe. Her lips were painted and unsmiling, though there was the slightest pout about them. Her wavy brown hair was carefully coiffed, but the glamour of the younger Amelia, the playful siren, was largely gone. She wore a scarf tied high around her neck, and a demure, buttoned-up, collared blouse. She had dark shadows under her eyes, suggesting exhaustion. From her US naturalisation papers, I knew her eyes were grey (her height was five foot six inches). In this picture, her steely eyes were knowing, piercing even. It was as though Amelia was play-acting another role here—one that

Amelia, 7 June 1945

required a veneer of respectability. Perhaps the photograph was taken for official purposes? I turned the photograph over. The writing on the back was German, and there was a business name, possibly a photographic shop, and an address: Adolf Hitler Platz. There was also a date: 7 June 1945. It was five weeks after Hitler committed suicide in his bunker, and six weeks after Alfredo's liberation from the POW camp, which was almost certainly in Berlin. Did this prove Amelia was in Germany at the end of the war?

Many streets and squares in Germany and elsewhere in Nazi-occupied Europe were renamed after Hitler during that period, including a square in the Charlottenburg district of Berlin that was given the name Adolf Hitler Platz after 1933 (its current name is Theodor Heuss Platz). I contacted the official archives in Berlin, who said they had no photographs of the city's Adolf Hitler Platz from 1945. A German colleague searched the phone directories from that period, and there was a photography shop listed in that square in Berlin, though it bore a different name to the one on the back of the photograph. That this photo, bearing this particular date and location, had found its way to me seemed extraordinary.

With each additional detail of Amelia's life, my great-aunt was becoming more real to me: a flesh-and-blood woman, not just a mythical figure from the distant past. My wonderment deepened: who was Amelia, this soul without peace? A woman courageous and resourceful enough to risk travelling into a Nazi lair to administer food to her little brother. A woman so desperate to escape devastated post-war Italy that she may have posed as a refugee and emigrated, alone, to America, leaving behind a wealthy man who loved her, who never loved anyone but her.

How could I begin to understand the character of such a person? How could I ever do her story justice? And what business did I have picking through the remnants of her life?

XVI

That afternoon, Michael and I caught a taxi to Teatro Rossetti in the centre of Trieste to see one of the locations where Amelia danced.

The theatre was built in 1878 and hosted a number of stars of the stage through the twentieth century: the conductor Arturo Toscanini, the opera singer Maria Callas, the actress Sarah Bernhardt. It also staged productions of *teatro di varietà*, or variety theatre. The genre was a form of light comedy popular from the 1930s through to the 1950s that drew its inspiration from the *café chantant* musical performances of La Belle Époque period in France. The revues combined music, dance and skits, and their lyrics and dialogue were full of irony and innuendo. The dancers had a freedom that women at home, in more traditional domestic roles, did not. One of the biggest names of the genre to perform in such shows at the Teatro Rossetti was Wanda Osiris, a platinum-haired showgirl and diva who wore lavish costumes and heavy make-up. Osiris partnered with Dapporto in the 1940s and was known as the queen of variety theatre.

When we arrived at the building, which sits on a corner at the foot of a hill, there was a wind stirring up the leaves and rubbish outside, and the theatre appeared to be closed. We found the box office, and I approached two staff at the counter, asking them if there was any historical archive of performances from around the time of the Second World War. I showed them the pictures of Amelia in her ballet costumes, and explained my interest. They couldn't help me, but one of them invited us to an upcoming show that he said concerned an important episode of Trieste's history. It was about the plight of the *esuli*, the exiles, and how they were forced to leave their houses and possessions behind when their homelands were given to Yugoslavia after the war. It was a curious coincidence, given the (questionable) connection I had only learnt of earlier that day between Amelia's migration to America and the displaced ethnic Italians from Istria.

I told the man that, unfortunately, we would not be in Trieste by the time of the show. He left his counter and asked Michael and me to follow him.

The attendant unlocked the doors to the building, took us into the foyer, across the carpet, into a lift and upstairs to the theatre entrance.

'I have a treat for you,' he told us in Italian.

Suddenly we found ourselves in the stalls of the grand theatre with azure blue walls, where a couple of men were performing a sound check. I wheeled up to the stage, which was framed in gold arches and set with furniture for a play. The attendant talked us through the three big restorations of the theatre that were under- taken in the twentieth century. He asked us to turn around so that we were facing the cerulean blue velvet theatre chairs, and to look up beyond the two levels of galleries to the ceiling, in the middle of which was a golden dome. Painted around the dome was the scene of a dark stormy sky with dirty grey clouds. The attendant flicked a switch and stars began to appear. Gradually, the whole ceiling lit up like a magical night sky full of sparkling constellations.

We thanked him, then wandered back to the hotel, marvelling all the way at our theatre experience. We passed street vendors selling roasted chestnuts and stopped for coffee at Caffé San Marco, a 1914 coffee house where Saba, Joyce and Svevo drank. It was full of old professor types and there was not a laptop in sight. Every table was taken, so we drank standing at the bar.

Back in Australia, I looked up Dapporto's biography, and saw that he met his wife, Augusta (Amelia's friend), performing in musical theatre in Rome in the early-to-mid-1940s. Like Amelia,

Inside Teatro Rossetti today

Augusta was a member of the *corpo di ballo*. Augusta and Carlo married in 1945. Dapporto's celebrated alter ego was Il Maliardo, the Enchanter. I found a copy of his book of the same title at a second-hand bookshop in Italy. Il Maliardo was a *viveur*, a pleasure seeker, who, with oil-slicked hair, a French accent and an elegant costume of coat-tail and top hat was irresistible to the female sex.

Augusta and Carlo had two sons together. One of them, Massimo, was an Italian actor of TV miniseries fame. I found the name of Massimo's agency and sent an email asking if he would speak to me.

Massimo was warm and obliging. Via email he told me his mother was born in Trieste and, though he had never heard of Amelia, he remembered his mother telling him the stories of the girls from Trieste who went to Rome to try to break into the *mondo dello spettacolo*, the world of show business. He sent me photos of his parents and their friends, hoping we'd find Amelia among them, but we didn't. Massimo also looked up the names of all the revues his father performed in during the 1940s. They had names like *Sognate con me* (*You Dream with Me*) and *L'isola delle sirene* (*The Island of Mermaids*). There were no cast lists in existence, however, and I could not verify which of the productions Amelia, a mere chorus girl, was in.

Our email correspondence continued and I discovered that not only was Augusta from Trieste, she was born in the suburb of Servola, where my family lived. It eventually transpired that Anna, Mum's cousin, had known Augusta's family and remembered Massimo and his brother visiting their grandparents when they were children. Most astonishing was when we discovered that Augusta's parents had lived in the very same apartment that Anna lives in today.

'One will see if, after a little while, we are all related!' Massimo emailed.

XVII

The Museo Nazionale Dell'Internamento, the National Museum of Internment, in Padua, two hours south-west of Trieste by car, is the only museum in Italy dedicated to Italian Military Internees. It is located in a modern-looking pale brick building that is easy to miss from the street. It opened in 1965 and is run by volunteers, many of whom have a parent who was imprisoned by the Germans after the 1943 armistice, as Alfredo was.

On our final full day in Italy, I sat at a table in the library's museum. I was surrounded by bookshelves and through the window could see a soccer field and an old rusty red wagon with a door but no windows and a series of numbers etched into a side panel. It stood on a piece of railway track. Up to 50 Italian prisoners were squashed into wagons like this one and transported north by the Nazis in large convoys.

Five men and a woman pored over the documents I had just placed on the white laminated table, enthusing about them. It was like I'd opened a big bag of lollies in a kindergarten. It was gratifying to finally meet people who were as fascinated as I was by these artefacts of Nonno's.

One of the men, General Maurizio Lenzi, the president of L'Associazione Nazionale Ex Internati (The Association of Ex-Internees) began explaining the significance of the documents— the metal POW tag, the Nazi-issued passport for foreigners, the Alkett tank factory pass, the Italian military records—in rapid Italian to the assembled gathering. Another volunteer telephoned his son who spoke English to come and help translate the technical military jargon.

I learnt that the faint 'St III A' etched into the tag, which I had failed to notice previously, signified that Alfredo was first registered as a POW with the Germans in Luckenwalde. I'd never heard of this town, located 60 kilometres south of Berlin. The 'Stalag III D' handwritten on the postcard he sent to his family meant he was in a POW camp in Berlin (in reality, there was no camp as such, just an administration centre in Berlin in charge of 200 separate labour commands). The 'AKDO887' handwritten on the same postcard was a workers camp, and probably referred to Alkett (IMIs, on arriving in Berlin, were sent directly to factories whose owners were responsible for providing camps and barracks for the forced labourers).

General Lenzi explained that the provisional alien's passport was issued after Mussolini complained about the situation of the Italian prisoners who were starving in the labour camps. The IMIs were treated more harshly than other POWs, given just 700 calories a day to live on, and up to 50,000 IMIs died during their imprisonment. In the passport, Alfredo's job description was listed as 'unskilled worker—pipe fitter', and General Lenzi speculated that his forced labour in Germany probably involved manufacturing tubes for military purposes.

The general then turned to the Italian military documents. Some were from the cupboard in my grandparents' house; others I had obtained from the state archives in Trieste. We were all hanging on his words. General Lenzi cleared his throat and began.

Before his capture, Alfredo was stationed in Pola, in artillery, where he was taught to fire cannons. He was deployed on coastal defence and was captured in Pireo (Piraeus), the Athens port.

Nobody in my family had mentioned anything about Greece before. Pola/Pula was a long way from Piraeus, and I wondered if this detail, though it appeared in official documents, might be incorrect.

(I asked Mum about this later. 'In all the years, he never mentioned Greece to me,' she said. All Mum knew of her father's capture was that he was pulled off a train at a railway station by German soldiers. A questionnaire Alfredo filled out after his repatriation in 1945 said he was on his way to Belgrade at the time of his capture, so perhaps he was on a train.)

Suddenly, the general's voice became excited. 'This is the most important part,' he said in Italian, reading from Alfredo's discharge papers. 'This line says he was positively judged by the military commission on his return.'

According to Alfredo's military papers, he was repatriated to Italy in early September 1945. He reported to the navy's collection centre in Venice, where returning IMIs were identified and had to complete a statement of their activities during their internment. All the returned Italian prisoners were interrogated as to whether they collaborated with the Nazis and the Fascists. Being positively judged meant Alfredo was deemed not to have been a collaborator.

It was now after midday, past the museum's closing hour, and time for the volunteers to go home for lunch.

'Would you like to see the tomb of the unknown soldier?' General Lenzi asked.

'*Sì*,' I replied and, before I could object, one of the volunteers, who looked like the late British actor Alan Rickman, grabbed the handles of my wheelchair and started pushing me briskly through the museum.

On the way to the temple next door, volunteers pointed out different relics: a prisoner's uniform, some utensils, a smuggled Italian flag.

Il Tempio Nazionale dell'Internato Ignoto (The National Temple of the Unknown Internee) was founded by a priest who, in 1943, gave refuge to some escaped English and New Zealander prisoners. The priest was betrayed by Fascists and deported to Dachau in Germany and, on his return to Italy, he dedicated the church to the Italian prisoners who died in the Nazi camps.

A volunteer unlocked the iron gates of the temple's atrium. The men pointed out the different plaques with the names of their deceased fathers and their comrades, all IMIs. I peered through the grate to a small chapel to the left of the atrium where there was a stone tomb with an emaciated figure—the dead Christ—laid out on top. Around him stained-glass windows portrayed images of suffering from the war: a man with his head thrown back in agony; a snake wrapped around the Nazi swastika; a series of hands gripping others' wrists in a circle formation.

We posed for photos outside with General Lenzi and a couple of other volunteers. Michael and I were apparently the first Australians to have visited this obscure but remarkable little museum.

We said our farewells and drove back to Trieste. Absorbing what I had learnt that day, my thoughts turned to our upcoming trip to Germany, and how I might fit in a visit to the town of Luckenwalde, not knowing what remains, if any, I'd find there of the POW camp.

At Caffé degli Specchi with my parents that afternoon, my mother listened to my latest findings about the IMIs.

'Nonno would think this was great, what you are doing,' she said. 'At least, I think he would.'

Upon our return to Australia from Europe, a letter was waiting for me from the Deutsche Dienststelle (WASt) in Berlin, the official agency that keeps the records of POWs in Germany in the Second World War. It confirmed that Alfredo, a sailor in the Italian navy, was an IMI and was held at camps in Luckenwalde and subsequently Berlin. The agency could not tell me where Alfredo was originally captured.

XVIII

Our week in Trieste, so brief, was over.

My parents flew home to Australia, leaving Michael, our son and I on our own to make our way north to Austria and Germany. As arranged, Romana and her daughter collected the three of us from our hotel and we drove to Cividale for coffee, then on to lunch at her sister's house in Udine.

I described my research to Romana on the drive. We talked about Victor Frankl's book, *Man's Search for Meaning*. Frankl was a psychiatrist and an Austrian Jew who survived Auschwitz. His observations on his experiences inside the concentration camps resonate with other kinds of human suffering. Such as: one retains the ability to 'choose one's attitude in a given set of circumstances', even when all other control over one's life has been taken away. And that one's mental health is based on the existence of a tension or the gap 'between what one is and what one should become'.[14] For me, this is the key to survival, when others in the same situation might think death is an easier option: a will to live that is based on a desire to keep achieving, to keep loving, to keep becoming.

Lunch was *pasticcio*, a word I hadn't heard for a long time, not since I last ate my nonna's rich lasagne, which she made with chicken wings and pork and plenty of butter. We sat at a large table of Romana's family and friends. Suddenly, Romana's mother, Rosie, pulled a sheaf of papers from under the table.

There were eleven pages of very thin paper with old-fashioned typing, stapled together, with an American address and the date '18 luglio [July] 1960' on the first page. Romana took the pages and began to read the Italian, translating as she went. My heart was pounding in my chest as I heard something I hadn't dared to believe I would ever hear: Amelia's voice, lifting off the paper like a ghostly vapour. It was not her complete diary, but typed extracts taken from the journal that her sister, Rosina, found in Amelia's house after she died.

The origins of this typed document were puzzling. It appeared to have been created by someone, a lawyer perhaps, as the basis for a claim for unpaid wages and exploitation by the abusive restaurant owner.

Finally, I had the names of Amelia's tormentor in America and his business. The man had owned a restaurant in a section of an American city where many Italians lived in the 1950s, on a street known for its Mafia hangouts. I later learnt that he was born in Sicily in the late 1800s and migrated to America shortly after the turn of the century. Coming from Trieste, it seemed unlikely Amelia would have known him or his associates before she arrived in America. The Sicilian Mafia was a powerful presence in certain US cities, where organised crime flourished during the era of Prohibition. From old newspaper clippings I discovered that shortly before Amelia arrived in the United States, a restaurant at the same location as her future boss's was linked to the bust of a counterfeiting ring by federal agents. Today a modern brick building stands on the site where the restaurant was once located. It's a laundromat.

The extracts covered a period of five months in 1954 (explaining the gap in Amelia's employers listed in the city directories: she must have been working in the Sicilian's restaurant) and were cross-referenced with page numbers from the original diary.

Accompanying the transcription was a page headed 'Explanation', and it read like a cast of characters from a play; even Amelia's cat was mentioned (her name was Lola). Amelia's vocabulary, her homespun Italianised American words (like 'scio' for show), were interpreted, and various locations that featured in the diary (mainly Art Deco cinemas—she adored the Hollywood movies) were specified.

The extract began on the first page of Amelia's original diary, on 1 January 1954, with the words: *'Il mio primo diario e forse sarà l'ultimo.'* ('My first diary and maybe my last.')

Amelia wrote that she knew she would find unhappiness in America. A stranger read her palm in Naples near the post office in 1950, a year before she emigrated, and warned her. She would always remember this prophecy. But Amelia was determined. She never lost her courage, she wrote. Her biggest wish was to leave Italy for America. She called it (in Italian) 'the big America, the place of dreams for many and many from the old continent'.

At nine o'clock one night in the Italian spring of 1951, a few weeks shy of her 34th birthday, Amelia sailed out of the port of

Naples on an Italian ocean liner that had spent the war transporting troops to North Africa, but now carried passengers on the Genoa–Naples–New York service. Her mysterious experiences during the war, when she helped her starving brother interned in Germany, were on her mind as Amelia departed Italy for the final time.

'I had a lot of faith in myself the same as I always had in the many sad and terrifying days that I passed during the war so that I never believed more unhappiness could happen to me,' she wrote.

What frightening things had happened to Amelia in the war? Did this refer to the 'work' she did for the Germans?

Amelia wrote that on the ship she was worried. 'Was I happy? I was preoccupied, I was anxious, I was sad. Yes, I did cry at the moment of separation when the scream of the vessel's siren frightened me.'

She found comfort in the fact that she was sailing in the Marion month, the month of 'cara Madonnina', the dear sweet Madonna.

Amelia wrote that a man, Angelo, who helped her 'in many things', came to the port to farewell her. Was Angelo the mysterious financier of whom Mum's cousin spoke? Did he help arrange her immigration papers?

From the passenger manifest of Amelia's ship, which I obtained when I returned home, I knew that Amelia travelled as a 'stateless' person, and used a slightly different name: it was her surname but she spelt it with a 'ch' at the end, rather than 'gh'. Was it intentional on her part? If so, the irony was not lost on me: with its Slavic spelling, so objectionable to my grandfather, the name may have made his sister's claim to be an Istrian exile more credible. Was this the reason why on board the ship Amelia kept to herself, avoiding the women who were too curious, and the men who spoke too much 'nonsense'?

'Alone alone on board I did not know anyone, I did not want to know anyone, too much talking, too many questions.'

Amelia stayed in her small cabin in second class, sleeping, reading and praying, only leaving it when the call came to eat, or to attend 6 am mass in the tiny chapel. She bought some rosary beads and returned to the chapel at 5 pm to recite prayers to her precious Mary.

'I had my heavenly Mother near,' she wrote.

Some mornings, Amelia woke before dawn and went out to the deck to wait for the sun, a *'bellissimo spettacolo per chi viaggia in Mare. Nel grande Mare'*, a 'beautiful sight for those who travel by sea. In the big sea.'

After a week, Amelia became sick. 'The sea was calm, but the waves under the water made the ship roll,' she wrote, her words laden with double meanings that are perhaps only apparent now.

By the time Amelia began keeping a diary, her life had taken an awful turn. She had settled in the United States, and within a few months met the man who would exploit, beat, humiliate and dominate her—and then (I later discovered) witnessed her application to become a US citizen. What exactly was the nature of their relationship? I saved the more disturbing parts of the extracts about her boss to read more closely when I returned home.

In her diary, the deeply faithful Amelia called her time in America her 'Calvary', and wrote that she had to pay penance for something. *'Il mio Calvario non è finito devo espiare per chi che ho fatto.'* 'My Calvary is not finished I have to make good for what I have done.'

What had she done?

Amelia saved her brother from near-death in a Nazi forced labour camp, and managed to flee the desolation of post-war Europe for her place of dreams, her *'posto di sogni'*. But when the American dream turned sour, there was no escape for Amelia.

XIX

It was late 2016 when I solved a small part of the mystery of Amelia's emigration.

I received a response from researchers at the ITS in Bad Arolsen: they had found an entry on Amelia among their records. It was an index card confirming that 'she left Germany for the USA' (the reference to Germany is a mystery) and that she was registered at the IRO's displaced persons camp at Bagnoli near Naples. Her surname was spelt with a 'ch'. An image of the yellowed index card contained Amelia's personal details—the first names of her parents, with 'Yug' next to their names, and Amelia's date and place of birth. Beneath that were listed Amelia's movements in 1951. First, she was listed at an address in Naples; next, she was in the Bagnoli DPC; then, after more than a month at Bagnoli, she emigrated to the United States.

What began as a hunch based on a casual comment from a relative in Trieste—all that I scrawled in my notebook at the time was 'made self go into refugee camp'—turned out to be true.

I tried to imagine what situation Amelia would have found at Bagnoli. How easy would it have been to blend in among the other displaced people trying to leave war-ravaged Europe via Naples after the end of the Second World War? There were, I learnt, various factors that may have worked in Amelia's favour.

First, Italy was unable to cope with the large number of refugees it found itself hosting after the war (in 1947, as many as half a million people). It feared the longer they stayed the more social and political instability would grow. As a result, it encouraged the exiles from Yugoslavia to emigrate, and signed an agreement with the IRO in 1947 authorising it to conduct activities in Italian territories for the care, repatriation and resettlement of refugees. The IRO operated seventeen camps for displaced persons in Italy. Bagnoli, run out of a former school 'with walled grounds and modern buildings', was the best of them. Bagnoli had easy access to supplies, adequate communication, facilities that included recreation rooms, laundry and a camp hospital, and was close to a port.[15]

In addition, the independent and worldly Amelia would have fitted in among the Istrian women who were regarded by the Italians as 'easy' ('*donne dai costume facili*', 'women of the easy customs'), because they rode bikes alone, wore pants and spoke directly to men.[16]

Some of the records relating to the Bagnoli camp are held in the archives of the UNHCR (which replaced the IRO) in Geneva. My Italian researcher spent a week in early 2017 at the organisation's modern offices there, copying old cables, minutes, letters and reports from the late 1940s and early 1950s. Many of them were about Italy's refugee problem, its reluctance to approve identity documents for the refugees from Yugoslavia in case they never left, and the problems this caused for international organisations and foreign governments trying to process the masses displaced by the war.

Among the UNHCR files were also official US documents outlining the protracted process that Amelia, as a displaced person seeking admission to America as a refugee, had to complete. To satisfy the eligibility criteria, she had to show she was either displaced from her country of birth or nationality or last residence as a result of events occasioned by the Second World War, and was unable to return because of fear of persecution on account of race, religion or political opinion. Amelia's claim first had to be approved by the IRO. She would have been interviewed by a US official and given a medical examination. The final decision to admit her to America would have been made by the US Displaced Persons Commission, consular services, and the Immigration and Naturalization Service: she had to satisfy all these officials, who were on alert for cases of fraud and misrepresentation. Amelia only just made the cut-off for the US displaced persons intake by a few months; the program finished in December 1951.

American politics would also have aided Amelia in her quest to emigrate to America after the war. The US displaced persons program was heavily slanted in favour of those fleeing Communism in Europe, and she was indisputably from a region of Italy that had just lost territory to a covetous Communist regime. America was a reluctant taker of refugees following the Second World War. America's Jewish community had lobbied lawmakers the hardest and earliest for a change of policy. It was deeply disappointing (and ironic) that, when Congress finally approved a limited displaced persons program—three years after the war's conclusion—its eligibility criteria were anti-Semitic, advantaged Christians, and permitted German collaborators and even Nazi war criminals (Jews were viewed in some quarters as pro-Communist). The Displaced Persons Act was amended two years later, in 1950, to become less discriminatory and more generous. Ultimately, 16 per cent of the 400,000 displaced persons admitted were Jewish, while almost half were Catholics—like Amelia.[17]

Still, I was mystified as to how Amelia came to be accepted as a displaced person. What events or relationships in her past would have lent credence to her claim to have had a connection strong enough to Istria to justify her emigration? Or had she simply embellished her circumstances? If so, hers would not have been an isolated case in the desperate and chaotic years that followed the end of the Second World War. Determined to flee the old continent, whether because of what happened there or because of what was left, would-be émigrés embroidered their circumstances and fudged identity documents to get over bureaucratic hurdles. It was also commonplace for displaced persons not to have identity documents at all, since a great majority had been in German concentration camps or were slave labourers.

What did Amelia tell her interviewers to convince them of her bona fides?

XX

I dared not look up at Michael, who was sitting at the other end of the lunch table, as I tried hard to contain my emotions.

Romana said she'd copy the document for me before our train left. I feared we'd run out of time and Amelia's diary, or at least this small part of it, would be lost to me again. Then my son fell off a chair and, amid his crying, Rosie and Romana told me to put the document in my bag. I did.

Two of Romana's other younger siblings arrived and we sat on the lounge. They wanted to talk about the plane crash—something I rarely agreed to do.

But then Romana's elder sister, Nadia, began talking about a dream she'd had shortly before the crash. She was on a plane flying to Rome when her plane crashed. In her dream she lay in a field, looking back at the aircraft. The plane was on fire, and she was trying to get back into it to get her handbag, but she could only use one arm—her right arm.

I sat on the sofa listening to Nadia describe to me a scene that she could not have known about, that almost nobody knew about, a scene that I had lived. Lying in a soaked field looking back at the burning plane, with my right arm the only limb that wasn't burnt: that was me. Nadia said when she heard the news of my plane crash, she knew she had dreamt about it before it happened.

Was there any hint in her dream that I was involved? I wanted to know. Nadia assured me that no, there wasn't.

Tears poured from my eyes as I fielded questions about the crash. I answered them, ignoring the concerned looks from Michael on the other side of the room. I wanted my Italian relatives to see what writing this book about our family, and my grandfather's and Amelia's stories, meant to me: that it was my way of working through my own traumatic experiences.

It was soon time to catch our train to Klagenfurt. Romana drove us to the station. On the way, we talked about Nadia's strange premonition. Romana told me that one day in early March 2007, she was on the phone to my mother's cousin, Gloria, who was weeping as she relayed what had just happened to me on the other side of the world. I was still in the coma. Suddenly, the song 'Amazing Grace' came on the radio, and Romana told Gloria that in that moment she knew I was going to live.

'Amazing Grace' was the song bagpipers played at Fairbairn RAAF base when the coffins of the five Australians killed in the plane crash arrived back in Canberra. It was also the day my family was informed I was going to be brought out of the coma.

Romana and her family waited with us at the station at Udine until our train arrived.

In the carriage, a grumpy Austrian father on his way to Vienna with his two sons told us we couldn't sit in his compartment, though we had tickets for that particular cabin in first class. I felt my intrepid traveller's instincts kick in. I had a three-year-old to look after and a wheelchair to worry about, and I wasn't going anywhere.

The scowling Austrian marshalled his sons and off they went to find a more agreeable place to sit. We never saw them again.

The train departed and I pulled Amelia's document out of my bag. 'I got the diary,' I said to Michael. 'I can't believe it.'

'I know,' he replied.

I looked through the pages. 'I have Amelia's voice, I can actually hear her voice,' I said, crying and laughing at the same time.

The sun was setting as we approached the Austrian border from Tarvisio, passing jagged mountains, snowy peaks and glowing church spires of the alpine towns along the way. A half-moon hovered above rocky-looking mountains and we watched the darkness envelop the landscape outside the train window.

Only while sitting on the train did it occur to me that I was tracing Alfredo's steps, following the same journey he had made from Pola to Trieste to the Nazi stalags of Austria and Germany.

3

Searching

I

I WAS FIRST INTRODUCED TO THE REHAB TRAINER, or arm ergometer, at the Royal Perth rehabilitation hospital in suburban Shenton Park.

I was appalled when I saw the contraption the first time, and the feeling has never left me. It's a little like the large winch that the grinder turns on a big yacht to control the sails, except the operator doesn't stand, and there's no big sea.

The rehab trainer sits on a table while I sit on my wheelchair, facing it. Around and around my arms go, my hands gripping the blue rubber handles. The piece of exercise equipment provides one of the few forms of aerobic exercise I can do now. Every time I sit before it I am reminded in the most visceral way of what I have lost.

Sometimes, if I close my eyes while I'm working out on the rehab trainer, in my mind I go places that I can't go to physically anymore—running places. As I push those handles harder, faster, as my heart rate increases, if I'm listening to the same upbeat music on my headphones that I did on my daily runs, I can find myself suddenly at the door of my old apartment in Campbell.

I stand at the top of my apartment stairs and bend down to do up my shoelaces. Then I'm bounding down the stairs onto the bitumen at the front of my carport. I do a few lunges, touch my toes, start the timer on my watch and off I jog down the driveway. I remember to stop at the road and check for cars before I turn right onto Blamey Crescent and run down towards Anzac Parade, Canberra's most beautiful street. Veering left, with the green copper dome of the Australian War Memorial at my back, Old Parliament House across Lake Burley Griffin ahead of me, the scent of Victorian blue gums that line the wide boulevard in my nostrils, I coast. My feet hit the pavement and I can feel the bounce of my Asics Kayanos propelling me forward.

Down Anzac Parade I run, passing the individual memorials as I go. There's the glass tribute to the nurses, the Rats of Tobruk obelisk, the upturned wings of the RAAF sculpture, the looping New Zealand basket handles. I breathe the sweet vapours from the eucalyptus leaves that were so fragrant during the four hot summers I lived and ran in Campbell from 2003, when their essence hung heavy in the drought-affected city's dry air. That was the year, 2003, when bush fires ravaged Canberra, killing four people and destroying 500 homes. I don't catch that smell so much anymore but, when I do, it is the smell of running in the Canberra summer.

I am running alone; my ponytail is flying behind me in the breeze I leave in my wake. I turn left off Anzac Parade, and cross the road to reach the lake. I run through the tunnel that brings me out to the vista of the High Court across the water, and my shoes hit the red gravel as I turn right again to begin my circuit around the lake.

All up, the path around the circumference of the lake is 33 kilometres. I know because before our three marathons, at our absolute fittest, Michael and I used to run the whole track, which stretches from Canberra Airport at one extremity to the National Zoo and Aquarium at the other.

I open my eyes and the images, the sensations, are gone, my run is over. I am back to myself as I am now, in my wheelchair, with no legs, in a room, sitting in front of the rehab trainer.

II

It was February 2003.

I was standing with a group of male colleagues in the Senate courtyard, downstairs from my newspaper's office in the Parliament House press gallery, eating a sausage and drinking a bottle of South Australian beer. Once every so often, during parliamentary sitting periods, Amanda Vanstone, a senator from that state, hosted 'Coopers and Kransky' barbecues for journalists.

We were discussing New Year's resolutions.

'I want to do my first marathon this year,' I said to no one in particular.

Michael, who I barely knew then, was in the group. He worked for News Limited, as the *Herald Sun*'s political editor; I worked for Fairfax. The rival media organisations were divided by a corridor and the journalists only infrequently crossed the ideological divide into the other's camp.

Everybody agreed that running a marathon was a great idea. The Sydney Marathon was in September. We had seven months to train for the 42-kilometre race. Only Michael followed through.

I met Michael soon after I arrived in Canberra in 2001 at Filthy McFadden's, a dark and somewhat seedy tavern in Kingston. Kingston is a suburb close to Parliament House to which journalists new to Canberra, sent by their head offices from the different capital cities, gravitated in those days. They shared rented apartments in Kingston, drank in its pubs and bars after work and ate breakfast in its cafes on the weekend. After two or three years working and living in the nation's capital, most returned to wherever they had come from.

I was at Filthy's with some press gallery colleagues. My memories of that first meeting are vague, but Michael remembers my glasses (I usually wore contact lenses), my overcoat and long hair. I seemed earnest, but he couldn't hear anything I said over the music and the chatter of other patrons.

After the 'Coopers and Kransky' lunch, I started training for the Sydney marathon. I got a weights program from an instructor at the Parliament House gym. I ran my long runs alone at the weekend, and my short runs before work with Michael. The Parliament House security staff got accustomed to safekeeping our passes as we left for our runs via the Senate doors. I thought Michael seemed like a nice person and, as we clocked up more kilometres, realised he was different to anyone I had known. He was smart and funny and had a humility that was atypical of journalists in his position. What struck me most, though, was that I could see, even then, that Michael had an exceptionally kind heart.

I was preoccupied in those early months of marathon training with my career and novel status as a first-time homeowner. I was studying a Master of International Relations and had my sights on an overseas posting with my newspaper. I was also busy painting the walls of my apartment (I experimented with different colours before settling for green and red).

It was the first time I had lived completely alone, and I revelled in my own space. I delighted in being able to play my own music (Norah Jones and Buddha Bar) whenever I wanted. I celebrated having my own fridge, which was filled with easy-to-prepare 'running' food (banana smoothies for breakfast, frozen fish and tins of five beans for dinner) that flatmates couldn't pilfer. The carpet was frayed, the furniture was mostly second-hand, and the place was freezing in winter. Yet I loved everything about that kooky 1960s, split-level, Harry Seidler-designed apartment that, with all its stairs, I couldn't live in now.

By the time the Sydney Marathon came around, after my 31st birthday, I loved Michael too (the knowledge of this hit me during a karaoke moment: he was singing a Bee Gees song at the end of the press gallery corridor one evening, at a farewell for an ABC colleague). Over the next three years we ran two more marathons together—one in Ushuaia, the southernmost city of Argentina, in 2005, and a 45-kilometre race on the Great Ocean Road in Victoria the following year.

I found the Fin del Mundo Marathon (literally, the end of the world marathon) while searching the internet for 'exotic marathons'. I wrote for my newspaper's travel section afterwards that I had selected it from a list of other possible marathons: 'Bangkok (too hot), Tibet (too high) and the Great Wall of China (too many stairs)'.

The highlight of the Argentine race was the start. We were transported at sunrise to the Tierra del Fuego National Park in a catamaran, across the chilly waters of the Beagle Channel. Our fellow runners were a bunch of eccentric athletes, some of whom had run hundreds of marathons, in the oddest of places, including a nuclear submarine and a mineshaft 700 metres underground. Spirits were high as we joined in the countdown before the starter's gun, 'Diez, nueve, ocho, siete . . .'

The first half of the race through the pretty national park on dirt and gravel paths was a breeze. The second, through the back streets of the hilly, dusty town, past gauchos on horseback, was much more challenging, especially for Michael. I offered encouragement as we shuffled up one particularly steep hill, where we were overtaken by a sprightly 70-something-year-old runner.

'Just think of the beer at the end,' I said.

'Stop talking,' Michael grunted.

We were beaten in that marathon by 42 minutes by a man in a wheelchair who broke a wheelchair record that day—he finished seven marathons on seven continents in 70 days.

Afterwards, we hiked the Inca Trail in the heights of Peru.

Michael and I ran the entire route of every one of our marathons together, step for step, no matter how the other was faring. But the Argentine race was the only one where I had to call on the Holy Spirit to get Michael across the line.

Our preparation for the marathon was hampered by a few late nights in Buenos Aires beforehand. We stayed in the apartment of one of my former Canberra flatmates who was working in the Australian embassy. Every night after work we joined her at a local *parilla* for steak, fried cheese and Malbec wine. My friend told us she was pleasantly surprised that we weren't like 'normal' marathon runners she knew, who insisted on bland pasta, water and early nights in the lead-up to the big run. But that was how we always trained. One of the best things about the Sydney Marathon was the celebratory meal we had at Golden Century in Chinatown afterwards: roasted duck, salt-and-pepper calamari and Tiger beer. We probably ran slower times for it, but being able to eat what we liked because we were running over 100 kilometres a week was one of the many benefits of all that training.

III

I had some exceptional, dedicated physiotherapists in Perth.

One of them, Dale Edgar, who worked with me in the burns unit, was on hand the day when, two months after the crash, I sat up for the first time with a spinal brace.

'That was the biggest day of my life,' he told me.

Another, Caroline Roffman, who worked with me in the rehabilitation hospital, accompanied me on the train ride home across the Nullarbor Plain after my discharge, just to make sure nothing went wrong.

But lying in the burns unit of Royal Perth Hospital less than a month after the crash, a different physiotherapist came to talk to me about my rehabilitation plan and quality of life beyond.

'You won't be active,' she told me.

Michael was with me when she delivered this judgement, and neither of us could work out why she felt it necessary to be so brutal at that time, or at all.

An unexpected illness or injury can make it harder than it already is for me to do physical activity, affecting not only my bodily well-being but my emotional reserves as well. It can take a while to pick myself up again after these setbacks. Despite the physiotherapist's discouragement, however, I have figured out for myself that I am as much of a prisoner of my altered body as I allow myself to be.

In 2008, a year after the crash, I returned to Perth for more surgery to release scar tissue under my left arm. I wanted to be able to put my hair up in a ponytail again. In Canberra I was swimming 40 laps of the 25-metre Parliament House pool, as I had done regularly before the crash. It would be some time following the 2008 surgery before I could get back in the water, and I decided I needed one last swim—this one in the sea.

We contacted a lifeguard at Perth's City Beach who arranged a beach wheelchair, specially designed for the sand, with four fat floating wheels. The lifeguard took me into the gloriously cool and clear ocean, and together with Michael and Mum we swam out past the breaking waves where it was easier for me to swim.

When Mum asked the lifeguard about sharks, he told us not to worry, he'd swim further out than us to make sure the shark got him first.

These days I swim and kayak when I can at Jervis Bay on the New South Wales south coast. To get to my kayak on the beach, Michael gives me a piggyback down to the water's edge. I am learning to ignore the stares of strangers on the beach as we trudge across the sand. Out on the water, I steer close to the land, where it's shallow enough to see stingrays moving beneath me and to hear kookaburras in the trees. I paddle out to a point where the water changes from aquamarine to near black and the open sea begins. I pause at a rocky platform to watch the resting seabirds— cormorants and oystercatchers and gannets—and the untamed swell lifts and lowers my boat. The headlands are in the distance and I experience a freedom I can't find on the shore. In a kayak, I don't feel different to anyone else.

It's not easy to be active, but it's not impossible.

IV

My endurance running was much commented on in the news coverage after the crash.

It was true that in the days afterwards the surgeon told my family that 'it was lucky that Cynthia was fit, not fat'. My fitness probably did increase my chances of survival, but newspaper descriptions of me as a 'champion endurance athlete' and an 'internationally competitive marathon runner' were written by reporters who had never seen me run.

My friend Lauren was at Narrabeen Lakes the day a search party had to be sent out when I failed to finish a triathlon.

It was a mini 'Maxim' triathlon, in the days when triathlons were not yet madly popular: a 500-metre swim, a 20-kilometre ride and a 5-kilometre run.

I had driven my car to Narrabeen Lakes on Sydney's northern beaches for the early morning start. Lauren remembers receiving a text message from me the night before. I was working as a solicitor in Sydney at the time, and I sometimes worked late into the night.

'There's no way she's coming,' Lauren said to her husband, Tim, when she saw the text.

Lauren and Tim were serious about their triathlons. Tim had competed multiple times in the Forster Ironman Triathlon (3.86-kilometre swim, 180-kilometre cycle and a marathon). Lauren had competed in the half Ironman.

'I texted you back and hoped desperately that you'd turn up and sure enough you did—you'd had three hours' sleep,' she recalled.

I had to be at Narrabeen by 6 am.

'Somehow you managed to get your bike into the car and get all your stuff together. I was always amazed how you did it.'

Lauren and I lined up at the start with the other female competitors. In their caps and goggles, these women were intimidating: jostling for position, straining to plunge into the murky body of water. They wouldn't hesitate to swim over any competitors who got in their way.

We completed the swim, and Lauren remembers spotting me in the early stages of the cycle track and waving. By the fourth and final lap of the cycle stage, I was nowhere to be seen. Lauren finished her run and waited.

'After a while, I thought, "Funny, Cynthia would normally be here by now."'

When the sweeper car (which follows the slowest of the bikes) returned, my friends assumed I must have been on the run. When the organisers started packing up and there was still no sign of me, Lauren started to panic.

'I was saying to the organisers, "You can't pack up, there's someone still on the course."'

Lauren sent Tim, who feared I'd somehow drowned in the lake, out to search for me on his bike. Meanwhile, she took hers back to her car, which was parked next to mine.

'As I raised my bike on top of the roof I glanced in your car and that's when I saw you in your seat, with the passenger seat right back. You were sleeping like a baby.'

She knocked on the window and asked me what I was doing.

'You said you did two laps of the bike and thought, "I can't be stuffed, I can't do any more, so I rode back to the car and fell asleep."'

Lauren informed the organisers everything was okay: the missing competitor had been located.

'I was so full of admiration that not only would you do the triathlon when you were so tired and had had so little sleep—you turned up with your bike and everything—but also that you were so willing to say goodbye to it,' she said. 'You had such determination and drive to get there but also such a lack of competitiveness!'

V

I go running in my dreams sometimes.

While they are pleasant dreams—I am so happy to be running again—there is an awareness that something isn't right.

How am I able to run on these prosthetic legs? I wonder.

In my confused sleep state, a conviction forms that, somehow, I've figured out how to run in spite of my injuries. It is always wrenching to wake up and remember.

I never took running for granted. I used to pray before the crash; I was in constant communication with God and talked to Him multiple times every day. Without exception, I said a small prayer of thanks after my runs. I was so grateful to be able to do them, and aware that not everybody was so lucky.

I had a tradition after finishing the 7-kilometre Bay Run near my parents' house in Sydney that I always ran when I was in town. I'd lie on the grass at the top of the small sloped path in the same park where my father taught me to ride a bike. Looking down I could see the rowing club where I rowed in my early twenties, and the public pool where I learnt to swim as a young child. As I did my stretches and sits-ups, I'd look out to the bay, and whisper: 'Thank you, God, for my health—thank you for letting me be fit and healthy enough to run.'

I felt close to God. Growing up, surrounded by Catholic nuns, I secretly feared God had me marked for a life in a convent. Though I desperately hoped it wasn't the case, I would end my talks with Him with words from the 'Our Father' ('The Lord's Prayer'): 'Thy will be done.'

I thought I meant it, too. But when I realised what God actually had in mind for me all those years—a life, not as a nun, but without legs—all I saw was abandonment.

My error was having what the Italian writer, Primo Levi, called a 'deep-rooted, foolish faith in the benevolence of fate'.[1] Yes, I was grateful for my bodily integrity and my health, but I also never entertained the idea that I could lose it all so soon and so completely. Even as the plane was crashing, even as I was thinking with some wonderment 'so this is how I'm going to die', there was another voice in my head assuring me it was impossible.

'Of course it'll be fine, this sort of thing doesn't happen to me, the plane will right itself,' this naive voice assured me.

In 2006 there was a hit-and-run crash in Victoria, outside Mildura, in which six high-school children were killed. The school chaplain who counselled their grieving classmates observed that the event did not destroy his faith, but it did alter his perspective on God.

'I've had to face the fact that religion, while it provides hope and assurance of something beyond their selves, it can't prevent these sorts of things from happening,' he said.[2]

When I emerged from the coma, I was on an intense high. I felt like God Himself had decided to let me live. As the plane was crashing I had prayed to God to spare me, and in those days immediately after waking up heavily drugged in hospital I felt euphoric, as if surviving had given me a special connection to Him.

The euphoria soon wore off and was replaced with anger. Why did God do this to me? Hadn't I prayed, hadn't I shown Him enough gratitude? Next came a frightening depression. How could I live like this? Would it not have been better if I'd died?

One of the doctors told me: 'You have passed through the stage of "I survived", now you have moved to the stage of "I survived but for what?"'

By the time I left hospital, after almost six months, my anger at God had transformed into a numbness. I didn't pray anymore. I wrote a piece for the newspaper at the end of 2008 which friends convinced me not to publish. It began: 'I have just spent my second Christmas without God.' I described the profound void that the crash had left in my life because I had lost my relationship with God. That relationship had sustained me through good times and more trying periods, but it had not survived the crash.

It was yet another thing I had lost.

VI

In clinical medical terms, this is what happened to me on 7 March 2007.

My doctors wrote this in a medical journal article published after my hospitalisation. I only came across it recently. I knew doctors were writing about my case because my survival, given my injuries, was remarkable. But, for a long time, I had no desire to see what they had written. I was only reminded of the article's existence when Michael and I transcribed his shorthand notebooks.

A 34-year-old patient was transferred to RPH [Royal Perth Hospital] after sustaining 60% TBSA full-thickness burns in a plane crash. Having escaped the burning plane wreckage, the flames were extinguished by muddy ground water. Escharotomies of the lower limbs and left hand were attempted at a local hospital prior to transfer. On presentation to RPH there were circum-ferential full-thickness burns to both legs and the whole of the left upper limb, and patchy full- and partial-thickness burns to the back and abdomen. Traumatic injuries included fractures of the vertebral body of L1 and left transverse process of L2, and traumatic pancreatitis.

The patient's feet and left hand were pale, cold and ischemic; therefore complete escharotomies, fasciotomies and vigorous burns scrubbing and lavage were [performed] urgently in theatre. Gram's stain of tissue showed mixed bacteria and intravenous (IV) meropenem was started empirically. The patient was trans-ferred to the intensive care unit (ICU), but developed signs of progressive wound sepsis with new expanding areas of necrosis, a vesiculo-bullous rash extending past burnt tissue and progressive myonecrosis; requiring multiple extensive debridements on days 2 and 3 post-admission, including left above knee and right below knee amputations.[3]

In my own words: 60 per cent of my body surface was completely burnt, gone. My back was broken, my pancreas was crushed, my body was attacked by an almost-fatal infection acquired from water in a rice paddy field that meant, in the end, doctors had to cut off my legs, including my left knee, to save my life. I was lucky not to lose my left arm as well, and only the ends of four fingers on my left hand were taken.

I got a shock when I saw the photographs accompanying the article. One showed my left leg as it was before doctors removed it from above the knee. It was resting against a blue hospital sheet; my foot wasn't visible. I had never seen my burnt legs before. I was not able to say goodbye to them: Michael had asked to after the first leg was taken, but it was too late. Before I left Perth, when my hospitalisation was over, I asked what became of my legs. The doctors didn't answer me directly; they were full of infection, was all they'd say.

In my mind I always pictured my left leg—the one I lost almost in its entirety—being unrecognisable, black and burnt to the bone. But it wasn't like that at all. It was sliced open underneath, a deep incision the entire length of the leg, where doctors had performed a surgical procedure to release the burns. Otherwise it was my leg as I remember it, covered by my still-recognisable skin, which was darker than normal, splotchy and brown and purple in parts. It was nothing like I had imagined. It was my leg and it was beautiful and it was gone.

I couldn't sleep for nights after seeing those photographs. I had nightmares in which I was standing and, looking down, I saw my legs as they looked in the pictures.

On one of her visits to Canberra in 2008, I asked the burns surgeon, Dr Fiona Wood, about my legs. Fiona is a plastic and reconstructive surgeon and invented skin technology for treating burns that she used on me ('spray-on skin', where skin cells are taken from an unburnt site, harvested, and used to spray onto a wound; it is critical where large donor sites are not available because the burns are so big).

How close did I come to dying before doctors removed my legs? I wanted to know. I needed reassurance that the amputations were completely necessary, that keeping my legs—even just a little more of them—had not been an option. Fiona told me I nearly died twice in hospital in Perth.

On the evening of the plane crash, Fiona, who treated Bali bombing victims in 2002, was sent on a RAAF plane to Indonesia to treat survivors. The same night, I was on a medivac going in the opposite direction back to Australia. My plane was originally headed to Darwin, but got diverted to Perth. It was a couple of days before Fiona saw me at RPH.

The first time I almost died, Fiona told me, occurred before she had returned to Perth. I was having CT scans after arriving at two in the morning following the crash, when I communicated to doctors that I could not breathe (my airway was swelling dangerously from the large burns). A quick-thinking anaesthetist saved me then. He intubated me, putting a baby-size tube down my throat to open my airways (after frantic attempts to insert an adult-size tube failed).

The second time occurred after Fiona arrived back at the hospital on the Friday, two days after the crash. She told me when she walked into the hospital the other doctors had just taken my dressings down to change them.

'I smelt you from down the hall. I went in and said, "What's that smell?", and they said, "Nothing." I said, "Something is wrong," and then I looked at you.'

Fiona took down my dressings again and says my flesh was melting.

'It was a flesh-eating infection; your skin melted under my touch. We told the hospital to clear the day in the operating theatre.'

Fiona had to keep two teams of doctors all working at the same time because the infection was consuming me so fast they could not keep up with it.

'We were working in one area and in the other the infection was eating you away.'

If Fiona hadn't walked in, hadn't taken down my dressings at that moment, I would have died then too.

I spent a week in an induced coma in ICU—this was necessary for me to tolerate the breathing tube, but also for all the surgeries. I was then transferred to the burns unit, where Fiona could keep a close watch on me. Whenever she stepped into my hospital room I felt safer; I felt that as long as she was there, I wouldn't die. I am still comforted when I hear a Yorkshire accent, with its 'stren'th' instead of 'strength'. She wore a set of colourful chunky beads when she came to see me, unless it was Saturday. On Saturdays she came in to see me in her lycra, having cycled through Kings Park to the hospital. It could be hard to keep up with Fiona in conversations. Her thoughts were delivered so fast and overflowed with such insights, I often wished I had a tape recorder so I could go back and replay them, slowly, after she'd gone.

I found it difficult to depart the burns unit and Perth because I felt like I was losing my lifeline to Fiona.

The German literary scholar Jan Philipp Reemtsma wrote a book about the month he spent chained in a cellar by kidnappers who held him for ransom (he was heir to a large family fortune). He described the 'atrocious' wish he sometimes felt subsequently to be in a very small room with a chain around his ankle again. Where did such a wish come from?

'Simple. In the cellar, feelings of no-longer-being-part-of-the-world had their place.'[4]

Similarly, in the burns unit, a place no one would ever want to find herself, I felt nurtured and protected from the outside world—from my mortality also—in a way I'd never experienced as an adult. Now sometimes if I enter a hospital, or hear a particular song from that time, I feel a pang, a nostalgia, to feel protected—safe, cared for—in that way again. It is a perverse wistfulness given the reason I was there and the daily indignities and extreme pain I experienced at RPH.

The burns unit was a kind of womb; leaving was like having one's umbilical cord cut again.

VII

The worst injury I had before 2007 was when I fractured both wrists after falling from a set of monkey bars in a park.

I ended up with my two arms in white plaster casts to the elbows. I was seven years old. I landed in the dirt on my wrists, which were both bent back. My mother was standing up a small hill from the play equipment when it happened and I can remember looking up towards her. The day I returned to school encased in fresh plaster, the other children were all sitting cross-legged on the floor. Sister Francis, the gentle second grade teacher, gave me two pillows, one to place under each forearm, so I could join them. The injuries were called 'greenstick fractures' because of the young bones, which were like green wood.

The language around broken and severed bones is ugly, and it unsettles me.

I was horrified to hear, after the amputations of my legs, physio-therapists refer to my residual limbs as 'stumps'. As if, after my injuries, my body had suddenly degenerated from something human into something inanimate—a piece of wood, the remains of a felled tree. I took exception to my diminished legs being described in this way, and have never used the word. I have a support attached to my wheelchair for my right limb. I refuse to call it a 'stump support'; it is my 'leg rest'.

But the talk continues around me. I saw an orthopaedic surgeon at the start of 2015 about recurring infections in my right leg, at the end of the bone below my knee. The doctor told me what he thought was wrong and said, chuckling, 'It looks like we won't have to do any carpentry for now.'

I winced. Carpentry. Like my bones were planks of timber ready to be sawed, filed away, at the surgeon's whim. I hated the thought of these people chopping away at me casually, bit by bit, as if it didn't bother me to think of my body getting smaller and smaller with every cut.

At what point would they remove so much of me that I would cease to be human?

VIII

It took minutes to destroy my 34-year-old self, but many years and much angst to make her.

I didn't always want to be a journalist. I was 27 when I found myself—almost by chance rather than any design on my part—in the profession. When I discovered journalism as a vocation, I loved it immediately. It was fun, it was meaningful, every day was different, I was paid to write! Journalism was a licence to challenge authority and injustice. It gave me a sense of freedom and a breadth of experiences and insights into different people's lives and professions normally out of reach to the average person. I got the people—journalists were a cynical bunch, socially and politically aware, all of them outsiders in a way—and the people got me. I was also quite good at it.

Journalism was the career I had been looking for, though I hadn't known it until it was literally staring me in the face. It was also where I found love.

Up until that point I was searching, never entirely happy with myself: my looks, weight, jobs or relationships. It was, reportedly, the American poet Frank O'Hara who said your twenties are the time for turning 'sharp corners', and that's exactly what I did.[5]

At 24, I left Australia and my job as a solicitor and went travelling in Nepal, Tibet, Europe, the United States and Africa over an eighteen-month period, working tedious jobs in London between adventures to save money for the next one.

Conducting this 'search for self' necessitated first putting a distance between my parents and me. This was a confronting process for my mother in particular. Mum's views on her relationship with her children are absolute: she sees us as extensions of herself, no matter our age or stage in life. Mum is still hurt that I moved out of home at 22, after getting my first full-time law firm job, saying it was too sudden. We argued the entire eighteen months I was overseas, with every one of our infrequent phone calls acrimonious, my mother convinced I was wasting my life.

Solicitors' jobs were scarce for new graduates when I got my final professional qualifications in 1995, after completing the College of Law at St Leonards in Sydney. I found a job as an insurance litigator at a large law firm at Circular Quay. I enjoyed the court work and the collegiality among the young solicitors and paralegals, but the subject matter—workers' compensation and public liability—left me empty.

Before long I was planning my escape from the law. I was interested in Tibetan culture, its Buddhist religion and traumatic political history since the Chinese invasion. I found a World Expeditions trek to the north-east face of Mount Everest that would take me overland from Nepal into Tibet and through the cities of Shigatse, Gyantse and Lhasa. I moved back in with my parents to save money, got a working visa for the UK, quit my job at the law firm and headed off overseas with a massive blue backpack and no return date.

I was rejecting my old life, 'cutting the strings' that bound me to that life, abandoning all my possessions and leaving my friends behind.

'The world is now my only friend,' I wrote, and headed to one of its remotest parts.

Everybody knew I was searching.

'I hope you find the answer,' my last boss wrote in my farewell card.

On my final day at work, I was doing court mentions in the NSW Supreme Court's commercial list and got talking to another solicitor. I later wrote in my travel diary: 'I remember the happiness of my heart when he said he was usually in construction and I told him I was leaving for Tibet the next day.'

In 1997, while working at my first law firm job in London, on Chancery Lane, I said to a friend that I had this constant feeling I was searching for something—'a place, a career, a person, a state of faith'.

She told me: 'You'll find it when you've learnt to like yourself.'

The remark seemed unkind at the time, though its perceptiveness is evident to me now. I did need to learn to like myself, but all I knew at that stage was that I didn't like being a lawyer. I was searching for an elusive non-lawyer me, a me I could like. Only then would I be able to open myself to others to like (and love) me too.

With each new continent during those eighteen months of wandering I got a little closer to figuring out what I wanted to do with my life. By the time I headed home from Europe, via Africa, where I spent two months travelling from Kenya to Zimbabwe, I had made the definitive decision to leave the law.

IX

Tibet's foreignness overwhelmed me.

I was in a small group of five hikers, three of whom were retirees. As we crossed the Friendship Bridge by foot from Nepal into Tibet I wrote in my diary that 'I wanted to cry out: "My God, I'm in Tibet."'

The small border town of Nyalam, where we stopped that afternoon to acclimatise to the high altitude, was freezing cold, barren, dusty. It was dominated by one dirt road lined by a gutter filled with rocks and rubbish, set against a backdrop of mocha-coloured mountains. What sounded like music from a *Kung Fu* movie soundtrack blared spookily from loudspeakers through the town. Tibetan women with serene faces walked along the road. I saw children playing, a few serious-looking monks, and many roving dogs. Our hotel, the Snow Land Hotel, was dark and dank, and had a patterned curtain for a door. The toilet was part way up the road from the hotel and consisted of a hole in a wooden platform, over a pit many metres below.

'I have complete awe and humility for something way beyond whatever I could have dreamed,' I wrote, wide-eyed, in Nyalam.

Then I had 'the worst night of my entire life to date'. We had ascended quickly that day to an altitude of 3750 metres and I was experiencing sensations I'd never felt before. I was woken by incredibly painful stomach cramps and when I stepped out of my room I blacked out, falling noisily to the floor, quite delirious. Two of the men in our group heard the thump and came out of their room to find me lying on the ground.

I spent a month in Tibet: four weeks of extremes, of sensory images so powerful I still summon them today if I need to calm my anxious mind. Prayer flags strewn between towers of stone, flapping in the chilly wind at the tops of high passes. Beautiful valleys where we camped by rocky streams, with mountains on one side and forest on the other. Snow leopard prints in the dirt. The constant roar of avalanches, crashing noisily like ocean waves. Glimpses of the majestic Makalu, the world's fifth-highest mountain, with its black, pyramid-shaped peak and, close by, Everest, the purest of whites, solemn, beautiful, terrifying.

'Barren, barren, barren,' I wrote in one diary entry in Tibet.

It is dust, rock after rock after rock, scorching sun, winds, all browns and yellows . . . There are little green streams all over the place. People—you pass them on donkeys herding yaks or cows or sheep or goats along the 'road'. Sometimes only a child, sometimes more. They all smile, are very dark with weather-beaten faces and dirt-encrusted bodies, the women in their colourful aprons, kids in ripped dirty jeans and jackets. You see the villages—not more than stone walls really, some are schools, one a hospital. Then there are the ruins—sometimes they blend so well with the mountains you'd think they were only rocks.

I experienced extreme cold in Tibet, sleeping in an orange tent on my own in snow storms at 5000 metres. My hands and fingers were frozen and aching and my thumbs became infected. My clothes were wet and caked with dirt. Sometimes I cried myself to sleep, then I'd wake repeatedly during the night unable to stay asleep on the cold, hard floor, hoping for daylight.

There was fear, but there was also exhilaration. I climbed mountains waist deep in snow, my legs weary and heavy, unable to carry the smallest of packs, breathing in oxygen from a can to keep moving. Other times I walked with shallow breath uphill across unstable scree. Below my feet and the perilous ground cover of broken rocks only mist was visible, so that I could not see how far down it was to the glacier if I fell. Suddenly, just the top of the mist would clear and out would poke incredible peaks of 6500 metres, so close it seemed as though if I threw a rock, it would hit one of them.

I felt a freedom I'd never experienced before. I was awed by the power of the Himalayas: by their spirituality and hostility.

After a month I was back in Europe, picking up mail from the Drifters Club in London (email was in its infancy). Three months of unplanned travel followed, sometimes with friends, but mostly alone. With a Eurail pass I journeyed through Germany, Italy, France and Spain.

I left friends in Pamplona after I was robbed while sleeping on a park bench one night, unable to find a spare hostel bed (I woke to find a man unzipping my jeans to get at my money belt). I regretted ever joining the masses of drunk and pot-smoking antipodean backpackers who descended for the 'running of the bulls' festival. I had a ticket to Switzerland stamped in my Eurail pass, but on the train I encountered a friendly American university student from North Carolina who convinced me to stop in Barcelona instead. Seeing him off at the airport in Madrid a few days later, at his suggestion I bought an aeroplane ticket on stand-by and flew home with him to Raleigh.

It was before September 11, but for such impulsive behaviour I was regarded with great suspicion by airport security staff leaving Spain.

'I have my doubts,' I heard one of them say to her co-worker as they inspected my passport.

No kidding, I thought. I have a few myself.

It wasn't romance that caused me to 'max out' my credit card on an expensive fare to America. I was reacting against the boundaries of a strict upbringing. I did it because I could. In the United States I hired a car and drove the Interstate 95 alone through South Carolina and Georgia. I immersed myself in civil war history in Charleston. In Savannah I visited the houses made popular at the time by the book *Midnight in the Garden of Good and Evil*. I listened to Blur and the Dave Matthews Band on a tape my American friend made me for the trip.

Back in North Carolina, I gave myself a 25th birthday present: a fuzzy green tattoo of a Celtic cross the American sketched on a paper napkin one night at a pancake parlour. We found the studio, Dogstar, in the phone book. The cross was inked into my skin by a young tattoo 'artist' who, going by his skill level, was probably the work experience kid. The tattoo was low on my back, behind my hip. Its location and diminutive size were indicative of the limited nature of my belated rebellion: it was a tattoo that nobody could see. (Somehow, with all that skin I lost in the crash ten years later, the unsightly tattoo survived the ordeal completely undisturbed.) I dyed my hair an ugly peroxide blonde and spent a weekend in Washington DC and New York with the American's father and stepmother and two of their friends, one of whom, a Frenchman, insisted on calling me 'Sheila' the whole time.

I flew back to Spain with crippling debts and commenced a marathon six-day solo trip by train, boat, bus and ferry to meet a friend from Sydney in the Greek islands. I slept on the train, and showered in the Nice train station. I arrived in Naxos grotty and in poor spirits, but cheered up once I located our camping ground and its amenities block. In Santorini I fell off a moped, twice. I got back on a boat to Brindisi, alone once again, with a bleeding leg and no medical supplies. I spent the night nursing my leg on the vessel's outer deck, where a kind backpacker from Manchester gave me some gauze to cover the weeping wound.

'After this I think I could be a foreign correspondent in Africa no problem,' I wrote in my diary.

This was the first mention I was contemplating a possible career in journalism (my travel companion in Greece had given me a book by a British foreign correspondent working in Africa).

I caught a train to Trieste, where I recuperated at my mother's cousin Giuliana's house. I spent time with Nonno's sisters, Assunta and Rosina. Rosina was distressed because she was losing her memory.

Then I headed back to the UK to find work.

X

In London, I dyed my hair brown and signed up with a temp agency, Australian Staff Connections.

I worked as a tea lady for one day in a public relations firm. I was introduced as a solicitor from Australia to an Englishman who replied without looking at me, 'Well, what's she doing *here?*' Next I worked as a shop assistant at a Dutch department store at Marble Arch for a week, before finding a paralegal job through a friend from Sydney. I wandered down to All Souls Church and saw an advertisement on the noticeboard at the back of the church for a room going in an apartment in the East London district of Bow.

Princess Diana died soon after I moved in to my new abode. I woke one Sunday morning to the news of her car crash. I mourned along with the rest of London. I walked down to Buckingham Palace to see the mountains of flowers stacked against the gates and shed tears on the Tube reading the newspapers filled with stories of her young sons.

I was miserable in Bow. Being unfamiliar with London's geography, I hadn't realised it was a rather depressed part of the city; its association with the famous gangsters, the Kray brothers, seemed apt once I had spent a few months there. There were evenings after work when I was followed home from the Tube station, and I once had to flag down a taxi to evade a pursuer. My lodgings were in a nondescript grey block of flats, the walls of which were thin enough that I could hear the violent domestic disputes occurring in the other apartments late at night. My landlord and housemate, an evangelical Christian from Oxford, was depressed too, a situation not helped by the doleful *Betty Blue* soundtrack she played repeatedly.

I avoided the apartment as much as possible, eating dinner out most nights at Indian restaurants in Sloane Square, at the opposite end of town. I made friends with an American banker from Toledo, who took me to Morrissey concerts and Wagner recitals, and let me house-sit his place in upmarket Parsons Green while he was away.

My gloomy surroundings and lack of solid connections to a home, job or people contributed to my existential uncertainty.

'I have this fear of loneliness,' I wrote in my diary. 'I'm so unsure about everything in my life, everything—love, how to express my faith, my personality, friendships, career, where I want to be, how I want to be.'

I did find things to like about London's East End. Most Sundays I went to Spitalfields Markets, where I ate felafels and trawled through racks of second-hand clothes. For twelve pounds I bought a heavy black-and-white houndstooth coat that I got relined and wore for the next ten years. I went for autumn runs among the squirrels in Victoria Park on foggy weekend mornings with the Smiths playing on my chunky yellow Sony Walkman.

Such days made me grateful for the path life had taken since I left Sydney.

'I envy nobody's, not one single person's, life, when I think about the things that have happened to me, especially in the past six months. Sometimes I even wonder why I have been *so* lucky?'

By the end of 1997, I was ready to leave the drabness of Bow and drudgery of my paralegal job doing data entry for pre-trial document discovery on a big shipping case. I loved the freedom of living in a foreign city but I was lonely and dissatisfied. Having made countless promises for self-improvement (such as vowing to 'stop apologising for myself' and 'finding the love of my life'), I left London to spend Christmas and New Year in Trieste. I ate the traditional good luck lentils on *capo d'anno* and said sad farewells to my great-aunts, Rosina and Assunta. It was the last time I saw them.

Bidding goodbye to 1997, I wrote in my diary: 'I feel like I'm really coming into myself.'

XI

My ideas about love were shaped by literary heroines and epic love stories that usually ended tragically.

Doomed couples like Catherine and Heathcliff, Voss and Laura and, in a book I adore, Vikram Seth's *An Equal Music*, Julia and Michael. Julia, a pianist, goes deaf and Michael, a violinist, breaks her heart. In *A Farewell to Arms*, another favourite, Ernest

Hemingway describes the scene just before Catherine Barkley dies in childbirth, leaving Frederic Henry, an American lieutenant in the Italian army in the First World War, behind. Henry bumps into a nurse in the hospital hall who tells him, 'Mrs Henry has had a haemorrhage.'

'Is it dangerous?'

'It is very dangerous.' The nurse went into the room and shut the door. I sat outside in the hall. Everything was gone inside of me. I did not think. I could not think. I knew she was going to die and I prayed that she would not. Don't let her die. Oh, God, please don't let her die. I'll do anything for you if you won't let her die.[6]

I believed in the existence of a love that transcended the material world, that in its most powerful, genuine form was otherworldly.

Travelling through Europe, I visited countless churches and cathedrals, as one does. In each new house of worship I performed a small ritual. I knelt down in a pew, or crossed myself standing at the door, and recited a variation of the same prayer: that one day, soon, I would find love.

I had been in (non-serious) relationships but, somehow, they felt forced, like they were being imposed on me either by others or by myself, agreeing to them because I thought I should. When I was fifteen, I had my year ten 'formal'. I didn't know any boys, having attended an all-girls Catholic school, and was content to go alone as my best friend was, but my mother had other ideas. Over my hysterical protests, Mum asked a boy who lived up the street to accompany me. Mum thought she was doing me a favour, but it felt like an arranged marriage. My sense of disempowerment was profound.

These relationships never lasted long (though the year ten formal with that unfortunate boy from my old primary school seemed to go on forever).

I had to find a version of myself that I liked, before I could share that person with somebody else.

XII

In 1998 I returned to London with a different job and a new place to live, on the other side of the city.

My goals, as always, were to save money and lose weight. I bought a set of electronic scales and wrote bizarre positive reinforcements to encourage better eating habits, such as 'I will dissociate myself from my body'. Beyond this, I resolved 'to be positive, tranquil, like myself'.

But my loneliness continued.

'Honest, no matter how independent I've become, I know I'll never be happy alone,' I wrote. 'Where are you, God? Why don't you hear my prayers about loneliness?'

And later, continuing a tedious theme: 'God, why can't I just find love and a lasting relationship? Why single me out for singledom?'

I moved into a furnished single room bedsit with a view of Wandsworth Bridge Road in Fulham. It was upstairs from an exotic cushion shop owned by the mother of the Hollywood actress Minnie Driver. She loved cats and chose her tenants on 'instinct'. I was among a steady stream of Australians and South Africans who occupied the other bedsits, one upstairs, one below mine. All my possessions—some crockery, a box of washing powder, a stack of magazines—fitted on the room's sole wooden table upon which also sat a small television set.

I could only afford the barest minimum of groceries, which I bought on social outings to the local Safeways with my fellow bedsitters. Most nights I ate potatoes cooked in the communal microwave with melted cheese or baked beans and broccoli. On weekends I devoured the London papers, which were far more interesting than those back home.

My new job carried greater responsibility than those I'd previously had in London. I was managing personal injury claims for British Rail. The agency's office at Paddington Station was located in a kind of disused warehouse. My co-workers were mostly stuffy Englishmen who brought to mind the characters from the BBC comedy *Are You Being Served?*, though there was nothing humorous about them at all. They regarded me, I'm sure, as an uncouth colonial subject (I was once reprimanded by one of them for scratching my thick woollen-stockinged knee during a meeting). I left after narrowly avoiding being fired for sitting too long on an old, impossible-looking summons that had clearly been ignored by many others before me.

My sister came to stay later that winter. We spent a few days in Paris, where we wandered for hours, entranced, among the statues in the sculpture garden at the Rodin Museum. I bought a pair of second-hand flared jeans at a flea market in east Paris in full knowledge that 'they will never fit until I start running marathons' (it was five years before I could do up the fly). In our hotel room we watched CNN's coverage of the diplomatic crisis in the Middle East that culminated, later that year, in 'Desert Fox', the US bombing of Iraqi military facilities. The idea of a career involving foreign politics and world travel began to take firmer hold.

'If I can't be married, then I want to be a diplomat,' I wrote.

Juliette and I also spent a week in Istanbul, where I heard my first Islamic call to prayer, its wail so piercing and jarring. In the

Spice Bazaar we bought bags of spices that we never cooked with, and marvelled at the sixth-century cathedral Aya Sofya, the abundance of cats and the 'women-less streets'.

Back in London, I dyed my hair black and started another job, my final one in that city, at a law firm located at London Bridge, working in construction law.

I liked this job. I was a senior paralegal on a court case that made news in the *Mail on Sunday*, involving European Union law and building contracts for the new Westminster building. I worked with a lovely group of English lawyers; it was my only job in London where I was treated like an intelligent professional. I travelled the city over, performing 'discovery' (inspecting documents produced by the opposing side under court order). Marylebone, Camden, Warren Street, Westminster: I was always in a great rush, dodging slow tourists in Tube stations. I worked long hours, from 9 am until 2 am many days, plus weekends, as the court case drew nearer.

There was a gym across the other side of London Bridge. In my breaks at the law firm I did punishing workouts to make up for all the Ben and Jerry's ice-cream I was eating alone in my little bedsit at night to console myself over my perennial singleness.

'God has me to Himself,' I wrote in my diary. 'If in a few years he wants me to join a convent I shall.'

It was in this last job, in May 1998, that I finally decided to leave the law for a new calling (not the convent).

I was enamoured of words and saved newspaper clippings with writing I admired, which I pasted into my journal. London's weather was a favourite topic of columnists—it was an unusually warm spring—and I cut out small articles about butterflies behaving in February as if it were already summer, and railway embankments carpeted in white flowers during May, following the downpours the city had received in April.

I had started a creative writing course with a friend every Wednesday evening at Munster Road. I wrote short stories and poetry about random subjects: homeless people, laundrettes, rooms full of cherries, Everest, dancers, spurned lovers, Portofino, teenage runaways. None of it was memorable and the course was cancelled when our teacher got a job writing for *The Big Breakfast*, a British television show. But the very act of writing fiction, words that didn't have to conform to a legal letter or university essay, unshackled my mind to new possibilities.

One day, sitting in my office in the London law firm—I remember the moment very clearly—I was writing an email to a friend in Sydney when I announced to her that I was going to be a writer.

Having made up my mind, I was ready to go home.

'It is never too late to be what you might have been,' I wrote in my diary, and next to it, 'Plans for Sydney'.

There were two: postgraduate study in journalism and marathons.

I had become friendly with a number of South Africans and started entertaining thoughts of returning home to Australia via Africa. I squeezed in as much travel as my job would permit before then: a trip to Chicago, another to Ireland, a final one to Portugal.

Sitting on a rock on a beach in Cork, I became philosophical about turning 26.

'This is the first real point in my life I've been able to stop and consider where I want to go next,' I mused. 'Until now it's been very subconscious—school, university, college, law firms, overseas to work. Really now it's in my hands to change my destiny or entrench it.'

In Lisbon my resolve to switch careers hardened.

'I don't give a damn what other people may or may not think.'

Each travel experience cemented my new dream to become a foreign correspondent. I would 'wear my writer's badge as a diplomatic entrance permit as I travel the world', I wrote.

In my final days in London, I did a couple of videoconference interviews for law firm jobs back in Sydney, knowing I'd need one to pay off the huge credit card debts from all the travelling.

I spent a day ambling about Portobello markets.

'I realise I possess the power to reinvent myself should I choose,' I wrote afterwards. 'I choose.'

I saw a fortune teller. Unlike the stranger who read my great-aunt Amelia's palm and predicted unhappiness before she sailed to America half a century before, mine was vague and I didn't record what he said.

I packed up my belongings and shipped the boxes back to Australia. I turned 26, and flew out of Heathrow to Kenya.

XIII

I arrived in Nairobi a week after terrorist bombings at the US embassy there killed 213 people.

A simultaneous bombing in Dar es Salaam in Tanzania, where I visited shortly after, killed eleven. The bombings were thought to be the work of Osama bin Laden, a name that meant little to most people at the time.

My introspection, so cringe-worthy to read back over now, continued in my Africa diaries—but something was different. I wrote about having a greater faith in myself, a greater optimism and peace.

'The time is ripe for me to listen to my heart, to turn my back on the law and get out there and find me a job that my soul is thirsting for. Please Lord send me a little tiny sign of how I can achieve this.'

I joined a group of travellers from Australia, New Zealand, the UK and America for an organised truck ride through south-east Africa. They were diary writers and book lovers like me. I shared a tent with a witty English woman, a solicitor from London who was also discontented with her legal career.

I spent the days on the open top of the truck with an orange scarf to protect me from the dust and let the wind blow wild in my face and hair. I relished wearing outdoors attire every day—hiking boots, khaki pants, baggy tops, a floppy hat, no mirrors—and being so close to the untamed natural world, among so few people. I saw my first giraffe while driving through the Serengeti; the animal's gangly grace was profoundly moving. The wildlife those first days in Kenya and Tanzania was astonishing: gazelles, zebras, warthogs, baboons, wildebeests, hartebeests, elephants, lions, hippos, vultures, mongooses, topis. The landscape was one of vast dry grassy plains, blue hills, waterholes and acacia trees. We weren't allowed to have showers after dark because of the risk of getting attacked by a wild animal. Life was reduced to its most elemental form, and I felt a rare kind of bliss.

In Tanzania we formed an expedition to climb Mount Kilimanjaro. It involved a three-day ascent to an altitude of 5895 metres—higher than I had climbed in Tibet. I was confident that, as an old hand, I would be able to cope better with the high altitude this time.

By the second day, at Horombo Hut (above 3700 metres), the familiar nausea and headache began. I took Panadol, drank litres of water and tea to keep hydrated and ate peanuts for energy. Late in the afternoon on day three, at Kibo Hut (above 4700 metres), my stomach felt like it was going to explode. It was cold and windy outside and the last half-hour of walking that day was gruelling.

'I want to make the summit so bad but I don't know if I can,' I wrote.

That night we were woken at midnight for the final ascent, up a rocky path, that eventually reached the snow. The plan was to arrive at the peak by early morning—but by 7.20 am I was back in the hut instead, documenting my failure. I had climbed until 2.41 am—a quarter of the way—when I fell for the first time, in tears. After falling again, I turned back with a guide, disappointed, disheartened, humbled, embarrassed.

On my miserable descent I pondered my career. Seeing all the United Nations World Food Programme trucks, I thought perhaps I'd enjoy working in the aid sector. I also swore I'd never return to high altitudes again. Then, back in the hut that afternoon, I began jotting down thoughts for what I would do differently the next time I went mountain climbing above 5000 metres.

We took the hydrofoil to Zanzibar for a few days. I wandered around the old Stone Town, with its confined littered alleyways teeming with small children, and its eighteenth- and nineteenth-century mosques and narrow two-storey houses with their intricately carved huge wooden doors and tiny first-floor balconies. At street stalls on the seafront I bought chapati and pieces of octopus that were barbecued in front of me on a hotplate. The London lawyer got talking to the laundry man at our hotel who told us his brother could arrange a boat to take some of us to nearby Prison Island for three pounds. We bought lunch for the trip—papayas, bananas, tomatoes—and found the vessel, a handmade wooden dhow piloted by two men. We picked up ten locals with their own food and building supplies and set off for the island, across the warm turquoise waters of the Indian Ocean that lapped white sands and palm trees and mud-brick huts. On the island I met a local artist, Salim, who (unknown to me) had sketched me lying on the beach. I admired his drawing, not because it was any good, but because he had made me look thin.

From Tanzania we went to Malawi, a country of vast potholes, swarming bugs, and a lake as blue and expansive as an ocean. On the road in we passed poignant signs on Caltex petrol tankers and roadside billboards.

'The meaning of life is struggle.'

'A government without women is like a pot sitting on a stone.'

Our campsite at the edge of Lake Malawi was patrolled by security guards with rifles and black Christian missionaries who wanted to talk about God. The lake was full of hippos and crocodiles and carried parasites that caused the disease bilharzia. Still, I (foolishly) went for a swim on my own at midnight on a dare from the London lawyer.

In Zambia, four nights later, I had my biggest scare of the trip.

We were camped by a river with a very steep embankment at the undeveloped Flatdogs campsite in the South Luangwa National Park. Zambia had a wild, frontier feeling about it. Poachers killed unchecked. We could hear snorting hippos and screeching baboons and our guide told us there were leopards nearby. Lions roared across the river and monkeys roamed our campsite. That night we had more terrible camp food for dinner, made palatable by the beer that I was learning to drink (a useful skill for my future in journalism). I set up the tent with the London lawyer and went to sleep around 11 pm.

At 1.21 am I was awoken by the startling noises of tree branches crashing on top of the tent. I reached for the zippered door, my immediate reaction being to run, and the London lawyer yanked me back. She was already awake and had figured out what was happening: elephants were feeding from the trees above our tent. Running from an elephant, we had been warned by our guide, who was sleeping in the truck with a rifle, was a sure way to get yourself killed (running apparently encourages elephants to charge).

My heart was pounding; I could feel blood pulsing in my shaking hands and body. For the next 30 minutes the pair of us sat motionless inside the tent in terror, watching the shadows of four huge elephants that were ambling about our tent demolishing the trees above us.

'Please, God . . . oh fuck, oh fuck,' I repeated over and over in my head.

We heard someone in the distance, a guard, trying to distract the elephants with whistling and clapping and gunshots. Eventually, the elephants moved on and we crept out of our tent. We were in shock: massive dollops of dung lay dumped around the tent where the elephants had been eating.

The last country we visited was Zimbabwe. In Bulawayo I met relatives of my mother: her cousin Alessandro's son, Aldo, and his family. My last act of madness was a terrifying bungee jump 111 metres down over Victoria Falls.

Just before flying out of Africa I rang home and discovered my interview with one of the law firms had gone better than I thought. I had a new job in Sydney, working in the construction litigation section of a big city law firm. I was back exactly where I had left off eighteen months before: in the NSW Supreme Court's commercial list.

But it wasn't for long.

XIV

Back in Sydney I started work at the law firm and enrolled in postgraduate journalism studies.

The next twelve months were arduous. I was regularly working past 10 pm at the law firm, eating the sandwiches that were delivered to our floor's kitchen at eight o'clock every night to encourage solicitors to work back late. One night a week I finished earlier and got a bus to the University of Technology Sydney to take my journalism classes.

On the weekends, living in a rented Art Deco apartment in Bondi, I was busy building a portfolio of news articles that were getting published in free suburban newspapers. The Sydney Olympics were approaching, and I wrote stories about the local residents' protests over plans to construct a beach volleyball stadium on iconic Bondi Beach.

Soon, I was being paid for my journalism. I got a part-time job with Richard Ackland, working out of his Law Press of Australia office in Kings Cross. The day I walked into Richard's tiny office on gritty Darlinghurst Road, with its strip clubs and junkies and greasy takeaways, I knew that I had, at last, found my calling. Another journalism job soon followed, at *The Eye* magazine, published by Eric Beecher's Text Media, then a third with Fairfax's *Good Weekend* magazine. I felt alive, unconstrained, thrilled by the task of reporting and crafting stories. I could hardly believe my luck, to have found people who thought enough of my writing abilities that they were willing to hire me as a proper journalist.

Sometime in 1999 I left the law firm job—even the promise of a stint in a legal office in New York could not keep me—as I had enough journalism work to keep me employed full-time. When *The Eye* closed (after a disappointingly short life) I was hired as a reporter at the *Sydney Morning Herald*.

In the space of a year, my reinvention from lawyer to newspaper reporter was complete. In all my wild imaginings about becoming a foreign correspondent, I never actually contemplated the possibility that—in order to get there—I might one day be writing daily news for a major metropolitan newspaper. It was simply outside my experience, not having ever actually known any journalists. But it turned out that newspaper reporting, and political reporting in particular, suited me.

Journalism picked me up like a novice surfer on a wave. Forces bigger than me were at work and I let them carry me, to where I knew not.

XV

I got my first front-page exclusive within the first couple of weeks at the *Herald*.

It was Friday, a story was unfolding out in the Ku-ring-gai Chase National Park in Sydney's north. A back-burning operation the previous afternoon had gone wrong and firefighters were caught in the blaze. The chief of staff sent two senior police reporters to the scene and told me to grab a taxi and go join them.

I arrived at the street where the fire had occurred: a line of houses backed onto the bush with a reserve at one end where the media had gathered. I felt redundant. The police reporters had the story covered and there wasn't much for me to do. The fire had long been put out and emergency crews had left. Some firefighters had died and others, badly burnt, had been taken by ambulance to hospitals around Sydney.

I figured my best chance was to find a resident who had seen something and interview them. But it was late morning on a weekday, and none of the locals appeared to be home. I drifted around the reserve, before deciding to wait on the footpath in front of the houses in case any occupants returned home. Every so often I knocked on a front door to see if anyone was inside.

Suddenly, one of the doors opened. A woman invited me in and I sat down on a chair, nervous, an intruder in her lounge room.

I could see the bush through the back glass doors and windows of the house. The woman began talking about the fire the day before. I turned the tape recorder on and listened.

She was home when the firefighters ran from the bush towards her house screaming, burning, their skin hanging off them. She and her husband tried to help them, hosing them down and wrapping them in sheets and blankets to put out the flames. They called for ambulances and tried to help the injured firefighters concentrate on their breathing after some started hyperventilating.

Mine was the only story that day. It ran on the front page of Saturday's paper, under the headline BURNING MAN'S PLEA: 'HELP, HOSE ME DOWN'.

The editor, Paul McGeough, wrote to me afterwards: 'What an impressive start to your career at the *Herald*.' My story, he said, was 'well-crafted to convey the emotion without becoming maudlin'. It was a three-line email, which I kept.

It was a day of multiple firsts: the adrenaline of a breaking story; being the star (for a few hours) of a newsroom; seeing my name on the front page of a newspaper; observing trauma and tragedy—nothing I'd known personally before—up close.

During my hospitalisation in Perth I received an email from a family member of one of the surviving firefighters. I don't know if this person had made the connection between myself and the front-page story I wrote about the back-burning tragedy seven years earlier. It was a generous note, with words of comfort for my family.

'BELIEVE that everything will be OK and Cynthia will survive and prosper, she will be different but she will be the most amazing person you know when she is through this and you will be so blessed that she is with you,' it said.

From the back-burning story and those that followed, I earned a reputation of sorts at the newspaper.

I was sent to cover unrest at the Woomera Detention Centre in baking outback South Australia. These were the days when the government hid refugees in remotest Australia rather than on distant islands offshore in the Pacific, when it was more difficult to stop journalists from reporting on their plight, as occurs today. A group of reporters, myself included, had set up in the red dirt just outside the front gates. We were reading placards held up by the hunger-striking asylum seekers and refugees inside the detention centre when the Howard government decided to move the public perimeter back 200 metres from the existing fence. The journalists all locked arms, refusing to move, and security personnel starting making arrests. An ABC journalist was carried off in a paddy wagon.

The chief of staff liked sending me on jobs, because things always happened.

XVI

Within eleven months of joining the *Herald*, I moved cities and joined the newspaper's Canberra bureau.

It was early 2001. As soon as I could, with my heart fixed on a foreign posting in one of the newspaper's overseas bureaus, I enrolled in a Master of International Affairs. Michelle Grattan, doyenne of political journalists, was my first boss in Canberra. I was given the communications and attorney-general's reporting rounds on account of my law background.

Michelle took me out to dinner at Portia's Place during my first week. Portia's was a favourite restaurant of journalists and politicians in Kingston. After the plane crash in 2007, the proprietor personally flew some of her food in plastic takeaway tubs to Perth for Michael.

As we sat at our table eating Chinese food, Michelle told me she kept horses. It was late in the evening in May and winter was not far off, but Michelle suggested I drive us out to see her animals, after stopping at Coles on the way to buy apples. I was unfamiliar with Canberra's geography, and I still don't know where Michelle took me that night, but we both climbed into my red Mazda 121 and puttered out to the paddock where her horses lived.

There was total darkness when we pulled up at our destination and, demonstrating my complete ignorance about cars, I suggested I leave the headlights on while I turned the engine off so as not to frighten the horses. It didn't take long for the car battery to go flat. Neither of us owned a mobile phone (they were rare at that time among journalists) so we walked to a neighbouring property, knocked on the door and asked to use their telephone to call the NRMA to come and replace the dead battery.

I covered two federal elections, in 2001 and 2004. After finishing the master's degree I was appointed foreign affairs and defence reporter. I loved pretty much everything about that job.

I travelled through Asia and the Pacific, to China, Laos, Malaysia, Indonesia, Fiji, East Timor, the Solomon Islands and Papua New Guinea, covering various regional forums and meetings and prime minister's and ministers' visits. I went to France, Germany, Poland and Belgium on different journalists' programs.

I interviewed Australian troops in the Middle East, including in Afghanistan and Iraq. On these highly managed trips it was a struggle to penetrate, in the short time available, the polished presentation of defence force commanders and their military personnel.

I visited Uruzgan Province in Afghanistan just after Australian troops arrived to establish their base at Tarin Kowt. We landed in a huge RAAF C-130 Hercules on an improvised runway—a stretch of flat dirt—because there was no tarmac in the remote province. I was not allowed to get off the plane.

'All one could see for miles were jagged mountain peaks, dust and hot, arid earth,' I wrote in a news article.

I flew in US Army Black Hawk helicopters up and down the streets of the Green Zone in occupied Baghdad, flak jacket on, watching soldiers fire flares from our aircraft to distract insurgents from shooting at us. I spent the night at one of Saddam Hussein's many palaces, where the Americans had set up their headquarters, at Camp Victory. Walking into the opulent, tacky Al-Faw Palace, located on an artificial lake, was unsettling: all those US soldiers amid all that elaborate marble. I felt uneasy being a guest of the occupying power, in a war I knew to be morally and legally wrong.

I arrived in Dhi Qar Province in southern Iraq with the defence minister, to visit soldiers deployed on Australia's largely symbolic mission in that tragically misguided war (the Australians were stationed in one of the safer parts of Iraq). We disembarked from a Hercules, where we had been fed messy Subway sandwiches for lunch while sitting strapped into four-point restraint harnesses on the aircraft. Fast food outlets were commonplace on the major American military bases in the Middle East.

The air was dry and scorching—around 50 degrees Celsius. There were hot winds carrying dust through the camp. After brief introductions, I interviewed some of the Australian soldiers stationed at the Ali Air Base, Tallil. There was some concern among troops over the lack of a cooling system for the soldiers' drinking water, and about gunners being exposed to enemy gunfire on the Bushmaster armoured troop carriers. I wore a white shirt. It was only later I realised that, from the moment I stepped out of the transport aircraft, the front of my shirt had been covered in bright yellow mustard from the Subway sandwich.

I was energetic and thirsty to learn, spurred on to succeed by the almost complete absence of other women reporting in the male-dominated foreign affairs and defence round.

I had barely started when it all came to an end.

XVII

As a journalist, you are an observer: of power and privilege, of ordinary people's lives, their triumphs, their tragedies.

As an observer, you feel protected. You are watching and the events you are watching are not happening to you. It is strange, therefore, to contemplate that my time as a journalist was bookended by two events that involved burns, that were stories about people burning to death.

The last major story of my career, the one that dominated my time as defence correspondent, involved the crash of a Royal Australian Navy Sea King helicopter in April 2005 on the island of Nias in Indonesia. The Australian flight crew and medical personnel on board were providing humanitarian assistance following the Nias earthquake, when the helicopter *Shark 02*, on final approach 'suddenly adopted an extreme nose-down attitude', lost height and crashed into the ground, eventually catching fire. Nine navy and air force members were killed. Two were injured but survived.[7]

I went along to the opening of the official Board of Inquiry in September 2005 at the Randwick Barracks in Sydney. Other media dropped off the inquiry after the first day, but I kept turning up. The newspaper paid for me to fly to Sydney for different parts of the evidence, and I got to know some of the families of the deceased personnel. They were originally wary of the presence of a journalist, but soon began to welcome my reports of the inquiry as evidence surfaced about the reasons for the crash.

The crash resulted from the faulty fitting of a tiny part—a split pin and nut—that caused the flight control system to fail. The error occurred during maintenance of the aircraft, some three months earlier, and its discovery exposed intractable problems at the 817 Squadron and a maintenance culture of 'shortcuts and workarounds' that developed during a period of high workload and operational tempo for the Australian Defence Force during the Howard government years.

Anger grew among the devastated families as, day after day, more information emerged. A realisation dawned that the tragedy might have been avoided, or its consequences mitigated, had senior commanders done more to address the problems at 817 Squadron, and had the helicopter been better equipped with crashworthy seating and restraints. I interviewed the families, some at their homes, others at a hotel in Coogee where they were put up by the Defence Department during the inquiry.

'The pain never goes away,' one of the grieving fathers told me.

The report of the Board of Inquiry was released in June 2007, when I was at the rehabilitation hospital in Perth. The Deputy Chief of Navy visited me just before the report's release. The wife of the Chief of Navy sent me a card on the day the Board of Inquiry published its findings.

The report found that at least four of the nine people killed had survived the initial impact of the crash but died in the post-accident fire. One of the deceased managed to free himself from his harness, but died from asphyxiation from inhaling toxic smoke and gas.

Two days after my plane crash, the family of one of the Sea King crash victims sent an email to my family, expressing sorrow for what I was going through, 'after she has heard all the dreadful details about the Nias crash at the Board of Inquiry'.

'I am sure that Cynthia would have been thinking of that when she was sitting in the plane.'

The email's premise was correct.

As I realised that the plane, and myself, were on fire, I remember thinking 'so this is what it feels like to burn to death'. Once I was out of the plane, and I saw the skin dripping off me like white honey, I recalled what the woman at Ku-ring-gai had told me about seeing the 'skin hanging' from the burning firefighter who ran out of the bushes towards her house.

What I had written about twice before—the most important stories of my career, two terrible tragedies—went and happened to me.

XVIII

I was happy being a journalist in a way I had never been before.

It wasn't just the job. I felt better about every aspect of myself, like I was finally the person I was meant to be. After years of searching—studying, changing jobs, travelling, dieting, dating the wrong people—at 34, I wanted for nothing more.

This was me before the crash in March 2007.

I was a foreign affairs and defence correspondent for a major newspaper. I got paid to fly around the world and ask people questions about things that mattered and then write about them. I even had my own work-issued satellite phone! I was, bosses had told me, a serious contender for a future posting in an overseas bureau.

I was healthy and super fit. I'd just had my road bike completely reconditioned and was due to pick it up from the bike shop before the trip to Indonesia. In January, Michael and I had started training for a fourth marathon.

That February I'd moved in with Michael: my one, and only, love. My clothes were hanging in a cupboard in his spare room. Getting dressed in the morning for work from a wardrobe in his house, rather than a bag on the floor, still felt like a novelty.

Michael got me, and I was crazy about him. He shared my values and passions: for journalism and social justice; for running, camping and hiking; for beer and chicken parmigiana. The previous September we had trekked together in India, fulfilling an ambition I'd carried since those afternoons spent daydreaming in Sydney Airport's coffee shops. Michael, in turn, introduced me to the best of Victoria: Australian rules football and Wilsons Promontory. I had just bought a new pair of brown leather hiking boots—I hadn't worn them yet—intended for our next camping trip to the Prom. I had also adopted the Sydney Swans as my AFL football team, though we missed their 2006 Grand Final loss because we were walking a remote Himalayan trail on the Indian–Tibetan border.

I had found it all—my true self and my life partner—when the plane crash happened.

My sister remembers talking to me on the phone the afternoon before. I was on a media bus with a group of journalists who had accompanied the Australian foreign minister to the inauguration ceremony of an Islamic school, the AusAID-funded Nural Huda boarding school in Bekasi. We were heading back to our hotel in Jakarta, having missed our flights to Yogyakarta that evening. The day's schedule was thrown out by a last-minute request from the Indonesian president to meet with the foreign minister.

It was an anxious bus ride. The bus driver was driving too fast, weaving erratically through the heavy Jakarta traffic, alarming us passengers. Meanwhile, Australian diplomats and journalists frantically altered their travel arrangements in order to get to Yogyakarta first thing in the morning, ahead of the foreign minister.

I can't remember whether I called my sister or she called me, but it was a brief and upbeat conversation. Juliette was living in Singapore. In the few minutes that we spoke, I told her how happy I was, that living with Michael felt so right. I was looking forward to joining him in Melbourne for the weekend after I got home from Indonesia (the head office of Michael's newspaper was located there). When Juliette got off the phone, she told her husband she had never heard me so joyful, so utterly content with life.

The next telephone call my sister received was from Michael himself, the following morning. He was calling from Melbourne. She was at home with her eight-month-old daughter. A couple of months prior I spent a day walking around a shopping mall in Bondi Junction with my young niece strapped to my chest in a BabyBjörn carrier (something I would never get to experience with my own baby).

'Hello?'

'It's Michael. I've rung you because I don't know who else to ring, but something bad has happened. Cynthia has been in a plane crash.'

'What?'

'The plane she was on has been in an accident. We don't know where she is or if she's okay.'

Michael told my sister that my newspaper had a correspondent in Indonesia who was trying to find me.

'I don't know the full details about it, but we just know we can't find her and we're looking for her.'

He asked my sister to call my parents.

XIX

I am no longer a journalist.

I went back to work for the newspaper for a brief period, after coming home from Perth. It took enormous effort to return to the press gallery in Parliament House, to see my colleagues again, to allow them to see me in my new altered body, so maimed, so fragile, so vulnerable—so much less of me. I had no strength and had to be pushed in a wheelchair along the thick pink carpet of the Parliament House corridors.

I didn't know what to wear. How do you dress a body with no lower limbs? I had returned to Michael's house in Canberra, to a wardrobe where a whole drawer—my sock drawer, full of stockings for work and sports socks for running—was now obsolete. (Michael, on a short trip back to Canberra while I was still in Perth, thoughtfully packed up my shoes—the dainty red-and-gold Tara Crystalle stilettos I wore to my sister's wedding in 2001, the cowboy boots I bought in Argentina in the early 1990s—into a plastic crate so I would not have to see them when I got home.)

One particular day stands out in my memory. It was February 2008, on the day Prime Minister Kevin Rudd made the apology to Indigenous Australians. This was one of those rare kind of days when one felt the privilege of working in Parliament House most keenly. In the press gallery overlooking the chamber in the House of Representatives, journalists literally do have a front row seat to history-making.

I wore a grey dress, an old favourite. It came to below my knees. Underneath it I wore the shiny, flesh-coloured full-body burns compression garments, which were made from a tough, woven medical-grade fabric that was meant to assist with scarring, pain and swelling. My longer right leg poked out from under the dress, and rested on a small leg support.

Sitting on the wheelchair in my newspaper's bureau, I felt diminished before my colleagues, among whom I had once walked with such confidence and self-assurance in knee-high boots and fitted skirts and jackets, though people couldn't have been nicer.

After the prime minister made the apology, Michael pushed my wheelchair down to the Members' Hall on the ground floor of Parliament House, with its high, light-filled ceiling and parquetry and stone floor. We said hello to some of the politicians we knew who welcomed us back, and stopped to chat to a few.

Then it happened. A group of people passed by us, and a man among them, looking at my amputated legs, called out something loud enough so that we'd hear.

'So this is what happens to people who work here,' he said, and laughed.

It was devastating. For myself and Michael, both of us barely emerged from months of the deepest trauma, to be the butt of the man's joke was crushing.

Michael confronted the man.

'How dare you,' he said. 'You are way out of line.'

But the damage was done, in that unfortunate moment, to my sense of self. I was humiliated and ashamed. I realised I had to prepare myself for the fact that this was how the outside world, strangers, would view me now: as a curiosity, if not worse. I vowed never to go out in public without prosthetic legs. Even if I couldn't walk (which I frequently can't), I would put them on to sit in my wheelchair, so the absence of my legs wouldn't be apparent. If I couldn't wear the legs at all because of wounds or pain, I simply wouldn't leave home.

I wrote about the shame I felt when people stared at my missing limbs in a column for the *Herald*. It provoked a confronting and divided response. I regretted writing the article because of the vulnerability it exposed in me, and the anger. I never wanted to write an angry piece like that again but, the truth is, when I read back over it now, little has changed.

I described how unprepared I was for 'how bad I would be made to feel by the outside world'. I wrote about the alienation caused by physical obstructions in shops where counters were too high and aisles were too narrow. I wrote about the offensive jokes about disabled parking spaces that suddenly seemed so prevalent in modern films and television shows. But worst of all was 'the people who stare', especially the adults 'who cannot seem to peel their eyes off' my altered body.

The article attracted some sympathetic and supportive readers, but also criticism and disapproval. I was scolded for my weakness in not wanting to go out without prostheses in order to prevent the staring. I was chided by those who had lived their whole lives with the stigma of disability and resented my having, and using, a public platform to express my shock at my new life as a disabled person.

Why go over this now?

A lot of people called me brave for surviving the crash and for living my life since so fully and with such optimism. But there are limits to my bravery and my capacity to endure rudeness and ridicule, to what I am willing to put myself through.

My friend, Lauren, wrote me a letter shortly after the plane crash.

I read today that the doctors in Indonesia had given you a six per cent chance of survival. I am so grateful to God for keeping you alive. You are an amazing person. I always knew you were. Not that it would make any difference to me if you weren't. I'd love you just as much if you were just an ordinary run-of-the-mill Cynthia Banham.

When I read this letter recently—it was in the boxes of documents from the crash—its words felt reassuring. So many other cards and letters from that time spoke of how I survived because I was 'clearly here for a higher purpose'. It's a huge burden to have thrust upon you.

In truth, from the moment I found myself in a burning plane, all I wanted to do was get back to the life I had before, the life I had only just found. I didn't survive because of some 'higher purpose'. I survived because I really, really loved life.

I loved my 'ordinary run-of-the-mill' life, and it's all I have wanted since.

4

Alfredo

I

WE WERE DRIVING DOWN A DARK, FORESTED ROAD, my driver Tomas and I, looking for a cemetery, 60 kilometres south of Berlin. I had arranged a driver for myself through the hotel concierge in Berlin, leaving Michael and our son behind to explore some of the city's landmarks.

The road was deep inside a biotechnology park, in the former East German town of Luckenwalde. On our way into the park, we passed a field of solar panels. It was an odd place to be looking for a Second World War cemetery, but this vast modern complex occupied the land on which the Nazi prisoner of war camp, Stalag III A, once stood. Some 200,000 POWs, including my grandfather, passed through here.

We spotted a sign, '*Zum Stalag Fritof*', literal translation 'peace yard', and kept driving until we came to a green metal gate, where Tomas stopped the car. It was so quiet and dark among the tall pine trees. There was nobody else around, but the gate was open, so we walked in.

It was lovely inside: tall linden trees with the golden foliage of autumn, and winding gravel paths carpeted in yellow and brown leaves that lay like scattered coins on the damp ground. Ahead

169

of me, as I entered the cemetery, was a large wooden Christ hanging from a crucifix, bathed in sunlight that broke through the surrounding trees. I walked closer to read the words on the plaque beneath His feet: 'A tous nos comrades decedes en captivite.' To all our comrades who died in captivity.

To my right, in a small green field of shady well-tended grass, was a series of grey headstones marking the graves of the Italian war dead. The bodies (215 of them) were exhumed and returned to Italy in 1992. The cemetery was divided into four sections: the Italian graves; the French section where the war dead of other Western allies were also buried; the Yugoslav section, which also contained Polish and Czech victims; and the Soviet graves.

Luckenwalde was where Alfredo was first registered as an Italian Military Internee (IMI) following his capture in September 1943. He likely stayed a short time; by January 1944 he was in Berlin. More than 15,000 Italian prisoners arrived at Luckenwalde in October 1943, most of whom were quickly transferred to other forced labour camps, as happened to Alfredo.

From the different testimonies of IMIs who passed through Luckenwalde, I have a fair idea of what the nineteen-year-old Alfredo would have experienced there.

After leaving Austria, Alfredo would have arrived at Luckenwalde's train station in an overcrowded, stinking, airless cattle wagon, feeling thirsty, weak, dirty. With fear in his heart, he'd have then marched the 3 kilometres through the town to the camp. That night he probably slept in a tent with other Italian prisoners, on the ground with no blanket. He would have been cold—the Italians were captured at the end of summer, and had only lightweight uniforms—and hungry. Prisoners were given a small piece of bread (80 grams) with a tiny amount of butter or jam (20 grams), a potato and thin soup each day. As time passed at Luckenwalde, Alfredo would have lost more and more weight. The prisoners were under constant guard: the camp was surrounded by a 4-metre-high barbed wire fence that was illuminated at night and had guard posts every 100 metres. Prisoners were beaten if they transgressed camp rules, kicked if they collapsed from hunger or cold. Around Alfredo, prisoners were dying; he himself may already have been sick. Tuberculosis was rampant, and bodies of the dead lay unburied in the mortuary for weeks.[1]

Before leaving Luckenwalde for Berlin, Alfredo would have been photographed, fingerprinted, vaccinated, disinfected and assigned his metal identity tag with his prisoner number, 111547. The rectangular piece of metal, the size of a couple of postage stamps, was divided into two identical parts split down the middle by a broken line. The number of the camp and his personal number appeared on both halves of the tag. If a prisoner died, one half stayed with the body; the other was broken off and sent to the International Committee of the Red Cross in Geneva, who notified authorities in Italy, who told the family.

I sat on a wooden bench to rest while Tomas took photos on my smartphone of the monuments that were too difficult for me to reach on my prostheses. The air smelt fresh and woody and cool. There was silence except for the occasional rustling of leaves in the breeze, the cracking of a falling branch, and a persistent woodpecker that hammered away from beyond the hedges marking the cemetery boundary. The sky through the canopy of treetops above was a clear pale blue.

It was unsettling to contemplate how this prettiness and tranquillity concealed a site of wartime brutality, the last ugly reminder of which was removed as recently as 2010. That was when the old military barracks (last used by the Soviets in the 1970s) were torn down.

Tomas returned with the photos and translated for me one of the German inscriptions he had come across, '*Die liebe höret rimmer auf*'. 'It means "Love never stops,"' he said.

I paused before we left to read the names of the dead, engraved in long lists on four metal pillars that stood in a semicircle at the cemetery's entrance. They were erected in 2009 as a part of restoration work on the cemetery commissioned by the Luckenwalde municipality. I wondered what Nonno would have thought of my visiting this place; a place that, until a week ago, his daughters had never heard of—that I only knew about because the volunteers at the museum in Padua told me my grandfather had been here.

Tomas drove back to Berlin through the grey town. Some of the buildings in the centre were rundown, empty, with broken windows. I noticed a discount store—a random assortment of its drab merchandise sat in baskets on the footpath. We passed along 'Peace Street', a reminder of Luckenwalde's years under the Soviets, and some fresh graffiti: 'Refugees welcome.' It was a month since the German chancellor, Angela Merkel, pledged to accept Syrian refugees—fleeing the violence and destruction of a protracted civil war—who made it to Germany.

Back on the Bundesstraße 101, we passed through corridors of chestnut trees, their yellow leaves fluttering like large snowflakes along the side of the road. Tomas told me how to recognise old West and East Berlin through the different shapes of the streetlamps.

Driving back from Luckenwalde that day, I felt for the first time in many years the rush of reporting an assignment overseas, though this one was very personal. I had visited Berlin before, on a work trip in 2006. For two or three days I walked the length and breadth of the city with an official guide. By the end, after I had seen the Berlin Wall, the concrete tombs of the Holocaust memorial and the Reichstag, and interviewed German foreign ministry officials about the war in Afghanistan, my feet—I walked it all in a business suit and heels—were covered in blisters. I was surprised at the time by how present the Second World War felt in modern-day Berlin, unaware that it was the city where my grandfather spent two years as a POW and forced labourer.

It was illusory, but driving in Germany with my 'fixer', I glimpsed my 34-year-old (whole) self again: independent, a working journalist, travelling the world.

II

When I picture my grandfather, he's wearing a blue Chesty Bonds singlet over his portly frame.

He always wore one, unless it was cold, in which case he threw an open flannelette shirt, sleeves rolled up, over the top of the singlet. I see him pottering around his vegetable garden or sitting at his place at the big table in the kitchen, facing the passage that led to the front door. He had a newspaper (the *Daily Mirror* or *Daily Telegraph*) or Italian crossword in his hand, and on his placemat sat a glass of wine. Behind his dining chair was a small shelf with Italian dictionaries. He had his own outhouse at the end of the backyard, next to his shed.

Nonno's preferred footwear was rubber thongs, which he wore with socks in winter. He had little hair, just a smattering of trimmed grey strands over his ears and around the base of his skull, exposing his high forehead, a family trait. He wore a tweed cap to keep his head warm when he went out in the afternoons to walk his dog. He was stocky, not tall, and he walked slowly, with a bit of a sway.

He drank Resch's Dinner Ale, or red wine with water, and smoked Marlboros or rolled his own cigarettes. He twirled his spaghetti with a fork and kept winding until he had the perfect mouthful. Then he'd wipe every last drop of sauce from his plate with a piece of bread speared onto the end of his fork. Nonno had the smell of his last drink about him, and he kept drinking even after he lost a toe to diabetes. He had an authoritarian manner which got worse when he drank; my mother says it was 'his way or no way'. He had a booming voice and called Mum by her full name, Loredana, rather than Lori, when they argued. But he also had a beautiful singing voice, which I never heard, and was in a choir when he was a boy in Italy.

My brother Sebastian, the youngest of us four kids, remembers once pulling on a cord dangling from the hot-water system in my grandparents' backyard, at the encouragement of our brother Anthony.

'What's this?' the younger brother asked.

'Pull it,' said Anthony, who knew better than to tamper with Nonno's things.

'You sure?'

'Yeah, pull it.'

Pulling the cord activated a pressure-relief valve.

'Nonno came flying out of the house,' recalled Sebastian. 'I never pulled on it again.'

Sebastian bears an uncanny likeness to a younger Alfredo, but Nonno—who had daughters but no sons—was particularly fond of Anthony, the eldest male grandchild. My father recalls Alfredo telling him with a heavy heart, as if he saw the future, that he wished he could be alive to see Anthony turn 21. Anthony was fifteen when Nonno died.

After lunch, Nonno watched us play cards or bingo with Nonna, then he'd call his dog and together the pair headed off to the bedroom for an afternoon sleep. Nonno's nap was non-negotiable, and he got cranky with my mother if we arrived late for lunch because it meant he got to spend less time with us.

Nonno made his own wine and preserved *melanzane* (eggplant). He marinated it in garlic, oil and herbs and we ate it with crusty bread rolls. He called my father 'boy'. Dad remembers from his days courting mum taking Alfredo to Paddy's Markets at Haymarket to buy grapes. Because Alfredo insisted they arrive at the markets before they opened at 5 am, my father—who lived on the other side of Sydney—slept the previous night in his truck near Central Station so as not to miss my grandfather's train. They bought wooden crates of fruit, which Dad loaded onto his truck, and drove back to Campsie. All that day my grandmother and her two daughters crushed grapes in the backyard in the rusty old bathtub. The bees came in large numbers for the skins.

Alfredo never went to church, but he had a strong faith. An incident when he was younger, when he ran into a priest he knew at a brothel in a town outside Trieste, meant he lost respect for the institution of the Catholic Church. But it was his deep faith in God that got him through his darkest hours as a POW in the war.

Nonno was a qualified plumber in Italy, and over many weekends he helped my father fix up my parents' old Federation-style house (when they moved into it in 1976, it had gas lighting and no bath). While they worked, Alfredo sometimes talked about how terrified he'd been as a teenager after he was captured by the Germans, not knowing what was going to happen to him. He had needed something to hold on to.

Just like his sister Amelia did a few years later on her frightening voyage to America, Alfredo prayed to Mary—that revered motherly figure with her special connection to God—to let him live.

'He said this prayer to the Virgin Mary all the time,' my father said.

'She let me live,' Alfredo told my father. 'Everything now is a just a gift.'

III

Before arriving in Germany, Michael, our son and I spent two nights in Klagenfurt, a small city in southern Austria.

We arrived at the station from Italy after dark. A kind guard helped us alight from the train with our luggage and directed us to the elevator. It was then that I realised the optimism—or folly— of our travel plans. How did I think we would be able to manage rapid train and platform changes with a wheelchair, a three-year-old child and all our luggage? Yet we would be required to do exactly this during the many train journeys that awaited us over the coming days.

We caught a taxi to our hotel and greeted the hotel receptionist. The officious blonde scowled as I inadvertently handed her the wrong piece of paper from our travel documents. Still reeling from our hostile Austrian welcome, we went off to find our room. Its distinguishing feature was a quirky string curtain that separated the bed from the bathroom. I ordered Weinerschnitzels from room service and read with bemusement the first page of the guest information book which listed the hotel's 'seven rules', including that staff be nice to guests.

The following morning, we woke to a heavy fog that didn't burn off until midday. In the hotel lobby after lunch we waited for a local historian, who had generously researched the history of Italian POWs in the area for me and offered to take us on a small tour. I had come to Klagenfurt on the insistence of relatives who were adamant Alfredo had been imprisoned here, despite the absence of documentary records verifying that he was.

Stalag XVIII A Wolfsberg, 50 kilometres outside Klagenfurt, was the main Nazi-run camp for POWs who were sent to work in different locations around the Carinthia region. A significant number of Italian POWs were transferred to Klagenfurt in large transports from north-east Italy in October 1943. If Alfredo did come to Klagenfurt, he wasn't here for long.

Paul Angerer, a Second World War history enthusiast, arrived and we climbed into his car. Paul drove us to Hirschenwirtstraße, where Italian prisoners who worked in the Wiener Neustadt Flugzeugwerke aircraft factory, making wing tips and tails for the German Messerschmitt fighter aircraft, lived. We stared through the metal mesh fence of what is today a bus and coach depot. The Karawanken mountain range separating Austria and Slovenia (where Yugoslav partisans fought the Germans in the war) was visible in the distance. Next we visited the site of the Messerschmitt factory, which was bombed in January 1944. A men's clothing store stands there now.

It was late afternoon by then, and we stopped for beer and coffee near the sixteenth-century Lindwurm fountain in Klagenfurt's central Neuer Platz, where Australian POWs gathered after they were freed by the Allies in April 1945. My son was underwhelmed by the giant stone dragon and fell asleep in my arms.

Klagenfurt was rich in Second World War history, yet today the city's wartime memories were largely indiscernible.

IV

The most complex part of our journey north to Berlin awaited us the next morning.

We had to get up at 4 am to drive a hire car to Salzburg, because trains weren't running between the two cities. We left plenty of time due to the uncertain situation in Salzburg, a major transit point for Syrian refugees. In Salzburg, we'd planned to take a train to Munich, where we had only minutes to change locomotives and platforms for our connection to Berlin.

For months leading up to the trip, I nervously followed the international news of the refugee crisis in Europe. Over a million asylum seekers crossed into Europe in 2015, many of them Syrian refugees. Desperate families and individuals were undertaking perilous voyages across the Mediterranean Sea from Turkey to Greece, before heading overland through the Balkans, Hungary and Austria, on to more welcoming countries like Germany and Sweden. As the crisis intensified, countries began closing borders, suspending train services, building walls. There were reports of thousands of people camped at some of Europe's major train stations—the same stations we would be travelling through.

It was the biggest refugee crisis since the Second World War. Rather than cancel affected parts of our trip, it seemed fitting that to research Alfredo's and Amelia's wartime experiences, we were heading into the maelstrom.

We set out with trepidation in the dark and watched the sun rise over snow-capped mountains and sleeping alpine hamlets as we wended our way north towards Salzburg. Thirty kilometres out from the city, we stopped at a petrol station. An attendant told us we would not be able to get anywhere near our Hertz car rental office at Salzburg train station because of the refugees. We returned the car to the rental company's airport office instead. There a clerk told us 7000 asylum seekers had arrived in Salzburg the day before, more than normal; usually they were receiving 3000 to 4000 arrivals a day. The asylum seekers were all at the train station, trying to board trains to Germany.

I pictured us at the train station: me trying to wheel myself through a crush of people and police and military barricades while Michael juggled our son and all our luggage.

We found a taxi at the airport and asked the driver to take us to the train station. As our taxi pulled out from the airport rank I had an idea.

'How much would it cost to drive us all the way to Munich?'

'Two hundred and thirty euros,' the driver replied after a pause.

'Okay, great, can you drive us to Munich, please?'

The driver turned the car around and we began our two-hour car ride into Germany. Later, I read about a Syrian law student who, after a car bomb killed his neighbour and his friends were snatched by government agents, fled to Sweden. The man made his way to Europe and, at the train station at Salzburg, three months before us, negotiated a fare for the same taxi ride to Munich—for *800* euros.

At the German border, our taxi was stopped. German police asked for our passports and searched the car. Suddenly one of the policemen began upbraiding us. In our haste, we had forgotten about a child seat.

'Next time it will be a 100-euro fine,' the policeman warned us in a disapproving tone.

I was mortified at our oversight. The taxi driver quickly converted one of the back seats into a booster seat and we got back on the road. We drove on the Autobahn through the idyllic Bavarian countryside, all shimmering lakes and green forests, but I barely noticed. The speed limit was 120 kilometres per hour and I sat in the front seat with my eyes fixed on the speedometer, which told me the car was doing over 160 kilometres per hour. I breathed deeply, gripped my walking stick like it was a magic handbrake, and prayed we'd make it to Munich unharmed.

Was I a bad parent for bringing my three-year-old on this research trip? I made a split-second judgement that morning, in a moment of uncertainty, that it would be less risky to travel by taxi rather than battle our way with a wheelchair through the train station in Salzburg. But, in doing so, I exposed my son to other dangers.

Sitting on the platform at the train station that afternoon in Munich, I watched my boy and our luggage while Michael organised our tickets to Berlin. I thought of the solitary hours spent guarding my backpack in train stations throughout Europe in my carefree twenties. I tried not to dwell on how dependent on others I was now, and how vulnerable that made me feel, especially with a young child to look after.

It was our last train journey. When we got to Berlin, as much as I dreaded more flying, I booked flights for our remaining travel in Europe.

V

Alfredo was 'davvero sfortunato', 'truly unlucky', to have been taken prisoner by the Germans, a Trieste historian told me.

My grandfather was certainly a casualty of poor timing. He was conscripted into the navy as a trainee gunner/cannon operator in mid-1942, after his eighteenth birthday, and was called up to enlist a year later, in August 1943. By then, the Italian government was secretly negotiating an armistice to secure the country's exit from the war, but the public announcement of this deal arrived too late for Alfredo. Nine days too late.

The year 1943 was one of deep crisis for Italy. Benito Mussolini, 'Il Duce', had dragged Italy into the war on Germany's side in 1940. The population had suffered since through years of widespread food shortages and the massive, devastating bombardments of villages, and had endured the humiliation of its military in Greece (Italy had to be bailed out by the Germans). Finally, in July 1943, the Allies invaded Sicily. Now Italy's monarch, military and political elites wanted out—at minimum cost to themselves and their country, with no further fighting, if possible. Italy's king, Victor Emmanuel III, dismissed the Fascist dictator on 25 July and had him arrested, and called out of retirement the ageing Marshal Pietro Badoglio to lead a new government. The Badoglio government secretly and nervously negotiated an armistice with the Allies that wasn't signed until 3 September, delaying out of fear of Hitler's reaction.[2]

For my grandfather, the timing was everything. Alfredo took his oath in Pola on 25 August, when Italy was technically still an ally of Nazi Germany. Along with the rest of Italy's servicemen, he was unprepared for the radio broadcast that came on 8 September, instructing them to immediately cease all hostilities against the Anglo–American forces. There was no forewarning for the trusting Italians, deployed alongside their newly turned enemies, the Germans, throughout France, the Balkans, Greece and Italy, and nobody to tell them what to do next. Just the ambiguous advice, proffered in that same radio message, to 'resist any eventual attacks coming from any other source', namely the Germans.

The Italian soldiers were abandoned to their fate. The prime minister and the king hastily vacated the capital for the south, where they could enjoy Allied protection. There were empty desks in Rome as military commanders on the ground made desperate telephone calls to their superiors seeking directives to allow them to prepare for the coming German onslaught. The Italian armed forces disintegrated, all military authority and discipline broke down, and soldiers and officers fled, almost all into the waiting arms of the Germans. Hitler, naturally, had anticipated Italy's betrayal, and bolstered German forces inside Italy and elsewhere the Italians were stationed. Immediately upon the announcement of the armistice, the Germans disarmed the Italians. There were massacres, with

25,000 Italians slaughtered throughout Yugoslavia, Albania and Greece, and over one million servicemen were captured.

The tragicomic nature of the situation the Italians found themselves in that day in September is captured by the black-and-white 1960 film starring Alberto Sordi, *Tutti a Casa* (*Everybody Go Home*). We see the Italian servicemen going about their normal business inside their military base on the Venetian coast, then comes the unexpected broadcast over the crackling radio about the armistice. Here are the soldiers' euphoric moments of celebration, halted when the Germans suddenly turn their guns onto the confused Italians. There go the futile telephone calls to superiors begging for clarification. Soldiers are falling, soldiers are running, soldiers are surrendering. Later come the northbound trains commandeered by Germans, pulling wagons of desperate men whose faces we cannot see but whose voices we hear begging through the grate for water. Was this what 8 September was like for my grandfather?

It is said the Italian captives were offered a choice. They could join the Italian Social Republic (Mussolini's new puppet government, re-established in the German-occupied north, at Salò), or be taken prisoner of the Third Reich. I came across a copy of a Nazi leadership directive from the time: '*Wer nicht für uns ist, ist gegen uns.*' ('The one who is not for us, is against us.') The words are eerily reminiscent of more modern wars.[3]

The next part of the story, historians describe as 'unusual, if not unique' in the history of the Nazi deportations. Of those million Italian servicemen, more than 600,000 refused to support Hitler or recognise the legitimacy of Mussolini's Fascist Republic, and consequently were interned in POW camps throughout Germany and Poland, to become forced labourers.[4]

Hitler refused to classify the Italians as POWs, arguing they could not be captives of an enemy state given the existence of the Fascist Republic. They were to be known as Italian Military Internees, with no entitlements to the protection of the 1929 Geneva Convention. Half the IMIs were put to work in the arms manufacturing industry (illegal under international law), as Alfredo was, and the rest in building, mining, forestry and agriculture. For two years, the Italian prisoners were treated like slaves: starved, frozen, beaten, humiliated, denied medical treatment for illness and disease, and worked to their deaths. This way, Hitler achieved two goals: he punished the Italian people for their betrayal, and simultaneously bolstered Germany's declining labour force.

What is said to be extraordinary about this situation is that the soldiers could have ended their torment themselves at any moment, but chose not to. There were of course different reasons why individual IMIs elected imprisonment over pledging allegiance to Hitler and Mussolini. The men feared being sent to the Eastern Front; some didn't want to fight anymore. But many were motivated by moral and political ideals—in refusing to capitulate they rejected Nazism and Fascism and Germany's ongoing war of aggression.

This is not the way the returning prisoners recounted their experiences once the war was over, however. It was not the way the ageing Italian former soldiers, like the grandfather of my childhood, recalled their memories for their descendants. I don't know what happened to Alfredo in those moments after the armistice. I don't know whether he felt those short-lived bursts of joy when he learnt the fighting was over for his countrymen. I don't know whether he saw comrades shot down in front of him. I don't know why he personally chose imprisonment rather than join the Germans, when or how that choice was put to him. Nor do I have his insights into how he felt, locked up in that crowded wagon with no food or water, not knowing where he was being taken.

The Italian soldiers' individual and collective acts of resistance were overlooked by Italian society for decades, and their stories, including my nonno's, were shaped, silenced, accordingly.

VI

When I first opened the box containing my grandparents' papers, before Christmas 2014, I had no idea that Nonno was a forced labourer. I had never heard of IMIs. The German Alkett factory pass was the clue and its former headquarters was the first place I visited in Berlin. I learnt what I could about Alkett from different local, scholarly, military and corporate histories: what it made, who worked there, the role it played in Hitler's war. The company that founded it in 1936—Rheinmetall-Borsig—still exists today, although under a slightly different name. Alkett built tanks for the German Reich and operated three factories around Berlin. When it ran out of German workers—first men, then women—it turned to foreigners and subsequently forced labourers. Alfredo, I knew from his permit, was forced to work at the company's main factory at Borsigwalde in north Berlin, though there were other sites at Tegel (near Berlin's small international airport today) and Spandau. A number of different German companies manufactured tanks in the Second World War, but Alkett, according to Hitler's armaments minister, was 'our most important tank factory'.[5]

I spent an afternoon with Tomas, the driver, exploring Borsigwalde, where Alkett's imposing red-brick administration building still stands on Breitenbachstraße. The suburb was named for a nineteenth-century railway engineer and entrepreneur who built Germany's first steam locomotives, August Borsig. A worn, heavy volume I found in a German second-hand book shop described how the locality was originally farming land, settled by the Borsig family company in the late 1800s to provide housing for workers. Today the suburb is a mix of prouder, more distinguished-looking buildings from the turn of the twentieth century, alongside the bland edifices of the immediate post-Second World War decades. Sitting in Tomas's car on Breitenbachstraße, I tried to imagine how, for nine years or so during the 1930s and 1940s, huge armoured tanks rumbled out of the Alkett gates and into Borsigwalde's streets, going for test runs.[6]

The Alkett factories developed, produced and repaired a range of German tanks. At the peak of production, ten to twenty new tanks left the Alkett factory every day. I looked up the different models in adulatory military history books: the 'light' Panzer II, the 'most numerous' Panzer IV, the 'legendary Tiger', the 'colossal', ironically named Maus (in English, mouse).[7] Joseph Goebbels, Hitler's propaganda minister, once visited Borsigwalde and was nearly knocked over by a small, remotely controlled Goliath, an unmanned tank normally used to carry mines into enemy bunkers and blow them up. He was saved by SS guards who flung their bodies onto the runaway vehicle. Alkett's engineers also examined captured foreign tanks for the Allies' design secrets, while damaged German tanks, the corpses of dead soldiers still inside, returned to the factories on trains from the frontline. The bodies were cut out of the vehicles and buried in a cemetery in nearby Tegel.

What sights, what experiences, would have greeted my terrified young grandfather at Borsigwalde, late in the war, in ravaged Berlin?

By the time of Alfredo's arrival, Alkett was a desperate place. Armaments production was collapsing because of targeted Allied bombings of factories, and the German arms industry was in trouble. The German armaments minister, Albert Speer, informed Hitler in August 1943 that any more attacks would bring it to a total halt.

In November, air raids burnt down the main Alkett workshop and Speer visited the site early the following morning. The factory fire was extinguished, but the surrounding streets were choked with fire trucks with nothing to do, as Hitler had directed all emergency vehicles within an 85-kilometre radius to attend Alkett.

The Borsigwalde factory employed 3000 to 4000 workers, among them hundreds of Russian and Italian POWs. Italian prisoners began arriving at Alkett from as early as October 1943; this is apparent from the sole account I found of an IMI at Alkett. Amid the different, always incomplete and wanting, histories was also a note that in January 1944, 381 new IMIs were 'examined' by Alkett bosses at Borsigwalde.[8]

Were the examinations for health reasons, to gauge workers' skills, or something else? I don't know. Nor do I know whether my grandfather was among this particular group. But Alfredo sent a postcard to his family that month from Alkett, the only one I found in his papers. It was dated 27 January 1944 and appears to have been his first communication home.

'Dear sister after such a long time I am back to you with this brief piece of writing,' he wrote in Italian. His handwriting was neat, careful.

Unknown to his family, for his heavily censored postcard revealed nothing of his frightening situation, Alfredo had been put to work inside Alkett's workshops. They were vast, noisy, often dangerous places. Enormous tanks hung suspended from the roofs, while on the floor the armoured vehicles were lined up side by side in long rows, waiting to be fitted with their suspension systems: rollers, wheels, tracks. Workers of different nationalities scurried between machines, carrying or pushing or fitting or welding materials and parts. The sounds of whirring, clanging, sparking machinery were deafening, the cacophony heightened by the radios and megaphones

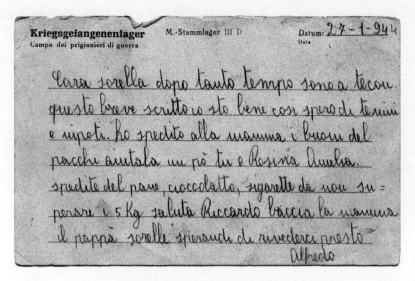

Alfredo's postcard from Alkett

that transmitted bulletins and music all day long. Accidents among the unprotected, untrained workers were common (warning signs were all in German).

Alfredo, as an IMI, was under the constant watch of armed SS guards. He was subjected to long, repeated rollcalls and had to work twelve-hour days, seven days a week, on almost no food. It was winter when he arrived and snow was falling over Berlin. The Italian prisoners, who had only whatever inadequate clothing they'd arrived with, often worked in the open, in below-zero temperatures, and many became sick. At some point, Alfredo fell ill. What little food Alfredo and his fellow prisoners were given was supplemented by scraps stolen from garbage bins. This was a risky endeavour, as prisoners caught doing this suffered demeaning, brutal punishments: slaps, beatings, whippings. Sometimes these were meted out by Italian capos, like the one so despised by Alfredo's fellow prisoners.

The forced labourers slept in locked barracks with bars on the windows in various locations throughout Borsigwalde. Many of the Italians lived in a camp in Gorkistraße, some streets away from the Breitenbachstraße factory; there were also barracks on Holzhauser Straße, closer by. Alfredo's nights were never restful— constantly interrupted by air-raid sirens and evacuations, filled with the terror of the Allied bombs that targeted Alkett. Forced labourers were not allowed to take cover in the factories' air-raid shelters and many were killed in bombings during October 1944.

Alfredo told my father in one of their conversations that the Germans made no provision for the safety of the Italian prisoners whatsoever.

'They were not considered worthy of protecting,' my father said.

My father did not know then that Alfredo was a forced labourer, and assumed Alfredo was talking about life inside a POW camp. However, with hindsight, I wonder whether my grandfather was talking about Alkett.

After the air raids, prisoners had to clean up the debris and bury the dead.

To minimise the loss of workers' lives, the company's forced labourers were housed two kilometres or more from their work-place. The journey to and from the factory each day was painful and demoralising. Prisoners had to walk the distance in wooden clogs to make escape more difficult, resulting in open sores on their feet. Compounding this, the Italians were spat at and insulted by the local German civilian population, who were encouraged to view the Italians as traitors.

Alfredo hinted at this to my father, though again he never mentioned Alkett or forced labour specifically.

There was no compassion from the locals, no offer of bread to the hungry, downtrodden prisoners who passed by them.

'They looked upon them as nothing,' my father said.

Today, Rheinmetall AG is one of Europe's largest defence contractors. The company has its own historian but my request for information about Alkett's forced labourers was unsuccessful. The historian told me the company archives held no documents regarding the forced labourers at Borsigwalde. He directed me to Rheinmetall's official, dry two-volume, 1000-page corporate history, which exists solely in German and notes that there are no exact numbers of how many forced labourers worked for the arms manufacturer. The Rheinmetall website makes no mention of Alkett's forced labourers specifically, though it does contain a sanitised account of forced labourers throughout the wider wartime Rheinmetall operation. It acknowledges that many forced labourers 'had to work for Rheinmetall-Borsig in World War II', and notes their 'great suffering'. But the official corporate account singles out the more palatable, 'touching' testimonies of forced labourers, such as the prisoner who was given pencils and paper to paint portraits for the Germans in exchange for bread, cigarettes and tinned food.[9]

My driver, Tomas, drove slowly along Breitenbachstraße, where I saw that the old Alkett administration building now housed a digital printing operation. I didn't attempt to go inside, assuming I'd only find modern offices today. Perhaps I should have asked the current occupants if I could look around and not let my immobility inhibit me, as it did.

The building evidently had a new top floor—the bombings in November 1943 destroyed its upper levels. Otherwise, Alkett's former headquarters stood silent about the past on a rather leafy suburban street with a wide footpath, bike path and grassy nature strip. Our car followed a driveway that ran down the side of the administration building, over bumpy cobblestones, before coming to a boom gate.

Alkett today

Back on the street I peered through the main building's spiked, red metal gate, through the towering red-brick arch above and into the paved yard behind. There was, apparently, nothing more to see.

What was I hoping to find there? What clues did I imagine would reveal themselves to me? The Russians dismantled Alkett in 1945. I was looking, 70 years after the fact, for signs that probably no longer existed of the suffering of Italian prisoners forced to work on Hitler's tank production line. How long did Alfredo spend at Alkett? I don't know. Given the damage to the Alkett factory from the heavy air raids, some IMIs were moved on to other work camps.

In the car on the way back to the hotel, I took out Alfredo's Alkett pass and looked at the photo of his nineteen-year-old self. He still wore his navy sailor's uniform, the one he was captured in. He did not look directly into the camera, but the despair in his eyes was plain.

VII

The following day I visited the Nazi Forced Labour Documentation Centre in Schöneweide, in old East Berlin.

I had high expectations for this museum, and hoped I'd learn something more about the Alkett operation. The Documentation Centre is located on the site of an original, preserved forced labour camp that housed IMIs and other prisoners. It's in the middle of a residential area, as many forced labour camps were. More than 3000 such camps were spread throughout Berlin.

No Berliner, no German, was unaware of foreign forced labourers, who were highly visible on their daily marches to work and toiling in factories and fields. Many millions of people, the largest groups from Poland and the Soviet Union, were kept by the Nazis under slave-like conditions to support German industry, business, agriculture and private households through the war. Forced labour kept Germany's war economy alive.

My driver this day was Flo, a Romanian refugee who had come to Germany 40 years earlier. On the way to the museum he described lingering sensitivities around the issue of forced labourers in Germany, and how they played into the current refugee debate. Germany's reasons for welcoming refugees during the 2015 Syrian crisis were complicated, derived not just out of guilt or a desire to affirm its post-Second World War identity as a good global citizen, but from a need for skilled workers to support the economy. For some, this rekindled memories of the Third Reich's solution to its labour needs.

I arrived at the Documentation Centre early and eager and, as soon as the doors opened, walked up to the reception desk and introduced myself. When the woman behind the counter proceeded to look up Alkett on Wikipedia, my disappointment was immense.

She suggested I visit the Landesarchiv Berlin (Berlin's state archives) to see what they held on Alkett, but warned me that most of the major German companies that used forced labour employed their own historians (something I had already discovered). Many had still not made public their archives from the war.

The museum curators were in a long meeting, the woman at the desk told me.

'I'll wait,' I said.

I wandered off to look through the Documentation Centre's permanent exhibition. I watched footage of the humiliation of a female Polish forced labourer who was punished for having a relationship with a German man. A barber shaved both their heads in public, leaving a chunk of hair at the front like a swine's tail. The couple was paraded through the town before the woman was hanged and the man imprisoned.

Suddenly, one of the curators appeared. She was overseeing an upcoming exhibition on the IMIs and told me I was lucky she was there—a day or so later and she would have been travelling. We sat down and the curator examined Alfredo's documents. She called his metal tag a *Stalag Marke*. The 'AKDO887' Nonno wrote on his POW postcard, beneath his identity number, was the identifier of the Arbeitskommando, or small working group, that he was assigned to in Berlin. We went to the curator's office, where she confirmed that 887 was indeed the number for the Alkett factory.

At this tiny piece of confirmation, emotion overwhelmed me. I tried to explain what this search for my grandfather's wartime past meant, how it was tied up in a quest to give some kind of meaning to difficult events in my own life. The curator looked at me and nodded.

We continued to discuss the IMI experience.

Alfredo was attached to Stalag III D, the POW camp located in the Berlin district of Kreuzberg. Camp officials there distributed Red Cross packages (where the Germans permitted), provided basic medical care, and farmed out prisoners to work details comprising 100 to 300 men. The curator believed Alfredo would have lived in the Alkett barracks on Holzhauser Straße, which I'd passed the day before and was now the site of a discount supermarket.

She then picked up the pink *Deutsches Reich Vorlaufiger Fremdenpass*, the provisional alien's passport with the Nazi crest on the cover and date-stamped 25 August 1944, and we talked about the events of that summer.

The IMIs were treated so harshly by the Germans that, by 1944, most were too weak to work. Mussolini, facing strong pressure

Alfredo's Deutsches Reich provisional alien's passport

from families of interned soldiers and the wider Italian public concerned about the poor treatment of IMIs, begged Hitler to improve their situation. Adding to the pressure, Hitler's ministers in charge of labour and armaments (Fritz Sauckel and Albert Speer) were lobbying for the same outcome, albeit out of a need for the Italians' continuing labour. Finally, in late July 1944, Hitler agreed to upgrade the living conditions of the Italians by changing their status to civilian workers. The Italians were no longer the responsibility of the Wehrmacht (the German armed forces) and under SS guard. It meant that they could now look for food and clothing outside the camp, in shops, on the black market or by looting German houses after air raids. A ceremony was held at a prison camp in Berlin to mark the new agreement where, in the presence of Mussolini's ambassador to Berlin, gates and barbed wire were removed to loud cheers.

My German researchers located a black-and-white propaganda video of the event. In a large hall, solemn-looking, thin-faced Italian prisoners listened passively to thumping, emotional speeches, to promises that by August the internees would be 'freed' to re-enter the National Socialist Germany. These images were juxtaposed with others of an armed German soldier uprooting a sign bearing an Arbeitskommando number from the ground and carting it off, as hordes of merry Italians ran amok through a prison camp, peeling off pieces of fence. Swastika flags flapped in the breeze.

In reality, these were cosmetic gestures. The poor conditions of the Italian prisoners barely changed with their new status, and any improvements were short-lived. Food rations dwindled, the long hours of work increased, prisoners still had inadequate clothing and blankets and poor living conditions. The punishments and beatings continued—including of the sick, who were forced to keep working—as did executions. The Papal Nuncio in Berlin (the

Pope's envoy) complained about the Italian prisoners' mistreatment, while Mussolini set up a special postal service so families could send their own food packages, though often they never arrived.

I thought of Alfredo's family in Trieste hearing stories about the starving IMIs, realising their parcels of flour and clothes were not making it to him, and Amelia vowing to deliver them to her brother herself. Did Amelia go to Berlin of her own accord, or was she asked by her family to undertake this parlous mission? I imagine it was her own doing. She must have made her way to Berlin sometime in 1944.

Before leaving the museum, I asked the curator about Amelia. 'Could Alfredo's sister have got food to him by working for the Germans?'

'Absolutely,' she told me.

Coming from German-annexed Trieste, Amelia was not the enemy, and she could very well have travelled to Germany to help her brother. Furthermore, camp guards were susceptible to bribery, particularly in the final stages of the war, when shortages were widespread and luxury items like chocolate, coffee and cigarettes were highly valued. I remembered how Alfredo, in his postcard home from Berlin in early 1944, asked his family to send chocolate and cigarettes. Italian prisoners from the north of Italy generally received more packages from their families than their compatriots from the south, which was under Allied control.

I realised that I had to stop judging my grandfather's experiences and the possibilities of life and survival during the war by standards that seemed reasonable today. I had to suspend the scepticism I'd quietly harboured about Amelia's role in saving Alfredo, which had always seemed—while inspiring and intriguing—slightly fantastical. Amelia was a woman from a different time.

VIII

That afternoon, my last in Berlin, I visited the state archives, a three-storey red-brick building on Eichborndamm, close to Borsigwalde.

'I am looking for any files on Alkett from 1943 to 1945,' I told the archivist as Flo, the driver, translated. 'I am especially interested in any information about forced labourers who worked there.'

A computer search revealed there were two files from that period, for the years 1944 and 1945. One contained information about damage caused by the Allied bombing raid on the Alkett premises; the other related to the addition of new railway tracks at Alkett. There was nothing that referred directly to forced labourers. The files could take weeks to retrieve, the archivist told me, and there was probably nothing of significance in there.

'I'd like to order the file on the Allied bombing raid,' I said, refusing to be discouraged.

While my request for the file was processed, I went into a separate room to view some photographs of Alkett that, I was told, I could access immediately. I sat waiting against a wall under a photograph of three German soldiers walking down a street. All of them were on crutches, two were missing a leg each, the third was missing a foot.

War wounds, I thought. How did I end up with war wounds?

A different archivist approached me. She had located the photographs of Alkett: they were taken in 1950, on Holzhauser Straße, where the workers' barracks were. They showed rubble, the remaining structures of burnt and bombed-out buildings, bare trees, a broken railway track, a wagon, stacks of bricks, and a couple of men sifting through the ruins with a wheelbarrow. My grandfather was long gone from this place, which looked like a wasteland five years after the war ended.

I returned to the reference desk where, amazingly, my file had been recovered already. Flo speculated it was the sensitive subject matter—Nazi forced labour—that resulted in such a speedy retrieval.

We went into the reading room. An elderly man sat watching the silent readers from an elevated desk, under a row of triangular grey pendant lights. For this task, I was reliant on Flo who, I was dismayed to see, was hurriedly flicking through the inch-thick file of yellowing frayed papers, assuring me there was nothing of interest.

'Please, can you translate it anyway,' I implored him.

I knew there could be a fragment in there, something to help me build my grandfather's story, and fragments were all I had. We were shushed by irritated readers and reprimanded like noisy schoolchildren by the man at the desk.

The Alkett file contained the company's compensation claims made to the German Reich over damage to its factories caused by the Allied bombings of November 1943, and January, March and April 1944. After the first bombing, on the night of 26 November 1943, which forced changes to Germany's tank production, the company claimed 1.619 million Reichsmark for the cost of cleaning up, rebuilding, and replacing machines, equipment and factory furniture. The letter included a statement from an architect appointed by Speer to reconstruct the damaged parts of the factory and the disquieting sign-off: 'Heil Hitler! Alkett.'

Another letter related to the Allied bombings of 22 March 1944, for which 1120 Reichsmark was claimed to replace a draught horse killed through hostile fire. In other correspondence, I came across mentions of the destruction of 800 sleeping spaces for workers and the need for more 'fremdarbeiter', foreign workers. There was no mention of any workers killed, though I knew from my research that many had died. It was as if such information had been edited out.

Why were these particular documents outlining the destruction of buildings, beds and animals preserved in the Berlin archives, but not others? Where were the documents about the forced labourers—details of their initial procurement, numbers, arrivals, accommodation needs, treatment, illnesses and deaths?

I took photocopies of some of the pages, and we left.

IX

I carried the poem I found in my grandparents' papers, 'La Mia Prigionia', around Europe, hoping somebody might recognise it.

I showed it to relatives in Italy.

'It was not written by someone who was good at typing,' Alfredo's nephew, Gigi, said.

I showed it to museum staff in Padua and Berlin, but nobody there had seen it before, either.

I pored over it with my Italian tutor. It was neither a complex nor sophisticated poem, and was written in simple Italian (not dialect), with minor spelling errors. But we agreed it was realistic and emotional and spoke of actual lived experiences; experiences that came to mean so much more to me as I learnt about Alkett and my grandfather's past as a forced labourer.

Triste—e questa prigionia, begins the poem, which is a heartbreaking lament for home and mother. 'Sad—is this imprisonment.'

It continues:

> I always think of my little home
> of mum who thinks only of me.

Alfredo

The poem was clearly written by a young man, too young to be married or have children, who was eighteen months into his imprisonment ('*son gia diciotto mesi*', 'it is already eighteen months'). It must have been written in early 1945.

The writer was forced to work on little food:

> Poor prisoner
> you must work
> carrots, turnips and cauliflowers
> you have only to eat,
> the good pasta you can only dream of.

His body, shoes and spirit were broken:

> with calluses on your hands
> broken shoes on your feet
> lost and without love.

He felt the hostility of the local population, including children:

> foreign children who pass
> why do you deny us a smile?

He was in a factory with heavy, noisy machinery, under constant threat of air raids:

> the roar of engines
> it makes the heart jump
> because of them
> you can only hear the vibrations
> of those awful bombs
> that make everything shake.

His greatest wish was to go home and embrace his mother again:

> when will it be over
> this wicked stubbornness
> and a steamed machine
> that will take us home
> we want our homes
> and a hug from mum.

Alfredo finished his education in the second year of intermediate school in the Italian system, at age thirteen. He was the youngest of five children, the baby of the family, and very close to his mother. It was common for IMIs to write poems. A number of former Italian prisoners wrote them as a form of psychological escape.

The poem was originally written in longhand, and there was also a typed version in my grandparents' personal effects. Only the typed copy had a title ('La Mia Prigionia'). The handwriting was my grandfather's: I recognised the same cursive style, and the way he formed certain letters, from the postcard he had sent from the POW camp in Berlin. The poem was written on a page that had been ripped out of a book or notebook. It had been folded into four, and the page's folded size bore the same dimensions as the Alkett pass. I imagine Alfredo must have carried the piece of paper home to Italy in a pocket and kept it, with his war papers, through the rest of his life.

Is it possible the poem was written by an IMI in Berlin, a forced labourer at Alkett? Was it written by Alfredo himself? If not, then one of his fellow Italian prisoners, a lost comrade perhaps, whose experiences of life and family and the deprivations of imprisonment and forced labour in a factory in Nazi Germany were identical?

Who, if anyone, did Alfredo show the poem to after the end of the war? Who knew of it, besides him?

What would Nonno tell me if I could ask him about the poem today?

X

Alfredo rarely talked about his experiences and his daughters mostly didn't ask him about them.

My mother and her sister only knew their father was imprisoned in a Nazi concentration camp in the war—not where it was, or what happened to him there. The only time they saw his metal POW tag was the day he brought it out to show me when I was a schoolgirl.

'He never mentioned working in a tank factory,' my mother said.

'He never spoke about life in prison, he never spoke about other prisoners, never about his capture, who used to look after him,' Mum's sister, Marina, said. 'I was never the type to ask questions.'

The little that Alfredo's daughters knew related to the cold and hunger he experienced in the camps. My aunt remembers her father telling her that it snowed and prisoners didn't have shoes or blankets. He told her he existed on scraps scavenged from the German officers' garbage bins when they were not looking, that he sucked on the juices of discarded chicken bones and boiled up potato peel in small tins to make soup. Alfredo also told a nephew that he killed rats with a slingshot for food.

This accords with the testimonies of other Italian prisoners, which are dominated by stories of hunger. Italy's most famous IMI, the journalist and cartoonist Giovannino Guareschi, wrote that hunger stalked the prisoners and sent men mad. The Nazis used hunger against the forced labourers not just to ruin them physically, but also to destroy their personalities, to gradually, ultimately, render the prisoners unhuman. Some prisoners recalled being so hungry that men ate the grass around their huts and the German shepherd pups belonging to their Nazi captors.[10]

I was shocked to read this at first, and thought of Nonno's German shepherds in Campsie. There was a series of them. When one died from illness or old age, my grandfather replaced it with another. He never kept any other kind of dog, and he always gave them the same name: Tommy.

Alfredo's silence was also a common theme among IMIs, many of whom returned traumatised by their experiences, unable to talk to their families about their imprisonment and forced labour. No effort was made for the social reintegration of these men in Italy, nor were they perceived as victims of Nazism at the time of their repatriation. Instead, they were met with hostility, viewed by some at home as Nazi collaborators, others as traitors of Italy's German ally, or as weak for having surrendered their arms. The IMIs also felt guilty for making their families suffer when they could have agreed to support the Germans and, possibly, been allowed to come home.

The marginalisation of the returned Italian prisoners was initially, for me, one of the most confounding parts of the IMI story. I hadn't appreciated how their treatment fitted with the construction of Italy's post-war identity, which was founded on the notion of a resisting Italy, and required denying or forgetting its Fascist past.

The Italian army was burdened by its history of having fought in the Fascist wars. Theirs was an inconvenient memory for Italian politicians, historians, teachers and filmmakers engaged in the post-war decades in nation-building and collective memory-making. Celebrating the armed resistance to Nazi Fascism—the bands of men and women that sprang up over Italy and formed the partisan movement—suited their nationalistic purposes much better. These armed, mostly Communist, guerrilla fighters, located largely in the mountains in northern Italy, helped the Allies by sabotaging and killing German soldiers and officers. Memorialising their story supported the identity of a resisting Italy. Fascism was conveniently portrayed as a 'parenthesis' in Italy's history, 'an external virus that had penetrated its healthy historical body'. Italy's inability to confront its Fascist past meant that, for many years, it was unable to reflect on and accept the deportation of its entire military forces. The IMIs, the hundreds of thousands of survivors of that deportation, were an uncomfortable reminder of Fascist Italy's role in the Second World War. The lack of interest in their fates was reflected in the fact that the first academic study only appeared in 1990.[11]

Alfredo's reluctance to talk about his wartime experiences raised questions for me about what he left out and why, and whether his silence should be disturbed. Alfredo exercised a choice in his lifetime not to speak about the stalag beyond small details, like the potato skins. Would he have wanted to talk about his other experiences with me now, after the passage of decades?

I personally felt every unexpected, uninvited request to talk about the plane crash—from media, acquaintances, even sometimes from friends and relatives—as a painful intrusion on my trauma that I guarded, for reasons of self-preservation, so protectively. Now that the politics around forced labourers and IMIs had shifted, would my grandfather have felt more able to talk about his internment? Or would the continuing pain and shame of his experiences have meant he didn't want to?

We often think that wellbeing after trauma relies on talking about what happened, on freeing one's voice. However, the silences that follow trauma can be viewed in another way—not as the repression of one's voice, but as a kind of voice in itself. Silence, in other words, can be a medium of expression, can tell us something about the traumatised person's experiences, if we listen. While sometimes not allowing a survivor of crime or wrongdoing to tell their story can be an injustice, not respecting silence can also cause harm.

There is another reason to observe and try to understand the silence that can follow trauma. The way someone chooses, or feels compelled, to live after surviving deep trauma can communicate in non-verbal ways. The anthropologist Carol Kidron, who has studied the effects of genocide on the children of survivors, calls this 'silent memory work'. Idiosyncratic behaviours adopted as a response to trauma are like scars: they can communicate the past without a survivor ever directly narrating their story.[12]

I think about bread, about its revered place in my grandparents' house, and the unspoken family history behind that. Bread had an almost holy quality to it. There were rules. A loaf of bread could never be placed upside down. Leftover bread was never thrown away, no matter how old or mouldy. If ever bread had to be thrown out, a rare occurrence, you kissed it first. Multiple uses were found for stale bread, like making breadcrumbs or tiny *gnocchetti* for soup or soaking it in milk for rissoles. Once it turned green, beyond human consumption, the bread was placed in string shopping bags that hung from cupboard door knobs in the sunroom for the birds. Nonna soaked the hard bread in water before feeding it to pigeons and sparrows in the park where she'd stop on her walks to the shops. Sometimes she found a pigeon with a broken wing, one that had survived a cat attack, and she brought it home, where it would recuperate under an old armchair, among the bags of bread and birdcages.

The reverent treatment of bread in my grandparents' house had religious connotations: bread as the body of Christ. But, in addition, my grandparents knew what it meant not to have bread, what bread represented. Nonno knew from the POW camp; Nonna knew from having to queue for food rations during and after the war. And they both knew from their experiences as new immigrants in Australia when they were unable to find work, when any food they had went to feed their young daughters, while they went without.

XI

Researching my grandfather's wartime experiences was not easy for my mother.

I assumed she would want to know as much as possible about her father's imprisonment, and I enlisted her to translate the IMI testimonies, thinking that involving her in such a way might give her a sense of personal investment in my project.

Instead I met with a resistance that initially exasperated and confounded me. I soon realised my discoveries were uncovering painful possibilities for Mum about her father's past, creating questions she would never be able to ask him.

At first, Mum complained that all the testimonies were the same. 'I don't connect it to my father because I never knew that side of him,' she said.

Then, when my mother came across testimonies that resonated more closely with what she knew about her father, she blamed me for breaking a silence her father had intentionally kept. When she finished one IMI's account of his liberation in Germany by Russian soldiers—a lawless period of violence, excess and retribution as the malnourished prisoners were released from two years of slavery and humiliation—she told me she wished she hadn't translated it.

'This is why Nonno never told us anything,' she said. 'He never wanted us to know.'

Alfredo was liberated on 24 April 1945 when the Russians entered the camps in Berlin.

The IMIs in Berlin had watched the front move closer through April from inside the camps. Food was scarcer than ever and, with daily bombings hammering the centre of the city and the noise of artillery close by in the suburbs, prisoners nervously anticipated their imminent freedom. One morning in April, the prisoners woke to find German guards had deserted their posts. A couple of days later, the Red Army arrived.

The Russian soldiers were feared by the German population as, drunken and vengeful, they carried out mass rapes and indiscriminate killings of local women on their way through Germany to Berlin. Alfredo told my father he had nothing personally against the Russians, who treated the IMIs quite well. He hinted to his family, however, at the brutality of that period.

'They had plenty of everything but it was an incredibly rough period when the Russians liberated them,' Mum recalled her father telling her, although he never elaborated.

My father said Alfredo described the liberation as a kind of party or banquet. 'They were treated like dogs in prison, the locals did not help them, they were bombed by the Allies and expected to die every day, then they were released, and it was like a holiday.'

In the immediate chaos of liberated Berlin, the freed IMIs began looking for food and clothes, first ransacking the storerooms and cellars of the camp, then the factories and houses around the horribly devastated city. Animals were slaughtered, sometimes with great cruelty, given most soldiers and officers had no idea how to do it humanely. The liberated prisoners killed and cooked herds of pigs, cows, rabbits and carts of chickens. Outside the city there were apocalyptic scenes of burnt villages and dying people. The

IMIs struggled to find accommodation and shelter from the rain and snow.

Alfredo told my father that he wandered around the countryside trying to find or steal food, as he made his way back to Italy.

The Italian prisoners were not a priority for the Allies after the war and they faced an interminable wait for repatriation, which was shambolic. Many months passed before Italian government representatives arrived to organise the IMIs' transports home. The returning prisoners travelled in lorries, buses and trains back to Italy, though train journeys were slow because bridges had been blown up and railway lines were in a poor state generally. Some of the Italians set off on foot or rode bicycles and made it to the border on their own.

Alfredo was repatriated to Italy four and a half months after his liberation, on 8 September 1945. According to his family, he walked home.

XII

After many translations of the stories of Italian prisoners, Mum and I read a testimony that was different to the others, most of which had dealt with Italian officers or camps in Poland.

The testimony was contained in a thin grey book that I picked up in Italy; it might have been at the museum in Padua. It brought us as close as we had come to understanding what Alfredo endured as a low-ranking conscript undergoing forced labour in Berlin. My mother translated it speaking into a tape recorder, so that I heard, as she spoke, the effect the story had on her.

Published in 1981, it was the story of an Italian chaplain, Father Vittorio Poloni, an IMI, number 122038. He was captured in Greece, aged 33. He was imprisoned for the duration of the war at Luckenwalde, but regularly visited the stalags and work camps in Berlin and its surrounds. He witnessed, first hand, the condition of the young Italian soldiers who were forced labourers.[13]

The chaplain described the initial familiar scenes of the convoys of IMIs travelling north on their wretched journey towards Germany; their miserable arrival in Luckenwalde; the degrading ritual of registration; the paltry rations; the inferior treatment of the IMIs compared to other POWs; the attempts by the Germans to entice the Italians to join their side with promises of better treatment and repatriation; the IMIs' dogged refusals. Then, Christmas 1943 arrived.

The Germans finally gave the chaplains permission to visit the factories, where the priest saw his first group of forced labourers. It was a group of 800 IMIs, most of them boys from the class of 1924, born the same year as Alfredo. They were working as forced labourers at the Mercedes-Benz factory, work camp number 483, in Ludwigsfelde, halfway between Luckenwalde and Berlin.

The young men, Poloni observed, were treated like beasts. If the prisoners made an error of some kind in the factory or the camp, they were beaten and condemned to carry a weight of 30 kilograms on their shoulders and run around the barracks until they collapsed on the ground.

As my mother translated these passages, her voice cracked. 'Cynthia, this is really hard.'

The IMIs were beaten until there was blood. A couple of Italian Alpini, specialist mountain troops, carried out the punishments of the IMIs. Prisoners were woken every day at 4.45 am, and worked through until 5 pm. They suffered immense hunger, they were tired and visibly malnourished, with many affected by tuberculosis. The chaplain took twenty of the sickest soldiers back to the hospital at Luckenwalde with him, and one succumbed shortly after to the disease.

Listening to the tape, I had to stop typing to wipe away the tears that were blocking my vision.

Reading and hearing Poloni's testimony, both of us knew, instinctively, that this was what Alfredo never spoke about.

Not all the factories around Berlin were as inhumane. The chaplain once encountered a German guard who took him home and offered him bread, salami and butter. But when Poloni returned to Ludwigsfelde the following Easter, in 1944, conditions had worsened and the young soldiers were even more malnourished, demoralised, battered and demeaned. They were *ombre vaganti, non piu uomini*, 'wandering shadows, no longer men', decimated by TB. There were more deaths. The priest witnessed beatings of many men with bayonets. He celebrated mass for the prisoners on an improvised altar in the camp.

'How many tears do I see falling from the sunken eyes, bathing sunken cheeks,' he wrote. 'I also cry, mixing my tears with theirs.'

Poloni's main work at Luckenwalde, apart from trying to bring spiritual comfort to the IMIs, was to bury the many Italian dead. After the Russians liberated the POW camp in April 1945, the Italians were last to be repatriated. During the six months he remained at Stalag III A waiting for the trains to transport him back to Italy with the sick, Poloni worked in the cemetery, which was in a pitiful state. Assisted by 30 volunteers, among them an architect and an engineer, and with the approval of the Russian command, he acquired timber to build caskets. Within 25 days, every tomb had a little wooden cross with a name.

Poloni also erected a monument to the lost Italians, inscribed with the words: *Morti per fame* ('Dead from hunger').

The priest's final act in the camp was to celebrate mass among the tombs—for the absent mothers, the wives and the orphans— and to say goodbye.

It was the same cemetery where I sat on the wooden bench in the biotechnology park.

My mother never dreamt about her father after his death in 1993. I did: after he passed away in hospital, he came to me in my sleep to say goodbye (the last time I saw him he was in a coma, and I hadn't known what to say to him). Hearing this upset my mother at the time; she wondered why she couldn't dream about him too.

After translating Poloni's testimony, Mum dreamt of her beloved father for the first time. She recognised him from his grey double-breasted suit. It was the same suit his mother bought him when he left Italy for Australia with his wife and two daughters.

A young Loredana with her father, Alfredo, in 1951

XIII

When I began looking into my grandfather's story, I didn't know that the traumatic experiences of the Italian prisoners in the Second World War were the subject of ongoing, present-day international legal and diplomatic disputes. I hadn't grasped how the hurt of family members continued, even after most of these men—their husbands and fathers—were dead.

As I delved more deeply into the story of the IMIs, I experienced a sad awakening around the suffering of Alfredo and the Italian POWs that extended beyond what they experienced in the stalags and factories in Germany and Poland to their treatment afterwards, once they got home and into their old age. It became so upsetting—I cried reading legal judgments about the struggle to have the IMIs' wartime torment recognised, some as recent as 2014—that Mum urged me to stop.

'You don't have to do this.'

But I did, of course.

Previously, I had been a little puzzled by my mother's sensitivity around the issue of compensation for my grandfather's imprisonment. As far as I knew, she had made a claim under a new German government scheme for former prisoners of the Nazis on her father's behalf sometime after his death, and it was knocked back. She was indignant about it—and continues to be. What did it matter, I thought to myself, when Alfredo was not here to benefit from any money were it paid, nor to have his feelings hurt when it wasn't?

How little I understood about the crime of Nazi forced labour—and about how a deep sense of injustice can travel across generations, across continents and time.

It took the German government to the 21st century to atone for the harms done to forced labourers during the war. In August 2000, it established a foundation—known in English as 'Remembrance, Responsibility and Future'—which paid out sums of money to more than 1.6 million individuals. It was a symbolic gesture rather than compensation, given the inadequate amounts (2500 to 7500 euros). The International Organization for Migration (IOM) administered payments for non-Jewish victims.[14] This was the same scheme under which my mother made the application for her father.

Why did it take Germany so long to recognise forced labourers? There were a number of reasons, but the general theme is this: forced labourers were seen as unworthy victims, and their collective experiences were an inconvenient memory for both the war's losers and victors, to be brushed aside. First, there was suspicion towards returning forced labourers by those at home (Russia imprisoned its survivors). In Germany, efforts were made immediately after the war to eliminate all traces of their presence, and the archives of the big companies that profited from forced labour remained completely closed to researchers until the 1980s (some still are). Cold War pressures meant the Allied powers wanted a Europe that was politically and economically stable. This required keeping Germany's industrial capability intact, so that companies who used forced labour were allowed to rebuild their enterprises and ignore victims' cries for recognition. (There were token settlements along the way; Rheinmetall, for example, was pressured into paying compensation to Jewish forced labourers when it tried to negotiate arms export deals with the United States in the 1960s.) Furthermore, under a 1953 international agreement on Germany's external debts, the country was allowed to postpone paying forced labourers compensation until a peace treaty was signed (no peace treaty eventuated).[15]

By the mid-1990s, after the Berlin Wall fell and following Germany's reunification, the international political and financial landscape finally shifted, and the issue of forced labour emerged into the open once again. With globalisation, large German firms were expanding into the United States, exposing them to American lawsuits and embarrassing, well-publicised accusations that they used slave labour during the war. This led a number of corporations concerned about their international reputation (car, electronics and arms manufacturers, banks, insurers and pharmaceutical giants) to contribute funds to the German government-supported foundation that was to be made available to all of Hitler's forced labourers.

For the Italian soldiers imprisoned by the Nazis and exploited as forced labourers there was, however, a cruel twist. I have a copy of my mother's application to the IOM on behalf of her father. It was rejected, as were all those submitted for the Italian forced labourers, living or dead. (At the time, my mother didn't know why.) IMIs were excluded from the scheme because in 2001, the German government decided that although Hitler had refused to recognise the captured Italian soldiers as POWs as punishment for Italy's betrayal of Germany, the Führer had no right to unilaterally change their status. And POWs may, according to the rules of international law, be put to work by the detaining power.

For IMIs, this was like being punished all over again. As prisoners they were given none of the special protections other POWs received (regular food parcels, visits from the Red Cross, the prohibition on working in armaments factories). Yet here was the German state, more than 50 years later, saying that for the purposes of this scheme, established to acknowledge the suffering of forced labourers—albeit in a small way—the Italians were actually POWs. One IMI, on having his application to the IOM rejected, said it would have been better if he had died rather than be told that his application for compensation had been denied.[16]

Germany's position was upheld by the International Court of Justice in The Hague in 2012. The court said it was a matter of 'surprise—and regret' that the German government had decided to deny compensation to the Italian prisoners on the grounds that they had been entitled to a status which the German state had, at the relevant time, refused to recognise. However, Germany's position was supported by an international law doctrine known as state immunity: essentially, countries can't be sued in other countries' courts without their consent. This meant that disaffected former IMIs refusing to be completely locked out of the German government's scheme for forced labourers could not then go and sue Germany for recognition in Italian courts. An act might be morally wrong, in other words, yet legally right, as was the situation with Germany's behaviour here. The International Court of Justice decision left a whole class of victims—of crimes against humanity, the gravest of international crimes—without legal remedy.[17]

Together, the international court's disregard for the entitlement of IMIs to justice, Germany's historical crimes and ongoing mean-spiritedness, and Italy's failure to make amends for its poor treatment of its imprisoned soldiers, means the suffering of these men continues to go unacknowledged.

This is why my mother still gets upset when she thinks about that rejection of her application to Germany for compensation for her father.

XIV

Writing this, I questioned myself constantly about my ability to deliver an accurate depiction of what happened to my grandfather in the war and my reliability as a narrator.

I felt acutely the impossibility of a mission that sought to restore memories that were never shared in the first place. The events happened more than 70 years ago. There was no one of Alfredo's generation left in his family, and any surviving IMIs, were I able to find them, would be in their mid-nineties. There were also the difficulties of working in multiple languages in five different countries and my physical limitations, which restricted my ability to travel independently and spontaneously.

Alfredo's story will never be whole again; all I have of his Second World War experiences are dubious fragments. My grandfather's military documents, so bureaucratic and sparse in their detail, beg to be filled in with his lived memories, which are forever lost to me. My mother can't tell me now whether certain recollections she has of her father's imprisonment—like the infernal lice and fleas—are based on what he told her, or on things she read while translating the various prisoners' accounts for me.

Distant memory, wrote Primo Levi, is a 'suspect source' that 'must be protected against itself'.[18] I am working with fragile memories, dealing in the second- and third-hand offerings of Alfredo's children and nieces and nephews. I have had to make judgements about which are reliable and which aren't.

In my conversations with relatives, I was asked again and again why I was doing this. Why was I asking all these questions about Alfredo and Amelia? Why was I visiting these distant places in Europe? Why did I want to know?

'Cosa serve?' Mum's cousins in Italy asked. 'How does it serve you?'

The repeated questioning of my motives made me uneasy about my project. What were my motives? Would there be consequences from uncovering these stories, of writing them down, of making that writing public? Sometimes, while reading about the Nazis and forced labour and POW camps and Mussolini and the armistice, I wondered myself about the tenuous connection of Alfredo's story to my own. Was I simply avoiding my story by writing about the others?

I tried to explain to my mother and her cousins why it mattered so much to me to write about my family's stories of suffering and surviving. In my limited Italian, I told relatives in Trieste, straining for the right words, that I wanted to go to the places Nonno went because he went there, that I wanted to understand Amelia because of what she did for her brother.

'I cannot write my story without writing his,' I told them.

It was the truth. I know I could not have read and processed the material about the plane crash and forced myself to write about it had I not been doing it as part of a bigger project about my family's history. Memory—our own, our family's, our community's—is central to identity. Bringing Alfredo's and Amelia's life stories into the present was the work of making sense of an otherwise unfathomable existence: my own. In gathering together and preserving the threads of our lives, I was deriving meaning when otherwise there seemed to be none. The deeper I went into the research on my grandfather, the more I realised how inseparable, for me, our stories were.[19]

Take something like thirst. The IMIs talked about spending days locked inside the cattle wagons after their capture and of going all that time without water. The excruciating thirst that follows from days of not drinking is described in different ways in the accounts of concentration camp survivors. One former prisoner explains how this kind of thirst is enraging, a sensation so horrific, so much worse than hunger even, that there can be no distracting from its all-powerful grip, no respite. For another survivor, such a thirst abolished all her senses.[20]

I do not know what it feels like to be deliberately denied water for days by sadistic captors, whether in a train or a camp. But reading the Second World War testimonies, I remembered lying abandoned on a trolley in the corridor of the hospital in Yogyakarta and begging passers-by for water. I had a thirst from the burns so violent that I wanted to scream, but I could barely whisper. Every atom in my burnt body cried out for liquid. The Indonesians ignored me. Maybe they didn't understand English. Perhaps they were unsure whether I was allowed water in my condition. Or they may have been preoccupied with other things.

While an individual's own experience of violence and suffering does not mean that they can understand another's experience of violence and suffering, it can build connections and ways of understanding. Ruth Kluger, an Austrian Jew who survived the Holocaust, made this observation after listening to German friends, years after the war, talk about claustrophobia caused by being trapped in elevators or new railway tunnels. It made her think of her own experience being stuck in a transport to Auschwitz.

'Isn't all reflection about the human condition (or conditions) a process of deducing from ourselves to others?' she asked.[21]

Reading about the suffering of the Italian prisoners, knowing my grandfather was one of them, somehow made me feel less alone with my own traumatic memories.

XV

There was a cousin of my mother in Trieste who I didn't see on our visit in 2015.

Andrea is the son of Alfredo's older brother, Silvio. I didn't know, until I was back in Australia, that Andrea was the one surviving relative who was present the day Alfredo arrived unannounced at his parents' house on his return from Germany. Andrea and I spoke on the telephone and later corresponded by letter. This is what he told me.

One day in September 1945, there was a knock at the front door of La Casa Rossa in Servola, Trieste.

Andrea, who was nine years old, was staying with his grandparents (Alfredo's parents), Amedeo and Anna-Maria, at the time. Someone opened the door and a young man appeared there whom Andrea didn't immediately recognise. Everybody stood rooted to the spot, in shock. It was Alfredo, arrived on foot from Germany.

I picture Alfredo in the garden outside La Casa Rossa, looking up towards the windows of his family's apartment, climbing the tall external staircase, gripping onto the wrought-iron railing as he slowly ascended the 30 or so steps to the blue wooden door. Did he pause to inhale the familiar smells of home, his mother's polenta and rabbit goulash, perhaps his father's cigarettes? Andrea told me that Alfredo embraced his parents and nephew for the first time in two years. His return was a huge surprise to his family, and they held a big celebration that night.

Alfredo told his parents about his imprisonment, and Andrea listened quietly to his every word. According to Andrea's recollection of how his uncle described his capture, Alfredo was on an Italian naval ship in the sea off Pola (perhaps this is why some of Alfredo's military documents say he was captured in Piraeus?). He was deported to Berlin where he worked in different camps, from the factories to the farms (suggesting he was not held only at Alkett).

Alfredo also spoke that day about his awful hunger in the camps. The Germans in Berlin did not feed the prisoners well, and he made soup with potato peelings. He told his family that—just as I'd read in some of the IMI testimonies—on multiple occasions he was so hungry that he ate his captors' German shepherds. He told Andrea that if the prisoners saw a dog, they would quickly grab it, kill it and cook it.

My grandfather was not underweight the day he arrived home, though. He was fat, and to the young Andrea did not look like somebody who had spent time in a work camp. Alfredo explained that his Russian liberators had moved him into another camp, where they fed the malnourished Italian prisoners so well that some died from overeating; their stomachs could not cope with the amount of food and they died of peritonitis. (When Andrea told me this, my mother suddenly remembered her father saying he had to skip to lose weight after his return to Italy after the war.)

Soon after being liberated, Alfredo started walking home towards Italy. He told his family he got cold on the way and some of his fellow ex-prisoners found a train wagon full of German currency, Reichsmarks, which they used as fuel for a fire to warm themselves. It was only later that they discovered the banknotes still had some value.

Andrea recalled there was one positive thing in Alfredo's story. It involved Amelia, and what she did to save his life. Here, Andrea confirmed what I had suspected, but no one else in the family had expressly said. In Germany, to help her brother, Amelia became the girlfriend of a German officer. She used him to get parcels to her brother. Andrea wrote in his letter to me:

> A good thing in this story is that Aunt Amelia, his sister, in order to help and save her brother, she had, let's say, a German officer in Berlin as a lover. So through this officer she arranged for her brother Alfredo to receive some parcels of food and clothing necessary for his survival, which he later shared among other prisoners.

Amelia would have been 26 or 27 at the time she took a German officer as a lover in order to alleviate her brother's suffering in the forced labour camp. According to Andrea, Amelia remained in Berlin for many years to help Alfredo. At most, by my calculations, Amelia's time in Germany could have overlapped with Alfredo's by eighteen months. I deduce this because Alfredo, in his postcard from Alkett in January 1944, asked that all his sisters, including Amelia, help their mother, suggesting she was not yet in Germany. The photograph I have locating Amelia in Berlin (possibly) was taken in June 1945. Where in burning, bombed-out Berlin did she live during this time? She was not listed in any of the city's directories during that period—but, then, why would she be?

Arriving in Berlin, Amelia, accustomed to performing on stage, would have had to assume a new role, one presumably fraught with danger but motivated by a profoundly deep love and concern for her younger sibling. I assume Alfredo was still at Alkett, though I don't know for certain. She had limited options as a single woman alone in Berlin in 1944/1945. As many other women did in similar situations at that desperate time, she used what bargaining power she had—her femininity, her youth, her companionship, her body perhaps—to reach her brother.

Nobody but Amelia, an untethered soul who did not feel bound to the accepted social mores of the period, could have done this for Alfredo. If Amelia's actions entailed moral ambiguities or compromises, she did not let this stop her. She believed in herself—she said this explicitly in her diary: 'I had a lot of faith in myself'—and her mission must have been deeply felt.

There was a personal emotional cost to what Amelia did, however, that was also evident in that line in her diary, the one direct insight I have from her about this time, the single fragment of her interior life from this extraordinary episode that exists today. Here is her Italian, and my English:

. . . tanti i giorni tristi e paurosi che passai durante la Guerra che non altra infelicita credevo che potesse avvenirmi.

. . . the many sad and terrifying days that I passed during the war so that I never believed more unhappiness could happen to me.

The comment tells me so little, and yet says so much. These days were so bad, Amelia dared to believe that she'd had her share of unhappiness and that she could never be that unhappy again.

How was Amelia's German lover connected to the sad and terrifying days that she wrote about? What kind of feelings did he invoke in her? Had the officer mistreated her? Or had others hurt her? What became of him? Did she leave him when the war ended? What sacrifices did she make, what indignities did she endure, in what manner had she been terrorised? How did Amelia's time in Germany—whatever untold dangers she'd faced—affect her?

My mother tells me I will never find out, that what happened between Amelia and her German officer boyfriend was private, between the two of them. Despite my best efforts, I know Mum is right. To uncover the secrets of Amelia's time in Berlin, I would have to find a still-living German guard or Italian prisoner connected with Alfredo's camp, a camp whose identity I do not know for certain, given that he was probably moved around.

Most of the attempts I made to learn about what happened to Alfredo and Amelia during the war resulted in disappointment. My grandfather's best man at his wedding, his closest friend, is deceased. So too is the author of the sole account I located of an Italian prisoner from Alkett (numerous emails to the former Alkett prisoner's son went unanswered). Alkett's parent company, Rheinmetall, was unhelpful and the official archives in Berlin were practically bare of information about the tank factory's forced labourers. The professional archival researchers I employed in Germany scoured the archives in Berlin, Brandenburg and Luckenwalde; they turned up very little. Most of the sources and files relating to Stalag III D in Berlin were destroyed at the end of the war, they informed me. Of Amelia, there was no trace at all.

My dream of finding someone who crossed paths with Amelia during the war remains forever out of reach. I was too young to ask my grandfather about Amelia—I knew little, if anything, of her story when he died in 1993. What might Alfredo have told me, had I asked?

Mum continues to be unconvinced of this part of her aunt's story, given her father never once mentioned to her what Amelia did for him while he was imprisoned in Germany. If Amelia took him food, why did he always tell his daughters that he was starving? Yet my mother is also aware there is much about Amelia she doesn't know.

'You don't know the half of it,' a cousin in Italy told her, when she pressed again on my behalf for more information about Amelia. The cousin would say no more.

I stared once more at the photograph of Amelia in Berlin in 1945, her pressed lips, her haunted eyes. There is nobody left who can answer my questions.

XVI

Andrea had other information about Amelia, concerning her life after the war.

Amelia, he said, went to Naples and other cities to dance in the variety theatre. This, Andrea said, was how she met her wealthy, much older American fiancé from America.

At first, when Andrea mentioned this detail, I dismissed it. A wealthy fiancé from America? I had heard much of the hapless and lovelorn Vincenzo, Amelia's wealthy Neapolitan boyfriend whom she left behind in Italy. I knew about the restaurant owner in the United States who abused Amelia, but this was the first mention of a wealthy American fiancé.

Then the American genealogists uncovered a marriage licence. In early 1952 (several months after she arrived in America), Amelia obtained a licence to marry a much older man. He was almost twice her age, in his sixties, Italian-born, and a widower with children Amelia's age (Amelia would have been his second wife). He owned a 'candy store'. The licence was valid for three months. Once again, a relative's small, seemingly unlikely detail about Amelia's complex existence had been verified. Before she left Italy, it was indeed possible that Amelia had attached herself to a wealthy single man, an American citizen.

At first, the American genealogists could find no trace that the marriage between Amelia and the elderly candy store owner had ever taken place. There was no 'return of marriage', whereby an official record is filed with a county clerk, and no newspaper notice. The man died in the late 1950s after a lengthy illness, around the same time as Amelia bought a house, the one she lived in at the time of her death.

How was this elderly fiancé connected to Amelia's emigration to America? How did it fit with her decision to leave Italy as a refugee? Immigrants at that time needed someone living in the United States to sponsor them, to guarantee them housing and a job. Was this man Amelia's sponsor? (I discovered later that he was not.) What became of their relationship? What did the man's adult children think of the liaison between Amelia and their father? Did they disapprove?

Not long after unearthing the marriage licence, the American researchers made another discovery. It was the man's will, made the same month they obtained their marriage licence. He left all his property to his children. Then he added this: 'I make no provision herein for my wife, AMELIA . . . by reason of the fact that she has abandoned me.'

So—the pair was married, after all. Amelia arrived in America in mid-1951. Within eight months, she had married the elderly American fiancé she first met while dancing in Naples and left him, and he immediately drafted a will to ensure she didn't make a future claim against his estate. There was no notice in the local newspapers of any divorce or annulment of their marriage but, after more digging, I found the precise date of Amelia's marriage in 1952 in her Alien File. It was 'annulled' twenty days later.

Why Amelia abandoned her husband so soon after marrying him is unclear. What is apparent is that Amelia had many boyfriends in her time, and that these relationships served a variety of different purposes. Which of these men, if any, did Amelia love?

Nothing about Amelia's life was straightforward.

XVII

While writing this chapter on my grandfather's imprisonment, I noticed something—a small detail—that I had previously missed.

Alfredo was born on 2 June 1924.

The date, 2 June, is Italy's national day, the Festa della Repubblica. It marks the day when (following the Second World War) Italy voted to become a republic and banished its king.

That's not all. That date, 2 June, was also the day Amelia died from breast cancer in America in 1960—on Alfredo's birthday.

Alfredo turned 36 that day. He didn't yet know the tragic details of the final years of his sister's life, and was unaware of how much

Amelia herself needed rescuing from what befell her in America. Why did Amelia never tell him? It is probable that she hadn't wanted to burden her family with her problems—certainly not Alfredo, who had himself already suffered so much.

Amelia's 'big America', the 'place of dreams', didn't work out as she had imagined. She had left a large family behind in Trieste and desperately hoped that some of them, including her brother Alfredo and one of her elder nieces, would join her in America, under the US laws permitting family reunification. This never happened and Amelia spent the final months of her life terminally ill and completely alone.

It wasn't long after Amelia's death though, with the discovery of her diary, that Alfredo knew everything.

5

Michael

I

I SENT MICHAEL A TEXT MESSAGE BEFORE MY FLIGHT left Jakarta
on the morning of 7 March 2007.

I wished him well for his interview with the prime minister later
that day, and told him I'd had a dream about him.

Michael was at Canberra Airport, waiting to fly to Melbourne.
He sent a reply: 'I hope it wasn't a nightmare.'

Michael arrived in Melbourne and went into his head office at
Southbank, on the Yarra River. He'd started working on a column
when two of his close friends, also senior *Herald Sun* journalists,
called him over and told him there had been a plane crash in
Yogyakarta. My plane.

Michael's phone started ringing and didn't stop. He went into
the editorial conference room and took calls from government officials from the prime minister's and foreign minister's offices and
the Department of Foreign Affairs and Trade.

'We think she is alive,' one official told him. 'A plane is taking
off from Jakarta. We hope to land in Yogyakarta. That means we
will have more resources on the ground.'

The airport in Yogyakarta was closed because of the crash.
Meanwhile, hospitals were being placed on alert in Darwin.

Later, Michael's colleagues read a story on the AAP wires confirming I was alive. He learnt that my newspaper's Jakarta correspondent had located me in Yogyakarta's Sardjito Hospital.

'They are X-raying her at the moment,' my colleague in Yogyakarta, Mark Forbes, told Michael when eventually they spoke. 'She has been badly knocked around. She is very distressed.'

I spoke to my father, many hours later, on someone's mobile phone.

'It's very bad, Dad,' I said as calmly as I could, trying to prepare him.

'What's very bad?' my father asked.

'I've been very badly burnt.'

'Can you wiggle your toes?'

'Yes.'

Dad was relieved, his main concern being for my damaged spine. He tried to get off the phone so that I could continue my treatment. He had no real grasp of what had happened to me; none of my family did at that point.

It was 5.30 pm Melbourne time when a consular official arranged for me to talk to Michael.

'My legs are burnt,' I told him. 'I thought I was going to die. I was crushed between two people but I couldn't breathe.'

The line was bad. Michael could not make out all my words.

'It's not good,' the consular official told Michael. 'They are concerned about her legs.'

II

Flags on the track, Joan Didion called them. And I saw them.[1]

They were warnings, 'notices of darkening', inklings that something was up in the month or so leading up to crash. On their own they were irritating, trivial matters—missteps—that you might have dismissed. Except that I didn't.

I remember one incident in particular. One morning I fell while running the Bay Run and split open my thumb. It was a day when I was due to cover the Sea King inquiry. I went to the GP's before work, but in the courtroom at Randwick Barracks my hand started bleeding and wouldn't stop. The army infirmary didn't want to help me because it broke with their protocols.

Somehow, minor though such episodes were, there were enough of them to cause me to tell two friends in January 2007: 'I feel like something bad is about to happen to me.'

We were talking early one warm evening outside the *Herald* offices at Darling Park, in Sydney. They told me not to be silly.

It was my moment of foreboding—like the stranger who read Amelia's palm near the post office in Naples. The universe sent me a signal, but it wasn't enough to cause me to alter my course.

The fact is I hadn't wanted to take this work trip to Indonesia, and I tried to get out of going.

I was originally invited to go by the foreign minister, Alexander Downer, but the invitation was retracted when the government VIP plane that we were meant to travel on had to be serviced. The trip was revived, but this time there was only space for me to travel with the foreign minister on his plane to and from Indonesia. I had to organise my own domestic flights inside Indonesia, as the VIP plane would be full.

All this trouble for what was, essentially, an interview with a cabinet minister on his plane ride home. There was a sub-regional ministerial counterterrorism conference in Jakarta but the proceedings would be conducted behind closed doors and my newspaper already had a correspondent in Indonesia. It sounded like a logistical nightmare for not much of a story at all. A colleague at *The Australian* had decided it was not worth the effort and pulled out. I asked my chief of staff in Canberra and one of the editors in Sydney if I could miss the trip. They said no.

On the day I flew out of Canberra to join the VIP plane in Adelaide for the flight to Indonesia, Michael and I went to watch an AFL football game at Manuka Oval. It was the pre-season NAB Cup, the Swans versus Richmond. I was the last one out of the house. Michael put my bags into the boot of his car and we drove to the football ground. It was a hot day. After the game Michael dropped me off at the airport, stopping for petrol and water on the way.

When I arrived in Adelaide, Michael rang me. I had left the front door of his house open. Not just unlocked, but completely wide open.

'How strange,' I said, embarrassed at my carelessness.

Looking back, I think I left the door open to guarantee my return. It was as if I was saying to the house, to my life, to the world: 'I am not ready to leave just yet—I will be back. And I am going to leave the door open just to be sure.'

III

The wait for the medivac in Yogyakarta dragged on and on.

Finally, in the middle of the night, I was wheeled across the bumpy tarmac to meet the air ambulance that was taking me back to Australia. I was conscious throughout the flight, petrified and powerless. I could hear two medical staff talking about themselves, trivial matters, over my stretcher in the Learjet.

Please don't let me die, I thought, as their conversation continued, like I wasn't there.

Michael's brother, Andrew, and his family lived in Perth. Andrew didn't sleep that night, after Michael told him I was being taken to Royal Perth Hospital. He was expecting me to arrive around 2 am (I arrived at 2.25 am local time). At 1.30 am Andrew got out of bed and headed to the hospital. Spotting a news crew outside the emergency department, he went inside.

Andrew called Michael to let him know he was at the hospital. Michael was at Melbourne Airport with my parents and brother, Sebastian, waiting for a flight to Perth.

After learning of the plane crash, my parents immediately began preparations to fly to Indonesia (when Mum rang Flight Centre, the consultant had never heard of Yogyakarta). Subsequently, they were told I was being evacuated to Darwin, so they headed there with Sebastian instead. Michael found them in a room at Darwin Airport when he arrived on a flight from Melbourne. The four were soon informed my medivac had been diverted to Perth and that their quickest way of getting to Perth from Darwin was to fly back to Melbourne and catch a flight from there.

Sebastian recalled how, on the flight from Darwin, the kind captain of the plane walked all the way down to the rear of the aircraft to find my father.

'Are you John Banham?' the captain asked, after introducing himself. He offered his sympathies, and told my father everything was going to be okay.

At the hospital in Perth, Andrew asked to see me. The nurses were at first suspicious, but asked him to fill in a form with my personal details. He guessed some of the answers (like the suburb of Michael's house in Canberra) and was allowed in to my room.

I was on a bed, surrounded by six or maybe eight nurses who all looked up at him. They moved away when they saw me recognise Andrew. He kissed me, held my right hand, and sat facing me. I was wide-eyed and lucid and we spoke rapidly, knowing I would be rushed off at any moment. There was black dirt and mud on the roots of the hair on my forehead and in my nostrils, and blood on my right earlobe and neck.

'Where is Michael?' I asked Andrew.

He told me Michael was only a few hours away. I told Andrew I got out of the plane and rolled myself in the water in the paddy field to soothe my burns.

'Did I do the right thing? I asked him.

'You absolutely did do the right thing,' Andrew told me.

'Am I going to lose my legs?'

Andrew told me to rest, that I would need every bit of energy I had now. I asked him to tell my friend Kathryn who lived in Perth that I was there (quite irrationally, I was concerned that her feelings would be hurt if I visited Perth and didn't let her know). Andrew didn't know Kathryn, but he promised to contact her. He reminded me that Michael and my parents were two or three hours away, then left.

We had four or five minutes together. Shortly after, I stopped breathing.

IV

My dreams in the coma were long, involved, vivid and disturbing. For days after waking up, I was convinced the events I dreamed had really happened.

Michael

There were two dreams. In both I was trapped and was trying, desperately, to get to Michael. The dreams have stayed with me. For years I have thought about them, although I never wrote down a word of what occurred in them until now.

In the first dream, I entered a huge fish tank that was sitting outside the hospital. It was the sort you might see large sharks swimming around in at the aquarium, though this one had rooms and furniture in it, and I lived there—it was my home. It was difficult to breathe under the water, and I had no breathing apparatus. An ABC crew was with me (a couple of journalists from ABC's *Australian Story* were on the trip to Indonesia following the foreign minister around). I remember seeing Chris Uhlmann, then a political correspondent for ABC Radio. He and a cameraman were there, in the tank, to film a domestic scene of my life with Michael, only Michael wasn't home yet, so we waited for him. I showed the journalists around the different rooms of the giant fish tank/house. I remember there was a vacuum cleaner; I must have been cleaning in preparation for the ABC crew's visit. I was uneasy about being filmed, though. Why was the ABC doing this? Had I agreed to being filmed? It got harder and harder to breathe. Where was Michael? I began to feel like I was suffocating. I needed oxygen and I desperately wanted to get out of the fish tank.

In the second dream, I was kidnapped by American spies who took me to Queensland. They put me in some kind of prison with high, windowless, concrete walls. I walked up and down these walls, searching for a way out. Michael was on the other side, but I couldn't find a way to him. It was cold and empty inside this vast, colourless prison, which felt a bit like a modern art gallery or museum, though one completely bare of artwork or installations.

I tried to negotiate my release with the captors, who wanted to recruit me to their agency.

'I don't want to be a spy,' I told them.

But they wouldn't let me go.

As my body fought death that week in the coma, my mind was waging its own battle to find a way back to the living, back to Michael. The enduring power of those two coma dreams tells me this.

Following one of the many rounds of surgery I had in Perth, after she was sure that I was going to live, the burns surgeon, Dr Fiona Wood, told my family that my 'determination for life' was extraordinary. 'I have never seen a patient worse attacked by infection who lived,' she said.

While there were other factors that no doubt contributed to why I am still here today, I believe the desire to return to Michael helped get me out of the burning plane and kept me alive in the coma. My youthful ideas about romantic love might have been inspired by the ill-fated heroines of unhappy novels, but when it came to the actual possibility of starring in my own tragic love story—dying young and leaving Michael behind—I pushed death away with all the mental and physical force I had.

Inside the burning plane, hearing the crackling fire and feeling it devour my legs, I thought of my future with Michael, a life together that had barely begun. I was not willing to let it go without a fight, one that continued through the coma with its exhausting dreams.

The full truth of what happened in the coma was, however, unknown to me until Michael finally transcribed his shorthand diary. As I lay dreaming about getting back to him, he was communicating things to me that my subconscious must have registered, even if I was unaware of them when I woke up.

V

My parents, Sebastian and Michael arrived in Perth together on Thursday morning, the day after the crash. Australian Federal Police cars were waiting at the airport to take them to the hospital.

My sister had arrived earlier after catching a midnight flight from Singapore with her husband, Dino, and young daughter. They were boarding a plane for Darwin when Juliette received a mobile phone call telling her that I was going to Perth. They left their luggage on the plane going to Darwin and ran to the other side of Changi Airport, just making the flight leaving for Perth.

None of my family knew the extent of my injuries. I was in the intensive care unit (ICU), but all my family saw when they looked through the window of my room 'was a big pile of sheets', Sebastian said. 'You were just wrapped up so much.'

They were given briefing after briefing from different doctors. In the morning they were told I was likely to survive, but then my situation and prognosis deteriorated over the course of the day. There was talk of pancreatitis. Someone mentioned the possibility of amputating a foot.

'Everyone was like, "What?"' Michael wrote in his notebook.

Michael and my family were allowed into my room. They were shocked by what they saw: my face and body were swollen beyond recognition. Only my face was exposed. I was hooked up to all sorts of instruments and tubes.

'I remember almost collapsing,' my sister said. 'I sat on the floor. I just couldn't believe it. There was soot in your nose, your ears, it was all black and you were so puffed up and swollen and you were lying like you were on a cross with huge bandages. Your hair was plaited up over your head, it was hanging over the top of the bed. I remember seeing you and falling onto the floor, just absolutely sobbing . . . I was just begging they would save you. "Please, God, please, God, don't let her die."'

Later in the day Michael did a brief doorstop outside the hospital for local journalists. He and my family and friend Kathryn had dinner at an Italian restaurant in Subiaco.

At breakfast on Friday morning Michael met my family at their hotel. My brother Anthony and his partner arrived from Europe. Anthony and Kate had found out about the crash when a friend texted them and told them to switch on the television. It was 3 am and they were in a hotel room in Switzerland. They spent the next 30 hours in the air trying to get home, wondering if I'd still be alive when they got there.

The mood in the breakfast room of the Hilton was more positive than the previous evening. My sister told Michael that, after this was all over, we might want to run our next marathon somewhere really challenging, like the Sahara Desert.

Then Michael's phone rang.

It was Dennis from the RPH media office. He sounded agitated. He told Michael my family needed to get back up to Wellington Street urgently. He wouldn't say why, but everyone knew Dr Wood was due back from Indonesia that day. They jumped in taxis and were taken to the boardroom to meet Fiona.

Two doctors came into the room. A young Irish doctor, Suzanne Rea, was with Fiona.

'Wow, that's Fiona Wood,' was Michael's first thought when he saw the famous burns surgeon.

Fiona's nervous demeanour quickly focused him.

'When she walked into the room, her body language was very wound up, tense, and we knew straight away something was very bad.'

My family and Michael sat around the boardroom table. Fiona was blunt. She told them I was growing an infection that she had found on the victims of the Bali bombings in 2002. I would not survive the night if doctors did not amputate my left leg.

Everybody was stunned. Until this moment, they all knew my situation was bad, but nobody had contemplated I might not survive.

'She put a choice to us, she told us what had to happen, which then was just one leg,' Michael wrote.

'It was either keep the leg or keep you,' my sister said. 'And it was just—keep you.'

My father, sister and brother agreed the doctors should take my left leg.

'If you don't do this, will she die?' my father asked Fiona.

'Yes,' she said.

'Do whatever you have to do to save her,' my father told her.

My mother saw things differently to the rest of the family. The others were prepared to let the doctors do what was necessary to save my life; they would deal with the consequences later. All Mum saw were the consequences: her daughter living a life without legs, a life my family's decisions had committed me to, in which I had no say.

Mum asked Michael what he thought. My parents at this point knew Michael as the boyfriend I'd been living with for barely five weeks, whom I'd broken up with at least three times over the past three years. Michael thought it was considerate of my mother. He didn't expect to be asked for his opinion, and would not have felt slighted if he hadn't been. Also, things were happening so quickly.

Michael agreed with my father.

Fiona left the room. Michael started thumping the walls, saying, 'Cynthia, Cynthia,' over and over. Juliette and Sebastian were crying. My mother started yelling at my father before storming out of the boardroom.

'You and your fucking prayers,' she told my father.

Dad had a faraway look on his face.

'They must have stayed up praying all night,' Michael told me later. 'I assumed your dad must have said, "We've got to pray." Your mum felt it didn't work—when maybe it saved your life.'

That Friday night at 8 or 9 pm, after putting her baby to sleep, Juliette returned to the hospital with Mum.

'I remember saying to Dino, "I have to get to hospital and tell Cynthia I love her because I may not get to see her again."'

Michael was at the ICU when they arrived. Only two people were allowed in my room at a time. Juliette and our mother went in to see me together.

'The nurses kept saying, "Just talk to her, she can hear you,"' my sister said.

VI

My family and Michael were in shock.

The hospital boardroom was set aside for them and, for the next two days, that's where they sat, around a huge table. At night they lay awake in their hotel rooms, unable to sleep.

The boardroom had a balcony overlooking the garden, and that's where my family went to talk and cry.

'We spent a lot of time outside talking about whether you were going to make it,' Sebastian recalled. 'I remember walking into that place every day wondering what was next.'

A group of five close friends and colleagues of Michael and myself flew into Perth from the east coast to help: Matt, Damon, Ferg, Alle, Cosi. They sat with Michael and my family. Together with Michael's brother, Andrew, they did the washing, kept people fed, bought them clothes, listened to them talk, held them when they cried, took them for walks.

Fiona returned in between surgeries to update my family. She couldn't say whether or not I would survive.

There was no call from the hospital Saturday morning, but at 10 am Michael and my family were back in the boardroom. Fiona told them Friday's surgeries on my left leg had gone well, but there were issues with my right calf. My right foot was already gone; the fire had burnt through the joint of the ankle. At first Fiona said she would save the heel, but later she returned to say it too was gone, that she couldn't save it. She was amputating my right leg from below the knee. Her brother, an orthopaedic surgeon, said I would be able to walk better without it, from a prosthetics point of view.

'It was incremental,' Juliette recalled. '"I had to take this, I had to take that" . . . Every time she came back she'd say, "I had to go further."'

The infection was spreading.

'Fiona thought she had got it with the last amputation, then she'd find the infection had moved further up the leg.'

My sister remembers Fiona telling them that if she hadn't experienced Bali four and a half years earlier, when more than 200 people died in terrorist bombings, she would not have known how to save my life.

'Fiona was pre-empting everything that was happening to you— she was growing cultures from your skin and treating your body with the appropriate antibiotic before you grew the bugs yourself.'

The bugs had killed some of the victims from Bali.

My mother was distraught at the ongoing amputations.

'I never said to take her leg, they shouldn't have taken her legs,' she told my father and siblings.

I asked Mum how that period in the coma unfolded for her.

'Every day they kept chopping off a bit more,' she sobbed, many years later. 'Every day it just got worse, worse, worse. It started off with one leg [the left]. So I adjusted my thoughts. She can work with one leg, I thought. She can drive an automatic car with one leg. She can walk with one leg. Then the next day it got worse. Fingers, your right foot.'

My mother said when the doctors emerged after more surgeries to tell my family they thought I was also going to lose my left arm, she told them to stop.

'I said, "No, she's not."'

'Well, we're going to try and save it,' the doctors said.

'They can't just keep taking pieces of Cynthia,' my mother told our family.

This time, my father agreed with her.

Sometime that Saturday my family received a delivery in the boardroom. It was hundreds of letters and emails that people—friends, acquaintances, members of the public—had written to me and my family. My siblings sat at the table with Michael going through them, making a pile of the ones I should see and another of ones to show me later. My family, who didn't know much about my journalism career, was staggered at the volume and sentiments of the mail.

'I remember going through a lot of stuff, being quite amazed how the public, everyone, was getting right behind you,' Sebastian said.

My parents went to sleep Saturday night in agreement that, if the doctors asked them for permission the following day to take another limb to keep me alive, they would refuse.

VII

On Sunday my family and Michael awoke to the unexpected news that the infection was under control.

'For the first time, she looks like a survivor,' Suzanne, the other burns doctor, told them.

They were moved out of the boardroom and into the waiting room of ICU, where they sat with our friends by a malfunctioning lift that kept opening spontaneously, even though no one was in it and no one had called it. In pairs they filed, day after day, past the medical staff at the desk on their way to see me in my room. It felt to my father as if everyone around them was so detached.

'What was happening in the room seemed monumental to us,' Dad said. 'Our whole world was being turned upside down and I just walked past these people carrying on with their mundane lives.'

In truth, the medical staff did care about my sad and traumatised family. One day an anaesthetist handed my father, who was sitting in the ICU waiting room, a small statue of a Buddha. His young daughter had asked him to give it to me.

Michael helped my family write a statement for the media. It was a difficult process for him. Michael felt my family should put out a statement because the media interest—given the circumstances of the crash and involvement of journalists—was intense. But neither my mother nor my sister wanted to.

'Cynthia wouldn't want it,' Juliette said.

Michael didn't want to get into an argument, and he backed off, leaving it to my parents to decide what to do.

Eventually my brothers decided the family should make a statement and asked Michael to write it. They baulked, though, at putting in too much detail about the amputations which, in medical terms, would be described as one leg above the knee, one leg below the knee. Nor did my father want anything about my broken back in there.

'What sort of father would put this statement out?' he asked Michael after reading an early draft that was accurate but too revealing for Dad.

243

In the end my father dictated a short statement, which was released on the Monday, four days after the crash. When I saw it, years later, I knew Michael couldn't have written it; a journalist would never describe what became of my legs in such an ambiguous and imprecise way. It read, in part:

> Our beloved Cynthia has suffered the most terrible injuries, which have resulted in the loss of one of her legs and part of the other . . . The losses were necessary to save her life.

It thanked the hospital staff in Perth and the 'two heroes who aided in her escape' from the plane wreckage in Yogyakarta, and asked the public to keep praying for me.

VIII

I woke from the coma on 14 March.

That morning, the bodies of the five Australians killed in the plane crash in Indonesia arrived home. The coffins of Morgan Mellish, Elizabeth O'Neill, Allison Sudradjat, Brice Steele and Mark Scott were unloaded from a RAAF C-130 Hercules at Fairbairn airbase in Canberra. Michael watched the footage on the television in his hotel room. He went into the hospital, too upset to have breakfast or do anything else.

Fiona advised my family later that morning that the doctors were preparing to bring me out of the induced coma.

Michael and my father were in the room when doctors pulled the breathing tube out. My eyes opened very suddenly. For a while I did not speak, and when I did it was difficult to hear me because of the oxygen mask. I said I wanted to put my feet up. I wondered why my legs felt so funny. Despite being in a hospital, I thought that I was lying on a sofa and my legs were hanging down over the side, resting on the floor.

I started to tell Michael where I believed I'd been—Queensland—and described how American spies had tried to recruit me. I told him about the crash, which I remembered happening before I was kidnapped by the spies. People were screaming, I told him. The pilot was going too fast. I rolled into a rice paddy field and screamed for help.

'I've been having a bit of bad luck,' I told Michael.

I didn't know that I'd been unconscious, and Michael tried to explain I'd been in a coma for a week, while I continued to insist that, no, I'd been in Queensland with the Americans.

None of my family knew who was going to tell me about my legs, when, or how.

'Telling you was such a huge thing,' my father says. 'Who was going to do it? Who was going to break this huge news to you? I didn't want to take it on board because I had as much to do with it happening, more to do with it happening, than anyone.'

My parents still carry enormous guilt from having given the doctors permission to take my legs.

There was no one to advise my family on how to break the news to me in hospital. They had to figure it out for themselves.

IX

In the end, my father was the one to tell me.

He had watched with dismay as what remained of my shorter left leg began to poke up awkwardly under the sheet while I was still in the coma. The medical staff eventually brought in a weight to hold my leg down.

'I thought, "She doesn't know yet what has happened to her,"' my father told me. 'That was really hard.'

My father has always been fiercely protective of his children and spent his life trying to keep us safe. Nothing was more important to him. Even as adults, we only have to cough in front of him and it sets off a probing interrogation into the state of our health. Dad's own father, Fred, left his wife Beryl Rose, my grandmother, and her four children when Dad, her eldest, was ten years old. His response to having a father who didn't care about his family was to smother his own with love and concern.

Fred was a womaniser and a bookie. He stole money from his eldest son's piggy bank to pay off his gambling debts and hit his wife, once knocking out all her teeth. Fred had another family that Beryl knew nothing about until after they married, and who my dad never wanted to know.

'He lived a lie to my mother,' Dad explained. 'That other family was separate from me.'

Dad loved his mother, Beryl, unconditionally. Beryl struggled as a single parent. She worked cleaning hospitals, drank too much, took too many painkillers and had to be hospitalised often because of the side effects. The family was poor and relied on the kindness of a good neighbour, Mrs Innes, who 'always made lovely stew', and Beryl's kind brother Herb, a school headmaster, and his 'lion-hearted' wife Edna. Occasionally the children would go to one of Herb's schools in the country for a while to give their mother some respite.

My strongest memory of Nanna Beryl is her long, well-manicured fingernails that were always painted a shiny bright red and matched her lipstick. Dad remembers his mother's bravery. As a schoolgirl,

Beryl swam from one headland of Freshwater (then Harbord) Beach to the other. When Dad was a preschooler, she saved a man's life.

There was an explosion at a plumber's shop near their house: a worker had welded a large empty petrol drum full of petrol fumes which blew up, the shattering steel destroying the man's legs. His co-workers dragged the bleeding, screaming man up the street and left him lying on the footpath near Beryl's house while they went to call an ambulance. Seeing him lying there bleeding to death, Beryl didn't hesitate. While her young son (my dad) looked on, she ran into her house to grab towels and calmly wrapped them tightly around the man's legs to slow the bleeding. The ambulance eventually arrived, but had Beryl not acted when she did, it would have been too late for the man.

Dad didn't see his father much after Fred left the family home. They had a chance encounter once, when dad was nineteen and working at Haymarket in Sydney. Spotting Fred, he went up to him.

'Is your name Frederick John Robert Banham?' Dad asked.

The pair of them shared the exact same names, though Dad's mother always called her son John.

'Yes,' Fred replied, looking at Dad suspiciously, as though he had been caught out doing something wrong.

'I share the same name with you.'

'Oh, John,' said his father, but shortly after he had to go.

The last time Dad saw Fred was in 1977, the year my brother, Anthony, was born. Dad tracked him down in the caravan park where he lived.

'Here, hold your grandson,' Dad told Fred as he tried to pass him his newborn, but Fred declined, saying his arm was sore. He went inside the caravan and came out with a cat with two different-coloured eyes, one blue, one green, and held it instead.

A couple of years later, Fred passed away. He died alone in a caravan park on the central coast of New South Wales. I was in primary school. I can still see Fred's dirty blue-and-grey caravan parked in our carport after his funeral. Its floors were stained—I remember there was a large brown circular stain, the colour of tea. Who would want the old caravan? I wondered. My father sold it for $900.

Dad was a surveyor, inventor and amateur pilot, who loved science and university study and got his Master of Hydrogeology when he was 57.

Born in 1942, Dad's dream, unfulfilled, was to be a RAAF pilot. He was in the Air Training Corps at Manly Boys High School, one of the 'intrepid bird men', as they were dubbed (tongue in cheek) by the head of the rival Australian Army Cadets, a Second World War veteran. In Dad's second year of high school he used to wag sports afternoons with four of his flying enthusiast friends. They took the Manly ferry into the city and hopped on one of the free airport buses that left from Phillip Street. At the terminal at Mascot the schoolboys got talking to the kindly air hostesses, who asked the pilots to let the boys onto the resting planes. Dad and his mates were allowed to sit in the cockpits of the DC-3s.

'You can sit in the seat, just don't touch any of the controls,' the TAA pilots told the boys.

Afterwards, Dad and his friends caught the bus back into the city, where they'd walk up to Dymocks on George Street. They spent the rest of their stolen afternoon looking through the shop's aeroplane books—glossy hardcover volumes full of photographs—that they could never afford.

Dad left school at the end of his fourth year of high school when it became too expensive for his mother to keep him there. My grandmother didn't ask Dad to leave, but he knew with his wages he could help her out with the grocery bills. There his dreams of joining the RAAF ended.

When we were growing up Dad's garage was off limits, filled ceiling-high with old motors, bits of discarded furniture, rusty pipes, hoses, rope and ancient tools that we weren't allowed to touch. He brought it all home from Sydney's tips, where he worked as the senior surveyor at the Metropolitan Waste Disposal Authority.

We never had much money, so Dad made things from the scrap in the garage. There was a primitive alarm system for the house made from an old clock rigged up to a long piece of fishing line which he threaded all over the front garden. It only ever caught one intruder—my brother-in-law-to-be. Dad made cleaning systems for our above-ground swimming pool. One involved using an old plastic hose as a siphon. It required us children to spend Saturday after-noons in summer running in circles through the water until we had created a whirlpool and a large pile of leaves formed in the centre of the pool which we, by now cold and wrinkled, then had to scoop up and throw over the sides of the pool. Mum used the plastic hose to suck up all the dirt. The other method used a small two-stroke petrol motor, the kind you see on a lawnmower, which drove a water pump. It was tied to the top of the guinea pig cage to hold it in place. Dad once made a muffler for my brother's dirt bike out of an empty can of dog food with holes punched in it. He invented an edge trimmer for the grass before you could buy one in a shop. It was fashioned out of a lawnmower turned on its side, on the bottom of which he attached extra wheels taken from other old, no longer functioning, mowers.

Each summer our family spent a week camping under the paperbarks at Smiths Lake, south of Forster, on the NSW mid-north coast, a four- or five-hour drive from Sydney. Everything, apart from the tent, which Dad always pitched right before sunset over a bull ant nest, came from items salvaged from the tip. This included an old ironing board that Dad converted into shelves for our food, and a tent awning made with old jam jars. For the awning, Dad propped up a piece of calico with sticks which had empty jars on the ends to stop them tearing the material. The best thing about the camping ground was the general store. We kids were allowed to ride our bikes there every day on our own to buy ice for Mum's esky and ice blocks for ourselves. Swimming in the lake made us itchy and we inevitably emerged from the water with red spots.

Dad's driving ability was more movie stuntman than suburban father of four. He'd driven semitrailers and motorbikes as a young man. I remember hair-raising journeys driving down rugged mountains in the NSW bush in our canary yellow Holden Kingswood. Through ice and snow in the wilds of Kosciuszko National Park, or thick mud slides in remote bushland at Worlds End near Mudgee, Dad steered the car, gearbox in neutral with the engine off, never once losing control of the vehicle. When conditions became too perilous, he forced us children out of the station wagon and we had to trudge through the blizzard or storm, following the Kingswood down the treacherous dirt road.

During one such emergency, with the car heading into a downward slide on a lonely, ice-covered back road in the Snowies, the call to evacuate came suddenly and I didn't have enough time to get my feet into my sandshoes. I had to walk down a rocky, wet and slippery road in the snow in my socks, with my heels hanging over the backs of my Dunlop Volleys (we never had money for proper snow gear). By the time I was allowed back into the car my toes were numb with cold.

Dad came into my room in the ICU the day I was brought out of the coma. We were alone. He hadn't yet decided how I was to be told my legs were gone.

'I went in and you said, "Dad, would you just check my feet?", because you must have had some strange sensation,' he recalled.

'I thought, "I have got to tell her now," but until that moment I had no idea who was going to do the job.'

'Cynthia, they had to take your legs,' he told me. 'The doctor said you had hours to live and they had to take your left leg and your right leg below the knee.'

'Far out, Dad,' I responded.

'Cynthia, I am the bogeyman. I was the one who gave them permission. I couldn't let you go.'

'No, Dad, you weren't the bogeyman.'

We didn't say anything more about it after that.

My sister tells a slightly different version of what transpired. She says when I asked my father to feel my legs, he pretended to feel them at first.

'Yeah, they're here, they're fine,' he told me.

But I kept asking. 'No, Dad, feel my legs. Can you feel my legs?'

Finally, my father could keep up the act no longer. It was then he told me.

Dad says when Fiona informed the family that she had to take my left leg, amid the urgency, gravity and shock of the news, he hadn't fully understood that it would be removed from above the knee. I assured him—and my mother too—that I was so grateful to have lived, that they made the correct decision for me.

How could they have possibly decided otherwise?

X

Michael stayed with me that first sleepless night out of the coma.

I had a craving for a vanilla milkshake; it was not something I'd ever wanted before (or since). Michael said he thought he could get one, and checked first with the nurses. Because of my broken back, I couldn't sit up. To get any kind of relief from being in the one position all the time, I had to be rolled onto my side. The nurses showed Michael how to roll me.

Later that night, I needed to go to the toilet, and the nurse must have been momentarily out of the room. I had a catheter, but Michael had to get me a bedpan for my first bowel movement. We had lived together for little more than a month, and suddenly he had to endure this indignity with me. I was mortified, but Michael told me not to worry.

'It is wonderful, because it is a sign of life,' he said.

I expected him to be revolted, but he showed me only love.

I was hallucinating wildly from all the drugs and grew increasingly disturbed. The walls were alive. Three-dimensional shapes were forming all around me, worms were crawling out of the paintwork on the hospital room walls. When I closed my eyes, I saw soldiers fighting. I was told this was caused by the ketamine and I asked the doctors to stop giving me the drug.

For the next day or so, when I closed my eyes I could see AAP news wire clicking over in my head, updating itself automatically like it had on my work computer as fresh stories came in. I was amazed, but believed the crash had given me supernatural powers to read news wires. The stories were mostly about the crash. Some of them were written by a former boss and colleague from *The Eye*. I was happy to see she was writing about what happened to me, gratified that the stories were critical of the Indonesians. If I closed my eyes I also heard a malicious male laugh, like a character from a horror movie, as if the person was happy this had happened to me.

Despite my exhaustion, I did not sleep for days, partly out of fear of seeing the violent images and hearing that demonic laugh.

Michael

The next day I was moved from ICU to the burns unit. I saw the senior burns physiotherapist, Dale Edgar, before I left ICU. We talked about how important it was for me to move my arms now, particularly my left arm, which was completely burnt from what remained of my fingers up to my shoulder. Because of the burns my arms were stretched out in a crucifix position, so the skin didn't fuse permanently under my armpits. I slept like this for a month.

One of Dale's friends in the RAAF was involved in the recovery of bodies from the plane crash in Yogyakarta.

'He says he doesn't know how you survived.'

Soon after I arrived in Perth, Dale saw the burns on my legs and mentally prepared himself for what he thought might happen.

'I thought there was a very good chance you were going to lose these because the burns were very deep.'

That last day in ICU, although Dale and I talked in my hospital room as I lay on the bed, I was certain—in my heavily drugged state—that we were sitting together chatting on the floor. I could feel the carpet beneath us, as I sat with my back propped up against the wall.

'If I can't run anymore, then I am going to swim,' I told Dale.

'That is fantastic,' he said.

My hallucinations continued when the orderlies came to take me to the burns unit. To get me there, I was sure they pushed my bed into a laundry or rubbish chute, similar to the one in my sister's apartment in Singapore (in reality, it was probably the hospital lift).

The first night in the burns unit was traumatic. The medical staff moved me out of the ICU quite suddenly, and the burns nurses were caught underprepared.

In those early days, a nurse was stationed in my room around the clock to monitor me in case my condition worsened. I was in terrible pain, heavily drugged, extremely tired but unable—too afraid and alert—to sleep. The casual nurse found at short notice to stay with me that night wanted to read her puzzle book and, unable to locate a power point for a lamp, crawled around on the floor under my bed looking for one. My family had left by then, and I could hear and feel the nurse crashing about, at one point knocking my arms off my makeshift cross. I was terrified: I felt utterly vulnerable and feared something bad was going to happen to me.

I was lucid enough to contrive a story, and told the night nurse in charge when she came into my room that I needed to call Michael to say goodnight to him.

'Michael, I am scared,' I whispered into the phone. 'Please can you come back up to the hospital?'

Michael was there within minutes.

When the head nurse realised what I'd done, she was annoyed, but let Michael on to the ward to see me. I wanted to go back to the ICU, believing I was going to die in the burns unit that night. A doctor was called and reassured me that I wouldn't die, and I stayed put.

That night Michael began a concerted effort to build a rapport with all the nurses and assistants in the burns unit so that they would let him come and go as he pleased, regardless of the hour. It's something Michael does with people—politicians, dog walkers in our neighbourhood, shopkeepers, the teachers and parents at school. He has a genuine openness and enthusiasm that endears and disarms.

Before my three months in the burns unit were up, all the medical staff loved Michael, and he loved them.

'Cynthia says she can't wait to get out,' Michael wrote in his diary in early May. 'I realise I am institutionalised, and can't bear to leave.'

XI

What happened to me in the burns unit over the next ten weeks remains beyond description, untellable, though I must try.

Michael wrote no notes for the first week and a half following my transfer there. On the trip home from Perth I tried to write down some of what had happened, but found the burden of recalling my experiences too enormous. I never, ever wanted to remember what I had endured. How can I go there now? And, yet, how can my son understand if I don't try?

What can I tell of this time of unspeakable suffering, when my mind tried so hard not to feel?

My senses were dulled by shock and narcotics and other powerful amnesia-causing drugs. The burns nurses included young women of my own age who were wonderful to me—like sisters—but I never let myself connect with them emotionally. My only way of coping with my losses was to close down part of my mind. I hadn't just lost body parts; I'd lost the life that went with having legs. I couldn't allow myself to contemplate the enormity of this.

The physiotherapist, Dale, told me that I responded to the physical aspects of my recovery but couldn't deal with the psychological side.

'You didn't show your emotion—that was part of the shock, part of dealing with everything by insulating yourself. You needed to get yourself better physically before you got to the mental stuff.'

The room in the burns unit was always hot. I had an oxygen mask over my mouth and a nasogastric feeding tube inserted through my nose, past my throat, into my stomach. When it got blocked the nurses had to pull it out and reinsert it, a painful procedure. I was on a high-calorie, high-protein diet, and liquid food was pumped into my stomach 24 hours a day. I was told if I didn't eat and put on weight I would not be allowed to leave, and was plied with foul-tasting high-energy drinks, like Ensure and Resource. Yet I couldn't eat, since I was always full from the nasogastric tube. The only breakfast I could stomach was the odd piece of melon, so every morning I got a plate of different-coloured melons. If I eat watermelon now, when I'm cutting it up for my son, I taste the burns unit in the morning.

Though I wasn't hungry, I had a thirst in those first days so intense I cried. I begged the nurses for water, but my liquids were restricted (probably because of the disturbance to blood electrolytes which follows big burns and can be life-threatening). They counted my intake in millilitres and drops, and I was lucky to get an ice cube to suck on. Some nights a sympathetic nurse gave me small sips of a sweet juice.

'What is this amazing drink?' I marvelled, thinking I had never tasted anything so glorious. I pleaded with the nurse, unsuccessfully, for a little bit more.

In time, I realised it was just diluted apple juice from one of those plastic cups with the foil on top. I never drink apple juice now, but being able to drink as much water as I want when I want is a luxury I will always savour.

The doctors took blood from me multiple times a day, testing for infection. I had regular blood transfusions (I received 88 litres of blood; the average person has eight litres in their body). I had daily insulin injections and finger pricking for diabetes every few hours. I had heparin injections to thin my blood because I was immobile for so long due to the spinal fracture. My 'obs' were taken every three hours (checking temperature, heart rate and breathing). There were daily X-rays, frequent CT scans and weekly photographs of the wounds. I was hooked up to around-the-clock IV antibiotics. My right arm and hand and fingers were a mess of bruises from the needles. I later had a central line inserted into my neck.

To go to the toilet, a nurse had to roll my body—I was always lying on my back—on to a bedpan. The skins grafts were maddeningly itchy, especially under my hot back, and became worse in the evenings. As I could not sit up to give them relief, I had to be rolled onto my side, first one way, then the other, while Michael fanned my back. The rolling always hurt so much more after skin graft operations, which I continued to have while in the burns unit.

One night the itching became so bad I started to panic. I felt my sanity slipping and Michael called for the nurses, who talked me through what was happening and calmed me down.

A change of nursing shift signalled the arrival of another day. I listened to the nurses' chatter, as regular as noisy birdsong at dawn, and anticipated with dread my daily dressings change. I wasn't allowed visitors until it was over, so I waited alone with the breakfast that I couldn't eat. Nurses brought my morning pills—I ingested upwards of 20 or 30 a day, so many that the nurses had to crush some of them and force them down the nasogastric tube, which often became blocked as a result. They switched on mindless commercial FM radio to keep me company, which I disliked, but lacked the presence of mind to ask for a change of station. I had nothing to do but lie in my bed and contemplate what was coming.

To transfer to a different bed for showering, I had to be rolled by two nurses onto plastic slide sheets: they pulled me with one of the sheets across the slippery surface of the second sheet and onto the showering trolley. The trolley had flip-up sides to stop me falling off during the shower. The dressings were removed and I was showered lying on my back, hooked up to an IV line that pumped powerful painkillers and drugs to make me forget the excruciating pain.

It was the only time I was uncovered and saw myself, though it was only ever my arms. I didn't have my glasses, so couldn't focus, and because I couldn't sit up I never saw my bottom half. But, after the shower, I glimpsed what lay beneath the bandages on my arms. The sight of my left arm dazzled me. It looked like a margherita pizza: red and yellow, all open, bleeding, weeping flesh, not a piece of skin left. My arm was hardly human, more like a butcher's bone, as thin as a broomstick.

During the day I had hours of excruciating physiotherapy, one session before and another after lunch. I screamed and cried from the agony of moving my burnt left hand and fingers. The physiotherapists warned me that if I didn't move them I'd end up with permanent contractions. Indeed, the little finger on my left hand, which hurt the most—I couldn't bear to have it touched and it wasn't as necessary for function as the other fingers—is now permanently bent at a right angle. I developed fevers in the afternoons, always at the same time: around 3 pm. Every time my temperature went above 38.5 degrees Celsius a doctor came to take more bloods. My family took turns fanning my face (electric fans were not allowed in the burns unit) and cooled my burning forehead with cold wet hospital Chux wipes which became scorching hot within seconds. Meanwhile I vomited up pills and nasogastric food.

My family suffered and grieved my losses alongside me. They spent the days sitting in a row of chairs outside the burns unit, which was accessed via double interlocking doors. Before entering the unit, because of the high infection risk to burns patients, visitors had to wash their hands with antiseptic gel and put on plastic gowns, hats and booties. Every time another medical person came into my room—to take blood, give me pills, do physiotherapy, make an assessment, take an X-ray, bring the bedpan—my family had to leave. There was always some member of my family sitting on the chairs outside, waiting to come back in.

Michael

My father fixated on a disturbed man who hung around the hospital and called himself 'the messenger from God'. Michael once spent an entire day searching through the boxes of cards and papers that had arrived for me, looking for a piece of paper the messenger had left behind, which had the man's phone number on it, just to placate my desperate dad.

A month into our time in Perth, my mother lost her job and her best friend, who died from a stroke in Sydney. When she wasn't in my room, Mum put her only grandchild in the BabyBjörn baby carrier, and went for long walks through the streets and parks of Perth.

I developed a schedule for my family's visits which, though I craved them and never wanted any other visitors, exhausted me. My mother was always first in to see me each day, immediately after my dressings change, when I felt reduced, like a child. Michael came to see me after lunch, then the rest of my family. In the afternoons I slept while my brothers sat in the room beside me. My mother returned to feed me dinner and we watched the nightly TV news with my father, whose sadness and fear drained me. My parents left at 8 pm, when Michael returned.

The nights after Michael left were my darkest times. I had never felt so alone, so abandoned. The lights stayed on in my room all night and I couldn't sleep. Every three hours I had pills, another finger-prick test and more obs. I imagined what my family would be doing in their hotel. Were they eating together? Doing the ironing? Watching television? Knowing they were doing 'normal' things, united under one roof, without me, left me with a terrible emptiness and longing. I thought about my colleagues at the newspaper, about my university friends who were getting on with their lives, starting families. I thought about the crash.

My head filled with the blackest of visions and I couldn't close my eyes for fear of the frightening images that were always close by.

XII

Twice during my time in the burns unit I underwent more skin graft surgery.

I had almost nowhere left to take the skin from. The unburnt parts of my body were bright red, raw and painful from where good skin had been stripped to make skin grafts. The first surgery was in late March. The doctors told me they'd need to shave my head and take the good skin from my scalp, because there was so little left of it anywhere else.

My hair was long, thick and dark brown. It was the only untouched part of me, along with my face. For my sister, it was too much. She told her husband if I lost my hair, she would shave off her long blonde hair too.

'Dino lost the plot,' she said.

Unexpectedly, I woke from the surgery with my hair intact; the doctors had found enough skin elsewhere, and didn't require my scalp.

Michael wrote in his diary: 'After five hours Fiona emerges. She clenches her fist and says, "It's good, it's good." Cynthia's body tolerates surgery, no infection issues. Only 15 per cent of the graft takes, though, and her fingertips may have to go further, but no more from the legs.'

Death always felt close by. My parents panicked about the infection coming back, and in April it did return. For ten days I had to be 'blasted' with antifungal antibiotics via an intravenous tube. The really serious antibiotics (there were so many different ones) arrived fresh every day from the lab in a black bag, like a sack of poison.

I feared dying.

'I don't know if I can keep hanging on to the promise of our life together,' I told Michael. 'All my life I just wanted someone to love me and now I won't get the chance to have it.'

'It's my life too and I want my life with you,' Michael said.

I had the second skin graft surgery in late April. It went well, and Fiona told us it was the last she would have to do; any further skin grafts would only happen to release scar tissue if I wanted more mobility.

I got upset the day after the surgery, though, when the doctors informed me I had lost more of the fingers on my left hand during the operation. The shortened digits were hidden under bandages so I hadn't known. It was too much to bear.

I was so afraid of my dependency on others now, I told Michael. He talked to me about the importance of having my full left thumb and left arm; how I would still be able to grip a car steering wheel, propel a wheelchair, hold on to the side of the pool. He also said he was taking six months leave from work.

'I have decided not to go back to work this year,' Michael said. 'It is more important for me to be with you.'

'Remember that scene in the movie *Notting Hill*?' I asked him. 'You know, the one where the husband picks up his wife out of her wheelchair and carries her upstairs to bed? I always loved that scene. And now you will be doing it for me.'

XIII

What does it mean to lose one's sense of identity?

Trauma, it is said, deprives the individual of all agency, and can lead to a deep fragmentation of the individual's self and soul. In this way, it is different to tragedy, which can entail moral agony, but leaves one's dignity undamaged.[2]

When the burns nurses told me, towards the end of my three-month stay, that I could start wearing underwear again—underpants first and, later, bras—I felt anxious, uncertain. Why did I need underwear, I thought, when I had so many bandages and a hospital gown to cover my body? Weren't they enough?

Is this what is meant by losing one's sense of self?

When my catheter malfunctioned, I wet my hospital bed. Sometimes I had diarrhoea and the nurse couldn't bring the bedpan in time for me to roll on top of it and I soiled myself and my sheets. Once a nurse reprimanded me for the way I wiped my bottom— which I had to do lying sideways on top of a bed pan.

To have this happen to you, over and over, in front of your family and partner, at age 34, could this cause a person to lose their sense of self?

I lost, in the crash, all the rituals associated with maintaining my adult self. I simply no longer remembered I once had them. Like brushing my teeth. It took days in the burns unit before I realised that I would have to start brushing my teeth again. I was given a hospital-issued toothbrush, and when it came time to ask my mother to go and buy me a normal one from a chemist, I felt uneasy about that too. I was more comfortable with the basic hospital variety.

Some days passed after the coma before I realised I couldn't see the faces of anyone around me. I had forgotten that I wore glasses or contact lenses. It was a week or two before a new pair of glasses could be made up for me, after friends and family had a script faxed from my optometrist in Sydney.

I couldn't wash my face, and forgot what skin products I had used before the crash—which cleanser, which moisturiser. Some things I forgot so completely it took years for me to realise they were gone. It took until 2011 for me to ask my sister which hand cream I had used before my injuries.

Years after the crash, I was still trying to restore bits of myself to me—those that could be restored.

Shortly after I arrived in the burns unit, a thoughtful nurse announced she was going to wash my hair. It was untouched since the crash, and still had soot and sticks and dirt in it. I could not reach up to feel it; my hands and arms were bandaged and splayed out on their cross. The nurse, Fran, devised a method for washing my hair as I lay on my back unable to move, so that the bed didn't get wet. It involved lots of plastic bags and buckets. I could not see what she was doing, and to me it seemed she was performing magic at the head of the hospital bed.

When I felt the water touch my head, a part of my humanity returned. The feeling of the nurse's fingers massaging my scalp reminded me of sitting in a chair in a hairdresser's salon. The sensation evoked for me the person I was before the crash and restored a slight, temporary sense of dignity.

From then on, nearly every day, I asked the nurses to wash my hair: it was the only way for me to feel human again. I couldn't ask my family, who were not allowed to do it. Some of the nurses were annoyed by my extravagant requests and refused. But on the days when my spirits were so low that I couldn't bear it, I begged them to wash my hair, and tried to explain how important this grooming routine was to me: my head was the only part of me that was untouched, complete. I had lost my legs and my entire body was an open festering wound bound in bandages and bulky dressings. I was unrecognisable to myself—every part of me except my hair.

In May I was fitted, painfully and slowly, with the full-body pressure garments that I had to wear 24 hours a day for a year or more. I was horrified when the first set of custom-made garments arrived. They were in one piece, except for the gloves which I also had to wear, and asymmetrically shaped, with the enclosed lower limbs of different lengths. After putting them on with great difficulty, the therapist realised the designers had not left an opening for me to go to the toilet.

'This is a nightmare, it is impossible,' I sobbed.

I had no dignity left but the tiniest shards and they were being assaulted daily. One of the burns doctors, Suzanne, came to see me and promised me I would start to see the 'chinks of light'.

Before the crash I took care with my appearance but now clothes no longer mattered. When the time came for me to venture out of the hospital in a wheelchair, it was almost winter. My mother and sister bought me clothes for this new phase, clothes that could fit over a bulky spinal brace and pressure garments, clothes that would cover my bandages, my missing limbs. I didn't care what they looked like; there seemed no point. Besides, everything I wore soon became stained with lanolin.

On these first expeditions out of the burns unit, towards the end of my time there, I travelled with my family in a slow-moving procession resembling a kind of nervous caravan. Michael gingerly pushed the wheelchair down the hill to a nearby park, while my father walked beside or in front of me, shielding my skin grafts from the sun and fretting about the bumps in the footpath causing more damage to my fractured spine.

We arrived at Wellington Square and planted the wheelchair in the dirt on the edge of the park. My family members sat on the ground around me and ate their lunch. It was during these moments that the enormity of the changes to my person and my life revealed themselves in the most confronting way. Grief hit me like a crashing 10-foot wave. I detested this new Cynthia: my physical self and childlike dependence.

On one such outing I couldn't contain the emotional pain. That morning my breakfast was left by the orderlies as it always was next to my bed, but the occupational therapists who were due to come and help feed me didn't show. I was left waiting, unable to butter my (often soggy) toast. In the park that afternoon the anguish overwhelmed me.

'Anyone who has 60 per cent burns should not have to live, it is too hard,' I wept.

Everyone—my parents, Michael, my brothers—cried too.

Our wretched picnic was broken up when Michael's mobile phone rang. It was the coach of the Sydney Swans AFL team, Paul Roos, ringing to see if there was anything he could do to help. We were all so shocked to hear from Roosy—the club had already sent a signed guernsey to the hospital, which to us seemed thoughtful enough—that the tears abruptly halted. A starstruck Michael (who had Roosy's autobiography on his bookshelves at home) told the Swans coach I might be up for a chat another day, but unfortunately today was too difficult for me.

Our caravan resumed its slow and wary journey back up the hill. I returned to the comforting familiarity of the sterilised environment of the burns unit. It was a place where I didn't have to wear ill-fitting clothes, where I could lie privately in my bandages in my hot room, surrounded by the caring nurses who were used to horrific injuries like mine.

XIV

Faced with such losses of my physical and future self, I had to hold on tightly to the belief in something.

That something was a life with Michael. Without his faith in our shared life together, I don't know that I could have gone on.

If the days in the burns unit were anguished, the pre-dawn hours lonely and tormented, my evenings with Michael, between 8 pm and midnight, were a time of hope, of intimacy, of feeling adult again. While my family worried about the quality of life I would have with no legs and feared for my future, Michael made me believe that, limbs or not, I had a good life ahead of me—with him.

'I mourn your legs that are gone, but I love the legs that are still here,' he told me.

Michael did not then, and has never since, made me feel any less attractive to him than I was the day he first saw me. While my feelings about my physical being tend to veer from self-loathing to a more detached pity, Michael has always made me feel every bit the woman he first fell in love with.

There is a line in a Frank O'Hara poem:

you are smiling, you are emptying the world so we can be alone.[3]

That's what Michael did, every night, in the burns unit for me.

Michael was my last visitor each day, and he stayed until it was time for me to go to sleep. These hours, just he and I in my room, were sacred, and got me through the difficult times I endured during the day. There were no bloods to be taken, no visitors other than the occasional nurse. The only sounds were of our quiet chatter or, later on, the football on TV, or a movie. *Love Actually* was a favourite. For four hours or so my life became almost recognisable to me again.

Michael and I talked about our future after I got out of hospital and what we would do to reclaim as much of the life we had before as possible. We would get a house on the coast—I could sell my little apartment—a beach shack of our own near the ocean. This was something I had often thought I'd do if I remained living in landlocked Canberra, where I missed the sea. Our favourite coastal town was Tathra on the far south coast, and we'd start looking there. For the first time ever, Michael talked about the possibility of our having children together, a prospect that filled me with joy.

'I just want to live a normal life,' I told Michael on one of these nights, in late April.

'What does that mean for you?' he asked.

'I want to walk, I want to swim, I want to have babies and I want to go back to work.'

The nurse assistant who worked during the evenings made Michael his own special plastic gown. In coloured markers she wrote: 'I ❤ Cynthia.'

Michael only ever showed me strength and resolve. His diary, however, revealed glimpses of his own pain and struggles, as well as his constant efforts to lift me.

On 11 April, he wrote: 'I have feelings about how hard it will be. For the first time in a long time I cry in the shower. It's too hard for Cynthia. Will we have to buy a new house? . . . I tell her I love her. "I need you, Pinguinos, and I want my life with you."'

('Pinguinos' was the name Michael gave me in Ushuaia, where we did our marathon—the town was full of people dressed as penguins. I called Michael 'Ponchito', for the poncho I made him buy in Bolivia against his protestations that ponchos were only for hippies.)

Two weeks later Michael wrote about walking through Murray Street mall in Perth's city centre one afternoon.

'There was a girl in a wheelchair singing for money. She had arthritis and a woman gave her one US dollar.'

One evening in early May, Michael went to get a television set from the recreation room and saw the new wheelchair that occupational therapists had ordered in anticipation of my sitting up with a back brace.

'There it is—the wheelchair,' he wrote. 'It was like seeing a new bicycle by the Christmas tree before Christmas. I stay there till 12.45 am. She wakes at 11.15 pm. "I'm quite calm." All is well.'

Michael saw my abdominal burns for the first time a few nights later.

'Despite having a big dip out of it, she is not embarrassed. It is a sign of life to me. The nurses were worried I'm not prepared for it.'

A couple of days later he wrote about seeing me during a physio-therapy session, sitting in the new wheelchair.

When I arrive you are seated in your chair and you look so brave and yet so vulnerable. You are trying so hard and you are so hurt and trampled. It's too hard for you today. It seems so unfair. You are questioning if it is worthwhile. You worry about the sort of life I am going to lead but my life is your life and I want our life together. We are two rowers in a double scull. Look at what we have achieved but you cry many times today. 'I want my legs back I want my old life back.' This is very hard. Can I do what she needs?

Michael thought carefully about the importance of 'not blurring my roles of carer with the intimate role of being a partner'.

One difficult day I told Michael, 'If I had a choice I would let me die. No one should have to live like this. Look what I've done to your life.'

'You will walk again and we will reclaim our lives bit by bit as the rays of light shine through,' he told me.

Towards the end of May, Michael lifted me again. 'I suggest we have been living in the here and now for a long time; that was when your very survival was at stake and in the balance. Now perhaps we should confidently start thinking about the future.'

We started to plan our first Christmas in his house, our house, back in Canberra, half a year away.

XV

It was mid-April when I realised that, for my survival to be worth anything, I had to change my mindset.

My spirits still fluctuated wildly, and I constantly had to fight back feelings of frustration, helplessness and bitterness that I knew were dangerous and destructive. At some deeper level—the level of my character and belief system, which the crash had not taken from me—I understood that I had not been grateful enough for the life I still had. I'd been given the chance to have a new life, when others hadn't. If I was going to lead it, I had to get better—I had to get through this slow period of recovery.

I cracked my first joke during a blood transfusion around this time. One of the young resident doctors, Franc, walked in to take some blood from my right arm for testing. The arm, one of the few unburnt parts of me, was black and blue from all the needles. As the doctor began the difficult search for a compliant vein, I looked up at the bag of blood hovering over the head of my bed.

'Are you really going to take my blood when there is blood going in?' I asked. 'Why not take it straight from the bag?'

Franc looked at the bag and hesitated, as if actually contemplating my suggestion.

Michael laughed. 'You made a joke!'

A few days later I made another. I was talking to a nurse, Anna, about diets and nutrition, and relayed a story about my early vegetarian years. My refusal to eat meat when I was sixteen and seventeen led to massive arguments with my father. Michael told

Anna my father believed this vegetarian phase was the reason I wasn't as tall as my sister and two brothers, who were all six foot and over (I was five foot five).

'She is not actually that short,' said Michael.

'Well, I am pretty short now,' I said.

As the days and weeks and months passed, one by one I lost a machine, a tube, a drug, some other restriction on my body's capacity to support itself. In late March, my right arm was uncovered. I was shifted to a room further down the hall, away from the central nurses' desk, which was reserved for the most critical of patients. There was no more need for oxygen. In April, there was no more crucifix position. I had my first shower without drugs. My left thumb was exposed for the first time. There were no more antibiotics.

In early May, I was allowed to sit up, with help, in a rigid back brace to support my mending spinal fracture. The brace had a denim pattern, a sort of camouflage, that was meant to blend in with my clothes. I got head spins the first time I sat upright and my scarred bottom meant I could not get my hips to flex at a 90-degree angle. I was only allowed to sit up for ten minutes initially.

'It was so wonderful, I was so happy,' I told Michael.

I continued to pass small milestones. I sat up unassisted for three seconds, then 90 seconds the following day. Dale helped me to transfer from the bed to a wheelchair, and we later went outside the hospital. I breathed fresh air for the first time in two months; the taste of it, just outside the hospital's front doors, was sweet and beautiful. I spent ten minutes on the footpath before cigarette smoke from other patients forced me back inside.

'This is just the start,' I told Michael after my third day of sitting in the wheelchair. 'My aim is to be walking.'

I was slowly building strength, spending lunchtimes with Michael and my family outside my hospital room—first downstairs in the hospital cafeteria, then in the parks and cafes outside the hospital. After the first week of May, discussions began about transferring me out of the RPH burns unit into the rehabilitation hospital at Shenton Park. Maybe in a couple of weeks.

More developments followed, more signs of my body's reclaimed independence. I started taking pills orally. The nasogastric tube was turned off during the day and, eventually, at night too. The insulin was reduced, then stopped.

One day in mid-May, Dale drove me to Shenton Park to have a look around at the facilities, at my new (temporary) home. Sitting in a moving car was a novelty: I gazed through the windscreen at Perth's streets, trying to recognise the world as I had known it before, but it all seemed so foreign to me.

On 23 May, feeling scared and apprehensive, I left the burns unit for the rehabilitation hospital and my parents returned to Sydney.

'I am going to do this. I am going to do it strongly and we are going to make it,' I told Michael that night, my first at Shenton Park.

XVI

I had a regular routine at the rehabilitation hospital at Shenton Park.

My room had two entrances, the main one via the ward and another through a small ground-level courtyard at the rear. Every day at 8.30 am, while I was eating breakfast, Michael's smiling face appeared at the courtyard door. He didn't leave until I went to sleep at night.

After breakfast, five days a week, Michael pushed my wheelchair from the hospital room along a winding path to the gymnasium for another full day of draining physiotherapy. I had a session before lunch and another after lunch. Physiotherapy was followed by an afternoon appointment with the occupational therapists, who made splints for my left arm and worked on giving me back some function in my left hand.

There were daily visits from different doctors, as well as burns nurses who came to help me shower and do my dressings. There were meetings with social workers and psychologists, and ongoing painful fittings for burns garments. Michael called these hideous—but necessary—costumes my 'golden corset'.

At Fiona's encouragement, after she told the more cautious rehabilitation doctors that she wanted me to get on with it, I had casts taken of my residual limbs for prostheses. (My youngest brother, Sebastian, recalls standing in the car park one day at Shenton Park when a van roared in, music thumping. Behind the wheel was Fiona. Her visits were always uplifting.)

Shortly after my arrival at the rehabilitation hospital, the nurses taught Michael how to help with my morning dressings.

'I go in and see Cynthia for the first time unwrapped and I have never seen so much injury, especially all the tissue debrided and stripped away. The bone in her calf, her knee blistering, the indentation and discolouration.'

Michael sat through endless gym sessions with me.

'Nine am at the gym and you are in tears,' he wrote in his diary one day in May.

I had woken that morning with tight skin—I felt as if I were encased in concrete—and awful pain.

'There is so much pain, I wish I had only lost my legs,' I told Michael after he arrived that morning.

Half an hour later I was sitting in the wheelchair, doing my lateral pull-downs and presses, my side raises and seated rows, followed by stomach raises with a medicine ball.

'I am not going to let this beat me,' I told Caroline, my passion-ately committed physiotherapist. 'I want my old life back and I'm going to get it. I loved my old life.'

Michael watched as I began another set of pulleys, tears streaming down my face.

Sebastian joined Michael and me every night after work for dinner at Shenton Park. My brother was the only family member to stay in Perth with Michael during my rehabilitation, and had shifted his job in IT from Sydney to Perth after the crash.

'I just made that decision, on the second or third day I was there [in Perth],' Sebastian told me years later. 'I decided I was going to see you through to recovery.'

I refused to eat hospital dinners—a defiant act that helped reclaim some small sense of control. Michael and Sebastian consumed my servings of beef and gravy, tubs of rice pudding and cartons of Sustagen, while I ate their takeaway Caesar salads.

One evening Sebastian brought my luggage from the Indonesia trip into the hospital. The big red suitcase had been stowed safely on the government's VIP plane, while I flew on the doomed commer-cial flight. I remember taking my bag to a conference room at the hotel the day we were supposed to leave Jakarta, and being gently teased by other members of the foreign minister's travelling party for bringing such a large suitcase.

Michael and Sebastian went through its contents for me, item by item: my brand-new hiking boots that had never been worn; my running shoes, gleaming white with orange and red stripes, also hardly worn. Michael imagined what it would have been like going through the bag had I not lived.

My parents wanted me to do my rehabilitation in Sydney. They couldn't understand why I wouldn't go back east with them and argued with me about my decision to stay. I told them I wasn't ready to leave Fiona or the protective bubble Michael and I had created in Perth. I also knew I had a greater chance of returning sooner to an adult life, life as a couple with Michael, if I stayed behind with him.

Meanwhile, my other brother, Anthony, and his builder friends in Sydney spent their weekends driving to Canberra. Without being asked to, they renovated Michael's house, making it accessible for my wheelchair, in time for our eventual return.

XVII

In the burns unit, the nursing care was intense. At Shenton Park, the protective cocoon disappeared.

When I wasn't undergoing therapy, I was left largely unbothered in my hospital room, with Michael for company. Without the constant interruptions for more tests or medicines or other interventions, and my survival a certainty, I had more time to think about my new reality.

I was in constant pain, missed my parents, and was deeply depressed. While my mornings in the gym with the physiotherapists were uplifting and positive—I drew on a fighting spirit that was reawakened with the new day—when I returned to my room at 4 pm, after a final session with the occupational therapists, a heavy darkness descended. Every afternoon, during those couple of hours before my brother arrived for dinner, I was in despair, inconsolable. The blackness invaded my thoughts with the same regularity and predictability as the fevers that had afflicted me each afternoon in the burns unit. Michael called it my 'let down'.

'I don't understand why God did this to me,' I told my mother during a phone call one such afternoon.

'He doesn't exist,' she replied.

The melancholy, the momentary ups followed by the dreadful downs, continued for the entire time I was an inpatient at Shenton Park. Nobody around me knew how to respond to these feelings, which were always lurking. The hospital psychologist thought I was 'only just hanging on'.

At night, after Sebastian and later Michael left me and I was alone once more in my hospital room, I dreamt I was walking.

My surroundings didn't help. Shenton Park, with its amputee gym and wheelchair track, was the saddest place I had ever known. The gated facility was built in the nineteenth century to quarantine smallpox patients. On my way to and from the gym each day I passed by the children's spinal cord injury ward. Through partly drawn curtains, I caught glimpses of beds decorated with colourful teddy bears and balloons: gifts to brighten the lives of recently paralysed teenagers. On the way back to my room each day, I tried to propel myself up a particularly steep path that Michael called the 'hill of hate'. The physiotherapists told me, 'If you can do this hill, you can do anything in the outside world.' It was 21 June before I could make it to the top on my own.

To have so much human misfortune contained in one place, and to find myself a part of it—knowing this was where I belonged now, like an inmate locked in an asylum and quickly forgotten by those outside—mystified me as much as it depressed me. How did I get here? Life as I had known it, fast-paced, filled with work and travel and pubs and dinners out with colleagues and friends, was beyond my reach now. It was as Virginia Woolf wrote about the different perspective one assumes during debilitating illness: the world had 'changed its shape', the landscape of life lay 'remote and fair, like the shore seen from a ship far out at sea'.[4]

I felt trapped, not just by the rehabilitation hospital gates, but by the injuries that had put me there, from which there was no escape.

'I'm not supposed to be here,' I told Michael in despair.

(Seven years after I left, the Shenton Park rehabilitation hospital was closed for good.)

XVIII

Little rituals Michael and I shared kept me from completely falling apart.

Like pizza and football in my room on Friday or Saturday nights.

'The Eagles go down to the Dockers—a perfect day,' Michael wrote after one such evening in August.

We watched multiple series of *The West Wing*.

When the doctors deemed me strong enough to transfer from the wheelchair (across a wooden slide board) into the car, we busted out of the Shenton Park gates. We didn't go far: just to nearby Swanbourne Beach where, for a couple of hours, we watched storms roll in over the Indian Ocean.

'I see this and there was no way I was going to die in that aeroplane,' I told Michael the first time I saw the ocean, from the passenger seat of his hire car.

It was on one of these outings, in June, when Michael wrote that I had my 'first day of not feeling sad all day'. We had gone for a drive to the beach, where we also attempted our first use of a public toilet. There was no disabled toilet, and the door of the cubicle was too narrow for my wheelchair, so Michael had to lift me onto the toilet seat. Later I told him I dreaded him dying first, that I was troubled because I would always be dependent on him.

'We will need each other, but we will be a team, and we were always going to need each other anyway,' Michael told me.

My first dinner outside the hospital occurred one night in June, at the home of Janet Holmes à Court, the businesswoman and philanthropist. During my early days in the burns unit, Janet had delivered a present from a mutual acquaintance, and ended up befriending my mother. After my transfer to Shenton Park, she brought me a lamp for my hospital room and new pyjamas. That night, for our special dinner, Janet cooked pumpkin soup, a salmon dish as a main course and an apple dessert, for Michael, Sebastian and me. I had my first sip of wine since the crash: it was Black Knight, named for Janet's 1984 Melbourne Cup winner. Janet continued to show us many kindnesses for the remainder of our time in Perth, including a night at the West Australian Symphony Orchestra (of which she is chair) when I was strong enough, in July.

The only time Michael left Perth was for his criminal trial in Melbourne.

In 2004, Michael and his *Herald Sun* colleague, Gerard McManus, wrote a story about veterans' entitlements which prompted the Howard government to launch an Australian Federal Police investigation into the source of the story. Michael and Gerard refused to reveal their source after a public servant was charged with leaking documents, and they were charged with contempt of court.

In June, Michael had to return to court. It was an anxious day. We both knew if Michael was convicted, he could receive a jail sentence, which was flagged by a judge at a previous court appearance. In the end, Michael and Gerard were convicted and fined.

Michael returned to Perth the same night after the sentencing. He said hello to a worker at the hospital who, hearing that Michael had been given a criminal conviction over a story he'd written in a newspaper, told him matter-of-factly: 'Next time you'd better get it right.'

One day in June, the doctors told me I could spend a night in Michael's apartment. We made my favourite dish—eggplant parmigiana. But the night, though affirming of a shared life beyond hospital, was trying. Michael had to lift me from the bed onto the commode chair to go to the toilet in the middle of the night.

'A normal night but not normal,' he wrote.

Michael bought a camera to document some of the more positive events at Shenton Park. Like my open-air bike rides on a hand cycle around a park near the hospital; my last time wearing a back brace; the day I was strapped on a 'tilt table' with blue poles for legs and elevated until I was vertical. There were also birthday lunches in the courtyard for my siblings with our parents; my first (unsanctioned) beer; and taking a call from the prime minister in the hospital gym on the day of the press gallery's Mid-Winter Ball in Canberra.

We encountered many caring medical professionals at Shenton Park whose generosity and thoughtfulness went well beyond what their jobs required. On my 35th birthday in July, I fronted up to my regular morning physiotherapy session to find Caroline and her team had decorated the hospital gym with brightly coloured stars and balloons. Later that night a kind doctor and occupational therapist, both young women, turned up with a bottle of champagne and hair dye. They coloured my hair and did my make-up before a special birthday dinner with Michael at an upmarket restaurant, Balthazar (on the menu: oysters, duck pie, Margaret River red and diamond earrings).

After the spinal brace came off in July I was discharged from the rehabilitation hospital. My therapists threw a small party. I was officially an outpatient. I stayed at Michael's apartment in the city for the rest of our time in Perth and we returned to Shenton Park for my daily appointments.

Soon after I saw my new prosthetic legs. They were fitted with the Asics running shoes from the big red suitcase. On seeing the short artificial limbs, with their metal poles and fake feet enclosed in my old sneakers—running shoes which not so long ago held my real feet—I burst into tears.

'It's not how you have made them,' I told the prosthetist, worried I had hurt his feelings. 'It is what they represent.'

There were more photographs as I made my first giddy attempt at standing on prostheses next to Michael, who embraced me upright. For a few days I stood stationary, getting my balance, adjusting to the pressure of feeling the artificial legs strapped onto the ends of my severed bones.

On my first day of walking I took 36 steps in the parallel bars; on day two I took 108 steps; on day five I walked outside the parallel bars; on day seven I walked out of the gym.

XIX

Without being asked, the Sydney Swans became a significant part of my rehabilitation.

On Michael's birthday (also in July), Paul Roos and three of the Swans players—Brett Kirk, Craig Bolton and Adam Goodes—took us out for a meal. They were in Perth to play the West Coast Eagles, fierce rivals of the Swans. A friend from the press gallery, Matt Price, had arranged a corporate box for the game the following evening, and I invited some of my medical team to join us.

After champagne and chocolate cake on the morning of Michael's birthday at his apartment arranged by Caroline, my ever-thoughtful physiotherapist, Roosy and his players took the two of us to the Blue Duck, a cafe at Cottesloe Beach.

The lunch came after a series of phone calls from Roosy, who rang regularly to check on how we were doing. Over lunch Michael regaled the Swans players with highlights from Roosy's playing career at Fitzroy. Fitzroy happened to be Michael's team until they folded in the mid-1990s, but he pledged readiness to support the Swans after the Blue Duck lunch.

The Swans offered an unexpected, beautiful gift to us: a lightness and an escape amid all the suffering and darkness. By reaching out, Roosy and the club gave Michael and me a special closeness to the game that we loved watching together. Roosy and the players didn't ask difficult questions; they hadn't known me before the crash and couldn't make painful comparisons to what I had been. We just talked about the Swans' football season and the state of Irish defender Tadhg Kennelly's knee.

I was an unlikely football fanatic: I'd never before supported any kind of organised sport or team. But the athleticism and tribalism of AFL appealed to me. And Roosy, an exceptional individual—generous, dependable, composed, good-humoured—genuinely cared about Michael and me. He and his wife Tami became our friends.

After lunch with the Swans, Michael and I went down a pedestrian ramp to get closer to the sand. Sitting in the wheelchair, I asked Michael to touch the ocean for me.

'I want to feel the water, can you put your hand in the water for me?' I asked.

Michael ran down to the water. With tears in his eyes—I was crying too—he scooped up some water and sand and rubbed it, smiling, in my face.

'More salt water for your salty tears.'

There were other unexpected visitors during my days at Shenton Park. Among them was the prime minister, John Howard, who dropped in to Michael's apartment one evening.

In the days leading up to the prime minister's visit, his security detail checked out the building on Victoria Avenue. Izzy and Bashir, the two men who ran the convenience store downstairs and whom Michael had got to know, were unaware of the special caller.

'Michael, I don't know what is going on, mate, but there's cops everywhere,' one of them said.

Michael's mother, a big fan of the prime minister, was in Perth and joined us that afternoon.

'It's just some bloke from work who wants to drop in,' Michael told her about the guest we were expecting that evening.

'That's so sneaky,' Laurel said to her son when he opened the door to the prime minister.

Michael hoped Howard didn't think she was talking about him.

A couple of nights later the Labor MP, Robert McClelland, dropped in for takeaway. We kept the political visits to a bipartisan minimum.

It was late August when we bid farewell to Perth. We had final pizzas with the burns nurses, a last round of medical photos with Fiona and Suzanne, and drinks at the Hula Bula Bar with doctors and physiotherapists from the burns unit.

XX

While I was in hospital, Matt Price wrote me a letter.

Matt had recently relocated with his family from Canberra back to Perth. He made a point of looking out for Michael after the crash. He took him for coffee and arranged gym access for him at News Limited's Perth offices. Matt and his family came to Michael's birthday dinner at his brother Andrew's house in July.

Matt's letter was dated 22 May and was three pages long. Matt didn't yet know he had cancer.

In it, Matt told me: 'I've been meaning to write this letter to you for several weeks. It will be slightly different, I think, from many of the other thousands of letters and calls you've doubtless received since the horrible accident. Its focus is Michael.'

This is what Matt wrote:

It was only after the crash that I learned you and Michael had decided to move in together—a huge step for both of you. When all this madness happened, many of us had two pressing concerns—how would you survive the accident, and how would Michael bear up under such hideously traumatic circumstances?

Now, after many fretful weeks, it's clear you've pulled through. Many prayers have been answered. As for Michael? Here, for whatever they're worth, are my observations.

I first caught up with Harvs in the first week after the crash. While he was clearly knocked around, he took time out to say the most beautiful things. He hinted that he was aware his friends were concerned about his sudden, awful circumstances. He told me not to worry, that he felt after many years of frigging about that he'd found a purpose for his life. He couldn't resist adding that he'd prefer this purpose was something less trau-matic—such as teaching an African tribe about 1980s music. But this was what life had dealt him and he was up to the task.

Michael spoke so powerfully and sincerely about being inspired by your courage and stamina. It was a relatively short conversation, but I felt proud and privileged to hear his words.

In the days and weeks ahead I confided with a few other friends, and wondered whether Harvs' commitment would survive the craziness of that initial period. As you well know, he has been an absolute champion.

Most of Harvs' friends have been concerned to make sure he stays fit and sane, to make sure he's best equipped to help you through the marathon recovery. I now know not to hassle him, that's he's not interested in much besides being around you and helping wherever necessary. There is no sense of martyrdom or service—rather, he seems to be knuckling down to that 'life's purpose' of getting you back to 'normality'.

I don't pretend to know or judge the ins and outs of your relationship. I do know that what has happened to you both would test a 20-year marriage . . . None of us can know how we'd react to such calamitous events.

Quite simply, I can't imagine anybody reacting more lovingly, sincerely and single-mindedly than Michael. He constantly humbles and inspires me when he speaks about you, conversations which ponder life 5, 10, 20 and 30 years ahead . . .

Without sounding too melodramatic, I think Harvs' response to your accident has been utterly heroic. By any measure you have been dreadfully unlucky, Cynthia, but if it's any consolation I think what you have tapped in Michael is golden and precious. I keep advising Harvs to concentrate on the 'little victories' that have and will present themselves during your recovery, but you should also be aware of something large and magical that your situation has produced—the love between you and Michael . . .

Matt signed off: 'Rest assured you and Michael have left an indelible—and in many ways wonderful—mark on my life.'

Matt was a talented, much-loved writer who worked for *The Australian* and wrote a witty parliamentary sketch column. Matt's letter was in one of the boxes I brought home from Perth. He was the only person moved by Michael's response to my situation to put his feelings about his friend on paper for me. Matt's permanent words were a beautiful gift. He died from multiple brain tumours the day after the November 2007 federal election.

How was I so lucky to love, to be loved, by Michael?

I will never feel worthy of Michael's love, his devotion and sacrifice. Michael shared every gruelling minute of my recovery and rehabilitation in Perth and later, for another year or so, in Canberra. He was with me every single day. I have never had to face any of it alone.

Sometimes I ask Michael why he gave up so much—including his journalism career, which he left when our son was born.

'Because you lost so much and I promised myself I would dedicate myself to giving you back as much as I could. You don't just promise that for one year then forget it.'

XXI

It was Saturday, 10 March 2007, the second night of the critical surgeries.

Both my legs were gone. If this last amputation didn't stop the infection from spreading, I was going to die.

My mother was saying I was not going to make it. Michael knew she was preparing herself for the worst. All my family was crying. Michael and his brother went into my room in the ICU, room 11, feeling grim.

It was early evening. Andrew stood silently in the corner. Michael saw my unwashed hair streaked with soot, my bandaged body, my arms in the crucifix position. So many machines, so many lines and tubes and monitors.

He began to talk to me.

'Pinguinos, it's me, Ponchito. Look at you, you look so strong. I was thinking about the Sydney Marathon. Remember all our training and remember how when we got to the last and hardest bit we said, "This is what we trained for"? Well, this *is* what we trained for. It's life, our life, our life together. I want to live our exciting lives together. I want to ask you something. Would you please marry me? Say yes, please.'

I was in a coma, but at this exact moment, a tear squeezed out of the corner of my eye.

Michael saw it.

'I felt it,' he said. 'I felt your strength. I think you said yes. But I want to hear you say it when you can. I got it, don't you worry, I got it.'

The ICU was full of strong light. But suddenly something else, an almighty surge of energy, filled the room.

'I felt such strength, I felt such power, I felt such energy. It's there, it's in the room, it's palpable, and I felt it,' he wrote afterwards.

Andrew felt it too.

'It was like 1000 watts in the room, all this energy, it was like you were powering the room yourself,' Michael wrote. 'I saw you gorging yourself on the feeding tubes, taking all the nourishment, churning away to fight off the infection and survive. All I could feel was that you were going at a million miles an hour, taking all the food and getting on with what you needed to do to survive.'

Michael told me later that at first he thought what he felt in that room was the Holy Spirit. Subsequently, he decided it was me, willing myself to survive, powered by love, in turn powering the room with an incredible light.

Michael emerged from my room punching the air. 'Everything is all right,' he told my family. 'Did you feel it? She is getting on with fighting the fight now.'

Michael had to repeat the story over and over to my devastated family. Their mindset was so negative, so defeated, he had gone into the room thinking, 'It must be awful in there'.

'After a few minutes I realised what was actually going on. You were fighting to live.'

He didn't sleep that night; he was too wide awake. In his diary, he wrote: 'I have found my purpose. Total devotion to Cynthia.'

Michael asked me to marry him the following year. He didn't tell me about his first proposal, while I was in the coma, until we transcribed his diary eight years later.

6

Loredana

I

TURNING ON THE TAPE RECORDER IN EARLY 2015, I had no idea
what my mother would say.

Would she remember much at all about her childhood? What
kind of interview subject would she make? I began by asking her
to go back in time to Trieste, before she left Italy at age nine.

'Do you remember when you first learnt that your family was
considering migrating?'

'No.'

'Can you remember how you found out?'

'No.'

'What *can* you remember about leaving Italy?'

Mum paused.

Then, suddenly, they came: words—astounding, lyrical words—
speaking of things I'd never heard before, and of a pain so deep,
so early, I could never have imagined it.

'The only thing I can remember is I was not allowed to take my
toys. I had to leave my rocking horse, I had to leave my Meccano
set, I had to leave my Christmas cribs. I was only allowed to bring
a doll.'

My mother's voice cracked. I was momentarily dumbfounded. Mum had not thought about this since she was a child, was not even aware that she still had the memory.

All of Loredana's toys bar one—a porcelain doll called Giorgetto —were given away to the children of friends of her parents, to people she didn't know. Her family's entire belongings—saucepans, plates, clothes, sheets—had to fit into a single green trunk that travelled with them on the ship to Australia, stored deep in the hold of the *Sydney*, where they could not access it for the long month of the voyage. There was no room for the girls' toys (mum's sister was six).

I remember Giorgetto. He was old, from another time: chipped, dark-skinned, with stiff limbs. He lived at my grandparents' house in Campsie. He had originally belonged to Nonno's sister, Assunta.

This revelation was remarkable to me for a number of reasons, but mostly because I always believed that the pain associated with my mother's emigration from Italy began in Australia, after she arrived. I assumed her hurt resulted from the prejudice she faced as an Italian immigrant in the 1950s. I hadn't imagined that it started at the point of rupture, of separation, from Trieste and the people and possessions that constituted the little girl's world.

There was much about my mother's childhood that I didn't know, I was about to discover. But from that moment of hearing my 67-year-old mother break down as she spoke about toys taken from her six decades ago, I began to understand her more deeply than I had before.

Once I started to exhume these early memories, it wasn't so hard to see why the child might have felt the need to construct defences of the kind that last a lifetime, defences that she herself could not see.

II

There is a photograph of my mother that I had framed the year I became pregnant with my son.

My mother was nine years old. In the photo she is leaning out of the window of a train. An older man in a black coat—her maternal grandfather, Antonio (Toni)—stands on the platform, holding her right hand in both of his.

Toni's neck is strained forward and he reaches with his lips to kiss Loredana's hand. Mum is elegantly dressed. She wears a patterned tunic and, over it, a pale, unbuttoned jacket with a rounded collar and breast pocket. Her dark brown hair is bobbed; a piece of fringe hangs over her left eye. She is crying. She and her grandfather are saying their final goodbyes before the train

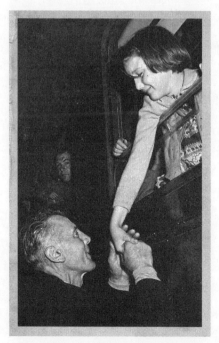

Loredana and her nonno Toni

departs Trieste for Naples, where her family will board the ship to Australia. To me it looks like her little heart is breaking.

The train left Trieste's main station at 7.30 pm on Friday, 24 May 1957; their ship departed for Australia four days later. (My mother's family was among the approximately 193,000 Italians who emigrated to Australia in the 1950s, the peak decade for Italian immigration. During the four decades following the Second World War, some 400,000 Italians settled in Australia.)

Mum didn't see Toni for another ten years, when she returned to Italy for the first time, as an adult.

For years this photo of my mother and her nonno Toni held a power over me. It shaped my limited understanding of Mum's migration to Australia and spoke about separation, about leaving and loss. It was the most wrenching family photo I had. Family photographs, it is said, can sometimes tell us more about our own needs and desires than about the past to which they bear witness.[1] The photograph of Mum on the train was not simply the image of a crying child—it was my mother saying goodbye to her life and extended family in Italy, her birthplace and, therefore, in my mind, my city too.

I asked my mother about her relationship with Toni. From the photograph, I imagined they were close.

Mum told me Toni lost his job as a school caretaker in the war and had to move his family—he had three daughters, including Anna, my grandmother—into public housing (it was called *sfrattai*, the evicted). He eventually found a new job as a garbage collector and the family moved to Sant'Anna, near the public cemetery. His wife, Natalina (Lina), was an orphan, a source of social stigma back then (most of Toni's family wanted nothing to do with her after they married).

Mum and her cousin, Giuliana, who were the same age, used to walk together from Servola, where they lived, to Sant'Anna to visit Toni and Lina (Giuliana was from my grandfather Alfredo's side of the family: she was his sister Rosina's daughter). On the way Loredana and Giuliana had to pass through 'some sort of scrub' inhabited by gypsies.

'Don't look at them, look straight ahead, because they'll give you the *malocchio*, the evil eye,' my grandmother told the girls.

The walk took the cousins almost an hour, but they loved visiting because Lina and Toni's two unmarried daughters, my grandmother's younger sisters, still lived with their parents and they owned high-heeled shoes. The little girls would race up the stairs to Toni and Lina's apartment to see who would get to the shoes first, then the pair would parade around in the high heels.

Lina died at 58 from a heart attack. Mum was eight.

'I remember having to go and give her a kiss, the body, and I remember the funeral and my mother was so distraught she almost threw herself after the coffin.'

After Lina's death, the three daughters left Trieste, one after the other, for Australia, and Toni remarried.

And Toni? Were he and my mum close, like I'd supposed? Mum says Toni was 'quite distant'; she was much closer to his wife, her nonna Lina.

III

As a child, a young adult even, I didn't press my mother for details about her emigration experiences.

I always sensed a brokenness there but had never pushed to understand it more deeply. In truth, I feared knowing how much Mum had been hurt, and by whom or what. Nothing was more painful as a child than thinking my parents were suffering. I couldn't bear to see my mother cry; it made my world feel so terrifyingly fragile, as its supports trembled. Sure, there were questions I had about Mum's girlhood, but I was content to let such mysteries lie.

Now, in my forties, I was ready to know my mother's story. I was convinced that the way I was brought up had something to do with my response to the crash, the fight that I had within, that so impressed people.

Emotions have a history. As the philosopher Martha Nussbaum writes, new objects of love, anger and fear bear traces of earlier objects, and our emotions towards them are therefore often also emotions towards our pasts.

'Past loves shadow present attachments, and take up residence within them.'[2]

If I wanted to understand my relationship with my mother, a relationship that shaped me, I had to open up her story—if she would let me.

My search for family history reopened old wounds for my mother.

Following our trip to Italy in 2015, I asked Mum to translate a book for me about emigration to Australia from Trieste and the Friuli Venezia Giulia region. We picked it up from the bookshop of La Risiera museum.

Mum read about a grandmother who had to be supported by relatives at the wharf where a ship was leaving with her grandson on board. The old woman asked incessantly whether the boy was on the ship. Did he have his red scarf? Was he waving? The nonna, her face drenched in tears, refused to leave, even when the ship was out of sight. The Trieste-born writer Giani Stuparich wrote at the time that 'tutto il cuore della città era là', 'all the heart of the city was there', in those farewells, in those bits of advice, in those final goodbyes.[3]

Reading the book made my mother recall the loss of her other grandmother, Anna-Maria, with whom she lived in Trieste.

Anna-Maria was present at the train station among the dozens of other relatives who assembled to say goodbye to her son, Alfredo, and his family that last night in Trieste.

'I didn't want to go back there, you made me go back there,' Mum, upset and accusing, told me.

Mum could not see how her story could possibly be relevant to mine.

'Why do you need to write about me?'

I tried to explain to her how her story was intrinsically connected to my own—to my survival.

'Who do you think made me, Mum?' I asked. 'You pushed me so hard all my life, that's why I am such an overachiever, that's why I have such a crazy work ethic.'

I told her that, growing up, I never felt good enough for her.

Mum denied ever thinking this and told me she had always felt proud of me—and I believed her. Even so, she had usually wanted more. I reminded her how hard she pushed me in high school. How the day after finishing the Higher School Certificate, for which I'd sat exams in physics, chemistry, and top-level mathematics and English, she yelled at me for being lazy when she came home from work to see me in front of the TV watching U2 music videos with a friend, and told me to get a job. The next day I found a full-time job as a supermarket checkout operator and I worked there through the holidays, until I found a job as a legal clerk.

I explained that today I saw a positive side to her lofty maternal expectations. I believed that this was part of the reason why I fought so hard after the accident. It was why I was so determined, even when I had lost so much, to succeed, to find fulfilment in my life. Because of her, I made high demands of myself.

Hearing this, my father cautioned me, 'Don't sell yourself short, Cynthia. You always had this in you.'

I tried a different tack. There was another reason why I wanted to include my mother's story and those of her family in my book, I told my parents. It was because these other stories had helped me to reach the point where I was ready, able, to write about what happened to me.

These conversations with my parents were on my mind when I visited the National Archives of Australia in Canberra and ordered Mum's family's immigration file. Immediately afterwards, I went down the road to the National Library of Australia and ordered a report that I had never wanted, never been able, to read before. It was the aircraft accident investigation report completed by Indonesia's National Transportation Safety Committee after the plane crash, my crash, in Yogyakarta in 2007.

I had a coffee in the library's crowded cafe while I waited for the report to be retrieved. A short time later, it was sitting on a trolley, ready for me. I placed the report on my lap and wheeled into one of the library's photocopier rooms. Glancing around me, I wondered whether the silent readers sitting at their desks sensed the magnitude of this act, which to me felt momentous.

In the cramped room, alone in front of a photocopier, I pulled myself upright and began to copy the 100 pages of the report, one by one.

IV

I'd always known that my mother had to leave school at the end of year nine, shortly after turning fifteen, to get a job.

I'd never known about the events leading up to it, though. I was unaware of the promises made that went unmet, the opportunities offered that went untaken. I hadn't appreciated how profound was the denial of Mum's chance to fulfil her potential, a potential that all those around her—parents and teachers—saw. Emigration, I knew, can threaten a person's sense of identity but, really, when it came to my own mother's experiences, I had no idea.

In one of our interviews I asked Mum about her education in Trieste, which was interrupted at the end of her fourth year of primary school, when her family left for Australia. She told me that she was 'very good at school'.

'School just came very easily for me.'

She recalled trudging up the hill to the school, Ezio De Marchi, with her father in the winter. If it was snowing, he would take her into a tavern on the way and buy her 'little glasses of advocaat', the yellow liqueur made from eggs, sugar and brandy, 'so that I'd keep warm during my school day'.

'I don't think he actually wanted to leave Italy, because he always used to say I was so good at school. He always used to say, "You are going to be one that's going to go on to high school and you're going to go on to university." I always remember that.'

Mum was so good at her schoolwork that other children were jealous. Once, when she was sick and had to miss school, my grandmother gave her daughter's completed homework assignment to another child to take to the teacher, and the child tried to pass it off as her own.

'It blew up into a huge thing and this girl was called a liar, which was the most horrific thing you could call anyone,' Mum told me.

After arriving in Sydney, Mum's family spent a month or two at the migrant camp in Greta, in the Hunter region of New South Wales, before moving into a boarding house in the Sydney suburb of Paddington. A priest on the ship on the way to Australia threatened my grandparents with excommunication if they didn't send their daughters to a Catholic school. Consequently, even though her parents couldn't afford the school fees and had no money to buy the uniforms—which included hats and gloves—they enrolled my mother and her sister at St Francis of Assisi Catholic Primary School on Oxford Street, where they also had to find money for elocution lessons.

In September, Mum was put into fifth grade and her sister Marina went into kindergarten. Soon afterwards, my grandparents started work in a tobacco factory at Waterloo and had to leave home every morning at seven-thirty. Loredana became her sister's minder. The sisters walked to and from school together every day, stopping to buy bread on their way home.

The first memory my mother has of her new school was being given a test in which she had to write the 'Our Father' in English. She didn't yet know the language. The first memory her sister, Marina, has is that for months she cried so much the teachers made her sit all day outside Mum's classroom. Because she couldn't speak English, and couldn't communicate with other children, Marina broke pieces of bread off her sandwiches and fed them to the ants, to whom she talked instead.

Mum (to her horror) was made to repeat year five and, though she struggled the first year, by year six she was coming first or second in her class.

'I've got all my reports at home,' she told me.

In high school Mum moved to Mt St Patrick's, run by the Sisters of Charity in Paddington, where, for two years, she excelled. Mum 'absolutely loved the nuns' (only recently she told me that she too harboured a belief she was marked for life in a convent, but my grandmother set her straight: 'Don't be ridiculous.').

Mum reeled off the nuns' names. Sister Francis taught her French.

'I was very good at French, being Italian, and oh—she was wonderful. Because I was so obedient, because I was brought up being so obedient, the teachers always liked me.'

Mum found for me the book, red and covered in protective plastic, that she won in 1961 for topping her French class: Victor Hugo's *Cosette*, a volume of *Les Misérables*.

Old Sister Stanislaus ran the tuckshop, where Mum worked 'because I could miss school and still come first'.

'I used to get to school early every morning and we'd have to go in and open the tins of beetroot and butter bread and cut tomatoes until the bell went for school. Then, at little lunch I'd go in there and, because I never had any friends, I used to love going into tuckshop and helping Sister Stanislaus and the mothers out.'

Mum loved Sister Stanislaus most of all because, when there were school excursions, the kindly nun let her select a bag of lollies to take with her.

'When there was an excursion on, because I never had any money, she'd give me a little paper bag and say, "Loredana, go and get a shilling's worth of lollies for the excursion." She always did that for me.'

After Mum finished primary school, her family moved to Newtown, where they lived for two years. In December 1961, after completing her second year of high school in Paddington, her parents bought a house in Campsie, in Sydney's south-west. Mum had to leave Mt St Patrick's, where she was coming first in her class and was 'the teacher's pet'.

'I used to get upset if I ever got a 99 and not 100. My report cards were always impeccable—it was always first or second. It used to annoy me when I came second.'

In the Christmas holidays my mother, in tears, went to say goodbye to the nuns in Paddington. She told one of them—it might have been Sister Amadeus, who taught her maths—that she was leaving the school.

'You don't have to leave, you can go to Potts Point,' the nun told her.

At Potts Point, one of Sydney's inner-city suburbs, was St Vincent's, a Catholic girls' high school with a reputation for academic excellence run by the Sisters of Charity. The nuns offered her a full scholarship.

'We will organise the uniforms, we'll organise everything for you.'

My mother was elated and went home to give her parents the happy news.

'I went home and I remember asking my dad, "Can I go to St Vincent's? It's not going to cost you anything." And he said, "I can't afford the train fares. You have to go to Campsie."'

Her father's word was, as always, final.

Mum spent her final year of high school, year nine, at a Catholic school in Campsie: St Mel's, run by the Josephite sisters. It was a horrible year, 'an absolute nightmare—that's where I came across real prejudice'. There was no French. She had to drop geography, history and high-level maths and pick up biology instead, not having done it before ('this biology was just a curse'), and typing.

'I hated every minute of it; I can't believe how dreadful it was.'

When, at the end of the year, she completed her Intermediate Certificate, there was no discussion about her continuing her schooling to obtain the Leaving Certificate (in the early 1960s there were five years of high school, not six as there are now).

'That was it, I had to go to work.'

My mother sat the public service exam and got a job at the Government Insurance Office (GIO). With my mother's wages— half of which she gave to her father—her parents could afford the mortgage repayments on their two-bedroom house and no longer needed their boarders. My grandmother's sister and her family, including three growing sons, moved out. Mum's parents were also able to renovate their house a couple of years later.

Loredana used to catch the train to work every day from her home in Campsie to the GIO's offices in the city. By chance, she shared the train with an Australian girl of the same age who wore the St Vincent's school uniform. My mother couldn't help but watch the girl on her journey to school at Potts Point each day and ponder what might have been.

'I thought how unfair that she was going to the school I was meant to go to and I was going to work.'

Any prospect of my mother finishing her schooling and attending university had evaporated. (She tried as an adult, while pregnant with me, to complete her schooling by correspondence but, once I was born, Mum found new motherhood overwhelming and gave study away.)

I finished high school. My parents supported me while I studied a double degree at university. They took out a loan to buy me a reliable, mustard-coloured 1976 Toyota Corolla so that I could drive the 30 or 40 minutes every day to Macquarie University in Sydney's north-west, which was not well-served by public transport. They continued to support me while I undertook legal training at the College of Law.

And I'd wondered why, after quitting my job as a solicitor to go travelling indefinitely, my mother didn't take it well.

V

There was a football field next door to La Casa Rossa, where Mum lived in Trieste.

She spent hours playing 'houses' in the football field with her friend, Alida. This game involved the girls sketching their dream homes with sticks in the dirt.

'We used to draw houses like an architect and we'd always have all these different rooms. You know: two bedrooms, a kitchen, a bathroom—things that we didn't have.'

While the friends fantasised about their make-believe mansions, Loredana's actual residence was uncomfortably cramped.

Loredana lived with her parents, sister and grandparents, Anna-Maria and Amedeo, on the top floor of the three-storey La Casa Rossa. Amedeo's pension paid the rent on the apartment. His son, Alfredo, an apprentice plumber before the war, couldn't find plumbing work when he returned from Germany (there was no financial support from the Italian government for returning Italian Military Internees). Eventually, he got a job at the steelworks across the road from La Casa Rossa, breaking up the pig iron with a 15-kilogram sledgehammer. It was too much for him physically (what permanent toll had forced labour taken on his young body?), and Alfredo was later given another position operating a crane.

Mum's grandparents had one bedroom, and her parents and the two girls slept in another. Mum's family's room was tiny but fitted one double and two single beds; the only way her parents could get to the wardrobe was by climbing onto Mum's bed. Being on the top floor, their room had a sloping ceiling which made it feel even smaller. There was a little window a metre high that Mum almost fell out of when she was three years old (her mother saved her, grabbing her by the legs). After this, her nonno Toni covered it over with chicken wire.

The apartment had a kitchen where the family congregated. Everything happened in that kitchen. Once a week, the girls had their baths in a small tub there. Loredana was allowed to draw maps in chalk on its walls for her geography homework.

'That's where we listened to the radio, that's where I did my homework, that's where we did the cooking, that's where they did the washing, the ironing—everything was done in this one little room, which they called the kitchen.'

There was one toilet down a 'great big hallway' which was shared between the five families that lived in the apartment block.

In the few black-and-white photographs that remain of La Casa Rossa in the 1940s and 1950s, it looks as rundown and dilapidated as it did when we visited in 2015. Then, as now, it was a patchwork of rusty metal and decaying timber sheds, crumbling stone walls and rocky dirt paths—though with better-tended garden beds than today.

Despite their modest circumstances, Mum told me, she had a 'wonderful childhood'.

'We had absolutely nothing but I never realised I was poor.'

Mum's grandparents kept chickens in the garden, which smelt of lilac in the spring and peaches in the summer. Her grandfather sometimes slaughtered a chicken for dinner. Afterwards, Loredana sat with her grandmother at the kitchen table while she plucked and cleaned it, watching and listening with fascination as her nonna explained how to remove the giblets without damaging the bile sac and poisoning the bird. When a chicken laid eggs, her parents took them to their bedroom to keep them warm.

'They'd keep this hen with all these eggs in their bedroom until the eggs hatched and then I'd see these little chickens before they took them out into the yard.'

A woman brought tubs of milk from cows in the countryside, which they poured into saucepans and boiled before drinking.

'When you boiled the milk it got this really thick, beautiful skin on top and we'd have sandwiches with this skin and sprinkled sugar.'

Her father grew radishes, peas and tomatoes in his brother-in-law's garden, allocated to him by the steelworks where the men worked. A pink climbing rose covered the gate to the vegetable patch. Her father let her pick sweet, young peas off the vine, while he collected the dainty radishes, which they dipped into a dish of oil, salt and pepper before eating.

The family kept rabbits, which her grandmother killed and cooked. There was also a compost heap.

'We'd put our bottoms over the bricks and do our business over this compost heap.' Her father covered it and 'we had the best vegetables ever'.

In the winter, Alfredo built a fire in a tin in the garden for his daughter and her cousin, Giuliana.

'We'd sit around and he'd give us little pieces of bread with butter and then a bit of anchovy on top.'

In the summer, Loredana went swimming at Le Saline, near the steelworks and the abattoirs, in the middle of the busy industrial zone. The abattoirs offloaded their waste—blood and guts from the animal carcasses—down a creek that came out right where the families of Servola swam.

'Sometimes it was clean, but sometimes it was dirty and there'd be oil from the oil refinery or there'd be rubbish from the steelworks or there'd be rubbish from the abattoir, but we used to absolutely love it.'

They just pushed the effluent away as they swam.

On weekends the family went for walks, stopping at different taverns around Servola for lunch. As a treat, the girls got an orange soft drink (at home, the children drank only wine and water). They ate platters of cold meats, cheese and fruit, and sometimes a man would come around with a huge basket of peanuts.

'You'd just buy a cup full of peanuts and he used to throw them on the table and then we'd just start shelling and eating peanuts.'

Occasionally they visited the cherry farm of one of Alfredo's friends from the steelworks, in a valley on the Italian–Yugoslavian border. They were each given their own cherry tree for a few hours.

'We'd all go up there and he'd say, "Right, that cherry tree is yours and that cherry tree is yours," and we'd climb this cherry tree and just eat our fill of the cherries.'

Mum's Aunt Rosina, a dressmaker, made the girls' clothes. Her grandmother, Anna-Maria, took Mum to San Lorenzo, Servola's church, every Sunday morning. She enjoyed it most for the sugar almonds that, when there was a wedding, were showered over the bride as she left down the front steps.

When Mum's cousins Andrea and Alessandro came to visit their grandparents at La Casa Rossa on Sundays with their sister Gloria, they brought their piano accordions and harmonicas and played in the tavern downstairs. Andrea, who is now 80, said when my mother's family left Trieste, this happy tradition ended. Their departure left a huge void and brought great sadness to the extended family, he told me.

Listening to Mum's nostalgic reflections on her life in Servola, so rich and colourful, so full of love for family and place, I questioned how she could claim to have felt 'nothing' on our visit there together.

Her reminiscences also cast a new light on certain rituals from my own childhood, such as how we celebrated Christmas.

Mum's early Christmases in Italy were spent with her father's parents, Anna-Maria and Amedeo. The feast of La Befana, the old woman who delivers presents to Italian children on a broomstick on the eve of the Epiphany (6 January), was spent with her mother's parents, Lina and Toni. Nonna Lina, a rotund woman who always wore a burgundy-coloured housecoat made of flannel, filled old stockings with dried fruit, nuts, lollies and fresh fruit for Loredana and Marina.

Mum did a similar thing for us growing up: we each had a small red or green felt stocking hung from the fireplace. Day after day, in the lead-up to Christmas, the stockings expanded as they were filled with chocolates, walnuts, hazelnuts and huge Brazil nuts that were impossible to crack.

The Italian Christmas tradition that captured my mother's imagination most was the nativity scene: what she referred to as 'my Christmas cribs'. Her cousin Giuliana's father made 'the most wonderful crib', Mum says. He set up the crib on a big table in the corner of Giuliana's bedroom (their apartment was close to La Casa Rossa).

'I always envied this wonderful crib. They used to go out and collect moss and he'd build mountains of moss—and the villages he used to build! That's why I loved cribs so much.'

At La Casa Rossa, there was only space for the tiniest of cribs, which sat on a table under a small tree behind the front door.

From my mother's descriptions of her Christmas cribs, I understood why, after I left home, she gave me so many nativity sets (bought year after year in the Christmas sales). We had a lovely one when we were children that Mum sent away to Italy for. It had a big stable that was sprinkled with bits of fake snow. At the start of December, with great excitement, my sister and brothers and I pulled out all the pieces from a big box in the garage and carefully placed the figurines of Mary and Joseph and the crib inside the stable. Around the outside went the three wise men, the angel and the shepherds. The crib sat empty under our tall artificial Christmas tree and we laid the baby Jesus in his bed of plastic hay on the morning of the 25th.

Having different Christmas traditions in Italy meant my mother's first Christmas in Australia was loaded with disappointment. Unlike the local children, she didn't receive a visit from Santa Claus on 25 December, since her parents knew nothing of the custom. In Italy in the 1950s, families didn't exchange presents at Christmas, but rather on the feast day of Saint Nicholas, on 6 December.

This was followed by a second, possibly greater disappointment, when Mum's parents tried to make it up to their daughters the next day, on 26 December. They assumed—erroneously—that on Boxing Day, the public holiday Australians celebrate the day after Christmas, people gave each other presents in boxes.

'I remember my mum and dad saying, "Well, you know, it's Boxing Day—we'll get you a present and put it in a box for Boxing Day."'

Off they all trotted that morning to Mark Foy's on Goulburn Street in the city, intending to buy the girls a special toy each to put in a box. They were dismayed when they arrived and not a single shop was open.

'Of course, in those days everything was closed on Boxing Day, so I ended up not getting anything.'

VI

My mother has always explained her parents' decision to emigrate as being for distinctly personal reasons: that, after a decade, her mother could no longer endure living with her parents-in-law.

My grandparents married out of necessity, though Alfredo adored Anna and couldn't wait to marry her. Anna wasn't as keen. On her wedding day, she was six months pregnant. Mum discovered that she had been conceived out of wedlock while looking through the family passports one day soon after arriving in Australia. Until then, her parents had told her they married the year before Mum was born.

Confronted by her daughter, Anna told the real story. She fell pregnant around New Year's Eve 1946 'because she'd drunk too much'. When Anna's father, Toni, found out, he wanted to throw his daughter out of the house.

Anna and Alfredo married in June 1947; they were both 22. Anna wasn't allowed to wear a white wedding dress (she wore grey). They had a wedding lunch afterwards at the home of Alfredo's older sister, Assunta. The pair moved in with Alfredo's parents, and Loredana was born that September.

I have a couple of photographs from Alfredo and Anna's honeymoon in romantic Venice. My grandfather's best friend and his wife went with them. The four are striding out, having ascended a set of steps somewhere in that labyrinthine city. Anna holds on to Alfredo's fingers and walks a step behind him. He wears an open-necked white shirt with the sleeves rolled up and darker pants; she wears a wraparound dress that doesn't quite disguise her growing stomach. Her wavy, shoulder-length hair is pulled across her face, and her brow is furrowed. Anna looks serious and troubled, unlike her new husband, who smiles contentedly. Mum said her mother was 'not a very expressive person', but her face in the honeymoon photo is quite revealing.

In 1952, Anna had a second daughter. Her increasing despair at her living situation wasn't due solely to the overcrowded conditions at La Casa Rossa, however.

Amedeo, Alfredo's father, was a violent alcoholic who hit his wife, Anna-Maria—including in front of their young grandchildren—and drank his pension money.

Anna and Alfredo on their honeymoon in 1947

'My father used to send me to the bedroom and then I'd always hear this terrible physical violence in the kitchen and sometimes Uncle Silvio was called over because my grandfather was incredibly strong and he'd help to control him.'

Anna-Maria used her granddaughter to prise money from her husband.

'I used to have to sit on his lap and ask him for money and then pass it on to her, because every bit of money that I got off him he wouldn't spend on drink.'

Anna 'just had enough' of her father-in-law.

'My mother just couldn't take it anymore,' Mum said.

While there's no doubt that my grandmother's intolerance for their living arrangements propelled her to want to emigrate, the family's domestic situation was shaped by the political forces of the day and the wider context of Trieste's vexed place in post-war Italy.

The year 1954 heralded the start of a brief but intense flow of migrants from Trieste, a city that had no real tradition of emigration before the Second World War, to Australia. It was brought on by the departure of the Allied caretaker government in place since the end of the German occupation, and the return of the city to Italy.

The period of the Allied presence was looked upon fondly by many Triestini, including my mother, who recalls a black American soldier, the 'first negro I ever saw in my life', giving her a packet of chewing gum. The withdrawal of Allied troops meant a huge loss of income for the city. But there were additional reasons why the local Triestini were left feeling so uncertain about the future.

Many Triestini felt overlooked by the central government in Rome, which to them seemed more interested in assisting the displaced ethnic Italians from the former Italian territory handed over to Yugoslavia after the war, than looking after the locals. Ethnic Italians (anti-Titoist *esuli*, or exiles) had been pouring into Trieste from Istria and Fiume since 1947. Civil servants posted to Trieste by Rome after 1954 were charged with Italianising the territory and, according to Gianfranco Cresciani, a Trieste-born, Sydney-based writer, they discriminated against native-born Triestini who did not fit the 'predominant nationalist pattern' and were not 'fervent supporters of the Italian cause'.[4]

There was an acute shortage of housing in post-war Trieste. Public housing was being constructed in the city, but from what the Triestini could tell, it was largely going to the exiles from Yugoslavia. The locals felt as though they were being forced out and became demoralised. My grandparents clearly felt this, because it's how Mum explains their housing predicament.

Mum recounts that, when her parents married after the war, they had to live with her father's parents because during the Allied occupation there was no construction and 'there was nowhere for people to live'. When Trieste was returned to Italy, people 'from Fiume [now Rijeka], from Pola [Pula] and Zara [Zadar], they all came to Trieste because that's when the Yugoslav fellow took over, Tito, and the Italian government gave all these people apartments, but not the people that actually lived in Trieste'. My grandparents 'never had the opportunity of getting their own apartment', even though there were apartments being built, including across the road from La Casa Rossa.

Meanwhile, on the other side of the world, Australia was busy engineering an ambitious post-war expansion of its population. The country had emerged from the Second World War feeling vulnerable, as a geographically vast yet significantly under-populated nation of seven million. Political leaders swiftly launched plans to expand Australia's population through immigration, the idea being to secure the defence of Australia, and grow and diversify the economy. The aim was to grow the population by 2 per cent per annum.[5]

To help achieve this, Australia offered assisted passage to Italian migrants. In 1951, Australia signed an agreement with the Italian government under which Australia paid one-quarter of the fare, Italy paid an equal sum, and the remaining 50 per cent was given as a loan to the migrant. The Australian government also agreed to provide temporary lodgings for migrants (free while not working) and employment opportunities for two years. This was the basis for my mother's family's migration.

So it was that disenchanted Triestini found themselves caught up in this heady rush to emigrate, with boatloads of people departing— many of whom, like my nonno, had jobs and were not leaving for economic motives—with no real idea of what awaited them. It is said 10 per cent of the population of Trieste left for Australia during a seven-year period from the mid-1950s to the early 1960s. It was a traumatic experience for many of those affected. The anguish of separation from family and their beloved city was reflected in local newspapers such as the *Corriere di Trieste*, which begged the native Triestini not to leave. Tellingly, there were Triestine flags flying in the crowds seeing off the first migrant-filled boats (red flags with a white halberd, Austria's colours), not Italian ones.[6]

Alfredo did not want to leave Italy. He was close to his mother and always said that, even if he was given his own apartment, he could never leave his parents. Alfredo did leave, though, because Anna wanted a home of her own. According to Mum, Alfredo was 'rapt in' his wife.

As soon as Alfredo left, Amedeo was placed in a nursing home, and Anna-Maria 'went from daughter to daughter' until she, too, went into a nursing home.

Mum's family's medical examinations, security vetting (for Fascists or Nazi collaborators) and preliminary interviews for immigration to Australia took place in early 1955. (I was slightly taken aback when the National Archives of Australia informed me they were withholding part of my grandfather's naturalisation papers on the advice of ASIO (the Australian Security Intelligence Organisation), Australia's domestic spy agency.)

On 12 April 1957, Alfredo signed the official immigration papers, according to which Australia, although not guaranteeing work, promised to 'render every assistance in finding such employment'.

VII

In Naples, where they spent three days before embarking on the *Sydney*, Mum and her family stayed in a big gymnasium-type building that had been converted into a dormitory.

The men and women slept separately, as they did on the ship. Mum's sister, Marina, remembers a rough passage to Australia, during which glasses and plates slid off tables, and the family sometimes slept outside on deckchairs with blankets because of seasickness. One night, Marina found herself on the floor of the cabin the girls shared with their mother, bleeding. She had fallen out of the bunk and cut her head open.

There were stops at Port Said, north of the Suez Canal, where Mum's parents bought the girls a stuffed toy camel from local boys with their baskets of trinkets, and Aden. The stopover in Ceylon (now Sri Lanka) was particularly eventful. The heat was intense, the girls saw their first elephants, the smell of the colourful fruit and vegetable market was overpowering, and Mum was followed through the crowded stalls by a man who, her father became convinced, was trying to kidnap his daughter. There was a pool party when the ship crossed the equator and English lessons for the new immigrants. The young Loredana believed that learning English was just a matter of mastering the pronunciation of its alphabet.

Alfredo and family on board the Sydney *in 1957*

Mum's earliest memory of Australia was eating her first tin of peaches. Their ship docked at the wharves at Woolloomooloo, in Sydney, on 26 June 1957. My grandmother's sister, who'd already come to Australia to be a domestic for a wealthy family in Sydney's eastern suburbs, was there to greet them. She took them to her home—a room in a boarding house in Paddington. There, Mum said, 'for the first time in my life I had peaches, canned peaches, and ice-cream'. (There was a peach tree in the vegetable garden near La Casa Rossa, but Mum had never seen the tinned variety before.)

Soon after, probably the same day, Mum's family took the train to Greta, about 18 kilometres north of Maitland in the Hunter Valley. The migrant camp had been an army training camp during the war. From 1949 to 1960, Greta housed thousands of newly arrived immigrants displaced from Europe. The population of the camp when Mum arrived was mainly Italians, Yugoslavians, Austrians and Dutch.[7]

The Greta camp was run by a quasi-military administration and facilities were primitive. The surrounding landscape was barren and there was, for many of Greta's inhabitants, a sense of social dislocation, desperation, depression and tedium.

According to Mum, the cooks at the camp were Polish, and 'Poles can't cook'. Her family 'absolutely hated the food', and her parents tried to get food elsewhere, which my grandmother cooked on a little portable stove that ran on methylated spirits. The Italian families walked into the town and, because none of them could speak English, they attempted to buy eggs by making chicken noises.

'Chiki, chika, quock, quock,' the men said to bewildered shopkeepers.

'No one could understand what the hell they wanted,' Mum said.

The family was housed in a kind of hangar, a 'very cold tin shed', the four of them in one room. It was winter and there were insufficient blankets. Mum's younger sister sat for hours on the wooden steps at the front of their hut. Marina didn't like going inside; she refused to eat the food and hated going to the school 'because people used to come and talk to you and I never understood what they said'.

'I could not understand why they always separated me from my parents, my sister,' she told me.

Food was not the only source of discontentment. In 1957, unemployment in Australia was increasing and work opportunities for new migrants were scarce. This led to a 'riot' at Greta, which one parliamentarian suggested was caused by the Australian government's failure to live up to its promises to help immigrants find work.[8] Some of the men at Greta found rural work in northern New South Wales and Queensland, including cane cutting, which led to long, difficult separations from their wives and children. For Triestini like Alfredo, who'd lived his whole life in an urban environment, the arduous farm work and separation from his family proved traumatic.

'He just couldn't cope with it,' Mum said.

For days before he left for the cane fields Alfredo practised chopping with an axe, trying to toughen his hands with calluses, but it never worked.

'He used to get these terrible blisters on his hands,' Marina said. 'He also hated being away from us.'

Their dad brought back big bunches of bananas to Greta along with stories about the snakes that were everywhere. Men chopped off their fingers after getting bitten by deadly taipans, Alfredo told his family. For their meals, workers dropped bombs into a dam, then collected and barbecued the dead fish.

After five weeks or so, the family found a room in a boarding house in Paddington. Anna and her daughters caught the train to

Sydney's Central Station, where Alfredo was due to meet them. When they arrived and he wasn't on the platform, my grandmother thought she'd taken the wrong train and started to cry.

Standing with her young sister and their suitcases watching my grandmother fall apart, Mum said she felt 'absolute fear'.

'Do you know what that does to your confidence if your mother doesn't know what she's doing? I was absolutely horrified to see my mother cry, not knowing where we were, not knowing anything, not understanding anything, not being able to read anything because everything was so foreign.'

They waited. Eventually, Alfredo appeared.

VIII

My parents first met in late 1965, in a jazz club in the Ironworkers Building near Circular Quay in Sydney. My mother was eighteen, my father had just turned 23, and neither liked jazz.

Mum had long dark hair to her shoulder blades and wore a short white dress cut with a high empire-line waist and a white ribbon down the front. She was with a girlfriend, out on the town for their regular Saturday night coffee in Kings Cross, followed by dancing at the jazz club or a discotheque. My father was out with a friend just returned from New Guinea.

My father, with a pipe in his mouth, pushed his way through a group of 'rough nuts', who were blocking the doorway to the club.

'I saw him coming through the door with the pipe in his mouth and I thought, "Wow, I wonder who he is,"' Mum said.

'I saw this young pretty girl looking at me,' Dad said.

That night he was feeling 'unusually confident'. 'I thought, bugger it, and walked right up to her and said, "Would you like to dance?"'

My father is six foot tall. My mother is five foot nine. When she stood up, in high heels, she came to my father's eye level. Dad was 'amazed'.

'I thought, "Wow, she's tall, isn't she?" We started dancing and I held her pretty tight.'

By the end of the night my father was besotted and asked if he could accompany Loredana home.

'No, my father won't let me go home with a boy,' she told him.

'Well, will you come out with me some time then?'

'John, there is something I have to tell you before you ask me to go out.'

My father listened, curious as to what this 'something' could possibly be.

'I'm Italian.'

Loredana expected that, hearing this, the young Australian man would say, 'I'll ring you,' and she'd never hear from him again. Instead, my father, a blue-eyed redhead who grew up on Sydney's northern beaches, said, 'So what? Will you marry me?'

Dad walked my mother to the station that night, kissed her, and asked her again if he could take her out.

'Well, you'll have to come home and meet my father first,' she told him.

He did—the following weekend.

'Boy,' Alfredo told my father that first meeting, 'any funny business I come after you.'

Dad was Mum's first boyfriend. She had met plenty of young Italian men at what Mum and her family knew as 'Club Trieste', the social club run by the Associazione Trieste on Rofe Street in Leichhardt, where her parents dragged her and her sister every weekend. But Mum wasn't interested in going out with an Italian.

'Why not?' I asked.

Loredana on my father's shoulders, taken at Campsie in 1967

'I was not going to be an Italian; I was not going to go out with an Italian.'

Why was being Italian such a negative for my mother, something she had to escape?

The feeling was not innate, but learnt.

IX

My mother's attitude, which seems so destructive to the self, was a logical consequence of the doctrine of assimilation.

It was through assimilationist policies that Australia's political leaders were able to encourage acceptance of large numbers of southern European immigrants after the Second World War, to make their presence more palatable to a nervous public, among whom anti-Italian prejudices were particularly strong.

Australia of the 1950s thought of itself as peopled by mostly British blood. White Australia was still official policy. Italians were few in number before the war and they were held in low regard. Some examples from the 1920s onwards illustrate: a university academic, a 'race' expert, from Melbourne said they were 'more likely than not to lower the social standard'; a national tabloid called them that 'greasy flood of Mediterranean scum'; the army said interned Italian prisoners in the Second World War had a 'child-like' mentality. Community leaders and government advisers on immigration planning after the war continued with their dislike of Italians. The Returned and Services League NSW branch argued Italians had a 'deplorable' military record, were not 'good mixers' and many were Communists. Northern Italians, Triestines like my mother's family, were regarded with slightly less disdain than their southern compatriots. While considered a greater security risk, they were said to be 'generally industrial and skilled types' with better education and hygiene standards.[9]

What were the country's leaders, striving to realise steep ambitions for rapidly growing Australia's population after the war, to do? They couldn't meet their objectives through British immigration alone. The Labor Chifley government tried to reassure Australians by falsely promising them that every 'foreign' arrival would be outnumbered by ten from Britain (in reality, more than half of immigrants admitted between 1947 and 1951 were from non-English-speaking backgrounds). By 1952, senior bureaucrats feared the increasing numbers of Italians could cause 'public alarm'. When the Italian component of Australia's immigration intake rose from below 1 to 28 per cent in the five years to 1951, the secretary of the Department of Immigration, Tasman Heyes, 'stressed the danger to Australian culture' and devised a plan to deter Italian immigrants while not appearing to discriminate. Rules were introduced forbidding immigrants from sponsoring friends from home; they were applied strictly to southern Europeans, but with wide discretion to northern and central Europeans.[10]

Migrants or their children had to 'meld into British Australia', so as to be indistinguishable from the rest of the population. They were expected to be grateful, to readily adopt the language and culture of mainstream Australia and abandon their own. This meant dispersing, forming relationships with Australians, doing away with foreign practices and beliefs. The indoctrination began on the boat to Australia. Brochures warned migrants that Australia was 'essentially a British nation . . . And we want to keep it that way.' Migrants were required to separate their new selves from their past, to shed their personal history.[11]

This was the Australia into which my grandparents unwittingly brought their young daughters. It was a time of immense, painful social change, and nine-year-old Loredana was thrust into the centre of it. The result was a permanent psychological wounding.

'I was made to feel that I shouldn't be Italian,' my mother said.

My sister wonders whether this was why Mum refused to speak her first language to us when we were children. Because she was ashamed of her heritage, were we denied ours?

Mum's sister, Marina, who has the broadest of Australian accents, responded to the bigotry in a different way from Loredana.

'I always said I was Italian, because that's who I am, and I never hid it. I always used to say, "If you don't like it, bad luck."'

For my mother, however, the experience left her exposed and painfully sensitive, forever unable to shed the hurt she experienced as a girl.

X

From Alfredo's immigration and naturalisation files, retrieved from the National Archives, I pieced together a rough timeline of the family's first few years in Australia.

Mum's family moved into the boarding house in Paddington at the end of July 1957. Alfredo was still cutting cane and travelling back and forth between Sydney and Richmond River in the state's north. The family lived in a room in a four-bedroom terrace owned by some Neapolitans, along with three other families. The families shared a bathroom and a refrigerator.

'You weren't allowed to have more than one shelf in the fridge,' Mum said.

It was common practice for more established (especially southern) Italian migrants to rent out their houses to pay off their mortgages. For newly arrived Triestini, owning one's home was not a familiar concept; it was an Australian dream, though one they soon bought into.

At some point in August or September Alfredo left his job cutting cane and returned to his family. The weeks following, with Alfredo out of work, grew increasingly desperate for the family. With no jobs and no money, my grandparents went out on foot, searching the city for work. They could not afford bus fares. Any food they had they gave to their daughters.

'They always used to say they weren't hungry so we would eat,' Marina says.

Mum remembers how when her parents were 'absolutely starving' they walked from Paddington to Surry Hills. A couple they'd met on the boat lived there, and gave Alfredo and Anna a plate of spaghetti each.

The year 1957 was not an easy one to be an Italian migrant arriving in Australia. The 1951 Italian–Australian migration agreement had fallen dormant after a year. This followed the eruption of violent protests at the Bonegilla migrant camp over poor living conditions and a lack of work opportunities for Italian immigrants. The government had called in the army. The agreement was revived after 1954, coinciding with the changing political situation in Trieste. By 1957, however, economic conditions in Australia were declining. Newspaper editorials thundered: the employment situation was incompatible with the rate of immigration. There were concerns over the detrimental effect southern Europeans were having on the country's British character. The Menzies government, keen to reassure Australians it was doing its utmost to make its migrant intake as British as possible, launched the 'Bring out a Briton' campaign. Sponsored Britons could migrate to Australia for a ten-pound fare.[12]

Things got so bad for my mother's family that my grandfather went to the Italian consulate and asked officials to ship them back to Italy, but they refused. Under the terms of the immigration agreement, he had to remain in Australia for two years. Instead, the consulate found Alfredo and his wife jobs at Leonard Norman's tobacco factory in Waterloo, which they commenced in October 1957. They worked there until the factory closed down, some 20 years later. The factory was on Amelia Street.

With their first pay cheques, my grandparents splurged. Alfredo bought four-litre flagons of red wine from Griffith. Anna and Alfredo also bought a record player for themselves, and a blue budgerigar for the girls. The family was soon able to move, for higher rent, from a small ground-floor bedroom in the Paddington boarding house into an upstairs room which had a balcony for the budgerigar.

The factory work was hard, involving long, tedious hours with minimal rest. Nonno used to stop at a hotel halfway between home and the factory every morning before work for a middy of beer and a brandy to fortify himself for the day.

My grandmother was a hairdresser in Trieste, but her qualifications weren't recognised in Australia and her English was too limited to requalify. Working with heavy machines every day would have been a difficult adjustment. One day Anna was rushed to hospital after her finger became caught in a machine and she lost her fingertip.

Thinking about my grandmother, a hairdresser, having to spend two decades cutting tobacco leaves in a factory, I recalled the other doll that, along with Giorgetto, came with Mum's family on the boat. Mum wasn't allowed to play with the doll and it didn't have a name. It had belonged to Livia, a good friend of my grandmother, who married an American soldier stationed in Trieste during the Allied occupation and later emigrated to the United States. As a young girl, Mum admired 'this most beautiful blonde doll' with rosebud red lips, which sat on a bed at Livia's house. When Mum's family left Trieste, Livia gave it to Loredana.

'I wasn't allowed to touch it,' said Mum.

My grandmother kept the doll for herself: she brushed the doll's blonde curls and starched her pink dress. Mum explained this was 'because, you know, Nonna was a hairdresser'.

Today the doll lives at Mum's house. Her hair is still pinned up in curls that Nonna styled with bobby pins, though the ringlets are a little bedraggled. Her painted red nails are also chipped, and her eyeballs have been pushed deep into their sockets.

I wondered if grooming the doll, carefully arranging its hair and dress, was my grandmother's way of holding on to her identity as

Anna the Triestine hairdresser, the woman she was before becoming a factory worker on a production line in Australia?

When the tobacco factory shut its doors, Anna stopped working and Alfredo got another job as a factory hand at Hotspring Heaters in Redfern, where he worked until his retirement. He found that job in 1976. I know because a clipping of the original job advertisement, from the newspaper classifieds, was preserved in my grandmother's papers. I showed it to my mother, who couldn't believe it was still there. The ad for 'Factory Hands' was circled in black pen.

Money was always tight during those early years in Australia. Mum gave up a promising future as a sprinter when her father couldn't afford the spiked running shoes. She was reprimanded for the times her mistakes cost her parents financially. Once she dropped ink on her school uniform and, trying to clean it, rubbed it so hard she made a hole in the fabric. Another time she knocked over the drainer in the communal kitchen and all the dishes her mother had brought from Italy rolled into the sink and smashed. Anna was so upset, she cried. A third time, Loredana, who was ten, travelled into the city on her own with money her mother had given her to buy a school uniform and, somehow, lost her wallet. With no money to buy the uniform or get home, Mum stood on George Street crying until she saw a policeman directing traffic and went up to him. He gave her two shillings.

'Oh, did I get into trouble for losing that money.'

Mum has some fond memories from her family's time in Paddington. There was a back lane where the girls learnt to play cricket. As a treat, every Friday night after their parents finished work the two sisters walked up to the top of Oxford Street to meet them for a meal of hot chips and potato scallops from a local fish-and-chip shop. Loredana accompanied her mother to

English classes at night with some of the other Italians they knew from Paddington. She babysat for families in the boarding house, including a family her parents knew from Trieste, and with her earnings bought herself a pair of school shoes. The families went on pleasant picnics in Centennial Park, where the children collected tadpoles in jars from the lake.

During that period, before Mum learnt to read English, my grandmother allowed her to read books from her romance fiction collection, given there were no other Italian language books for her daughter to read. Although Mum was only nine, she read scores of breathless novels about handsome Italian air force pilots. A favourite author was an Italian writer who wrote under the name Liala; she began writing escapist novels after her aviator lover died in tragic circumstances.

Nonna loved romance novels. I remember seeing books with racy Mills & Boon-style covers lying around on coffee tables in my grandparents' lounge room on our visits. Among the papers I salvaged from their house in Campsie was a black, vinyl-covered notebook, in which Anna recorded in alphabetical order the names of all the Italian-language romance novels she had read in the last twenty years or so. They had titles like *Amore Odio Desideio* (*Love, Hate, Desire*), *Batte il Cuore* (*Beat the Heart*), *Dove e Andato l'Amore* (*Where Has the Love Gone*). There were more than a thousand books on the list. Her daughters didn't know she'd kept this notebook.

The period living in the Paddington terrace was a testing one for my grandparents' marriage, brought on by Alfredo's absences from the family cutting cane. In our interviews my mother revealed painful, deeply private incidents involving my grandparents during their early years in Australia. These episodes exposed the intense emotional stresses Anna and Alfredo were under as they navigated a foreign country and desperately tried to hold their young family together. These revelations allowed me to see for the first time the heavy burdens my mother had to carry as a child, not only because her parents didn't speak English, but because they were so isolated, without adult friends or family to confide in and lean on for emotional support. Her father in particular turned to his eldest daughter for comfort during a particularly distressing time, when there was no one else.

In 1960, my mother's family moved away from Paddington, to another terrace in Newtown.

XI

The only time I had to terminate the interview with my mother because she was too upset to continue was when I asked her about the prejudice she faced as a child in Australia.

She was ridiculed over her food, her clothes, her poverty, her name—essentially, her entire person and personality. She changed her name to the more anglicised Lori, hid her school lunches, pretended the bed bugs on her uniform were something else—but it was never enough to mask her differences.

There was the bread.

My grandmother gave her daughters school lunches of mortadella sandwiches on thick-cut slices of Vienna loaf, because Alfredo would not eat the Australian-style sliced bread. She wrapped them in 'strange paper' because she never had normal sandwich wrap.

'I used to try to hide my food. It used to stink, they [the Australian children] reckoned, but the bread—the bread was dreadful—because it was a Vienna loaf. They never ate Vienna loaf, they only ate sliced bread, and I had this huge sandwich of

Vienna loaf. You know, you don't have sandwiches in Italy, you have bread rolls. It was the most shameful thing to have these Vienna sandwiches.'

There was the strudel.

'I used to love my mother's strudel,' Mum told me.

One day, she took a piece of strudel to school and another girl asked Mum if she could taste it.

'I said, "Oh no, you won't like it." She said, "Let me taste it." Strudel. She tasted it and she said, "Oh my God, did she put wine in it? It's disgusting." And I thought, "Oh jeez, I should never have given her a taste of my strudel." And it just made me ashamed of having a strudel.'

There were the bed bugs.

'The house in Paddington was full of bed bugs. We used to wake up in the middle of the night and try to kill them, squash them, and all this blood would come out, and in the morning we'd have to go through the mattress and see if we could find them and kill them.'

Mum recalls one incident when she was sitting in church.

'The girl behind me tapped me on the shoulder and said, "You've got a bed bug crawling on your blazer." Oh my God, the shame, the shame was unbelievable. I'm still ashamed of it. I tried to convince her it wasn't a bed bug, that it was a fly . . . She treated me as if I was some disgusting creature. "Don't go near her, she's got bed bugs." Oh, they all pulled away from me; oh, the shame.'

Mum was so distressed by this point that I asked her if she wanted to stop. She said yes, but first told me: 'See, they make you ashamed, ashamed of being Italian, ashamed of having Loredana as a name—the kids could never pronounce it.'

Then, sobbing now: 'I shouldn't have been ashamed of my mother.'

The prejudice did not only occur on the playground. It happened in my grandparents' workplace, on public transport and in public places. The whole family adopted defences to try to make themselves as invisible as possible.

On the train, the family kept silent, so that other passengers wouldn't hear them speaking Italian.

My grandfather was told not to leave the house on Anzac Day or he would be picked on for being a 'dago'.

If the family went to their favourite park or beach—Clifton Gardens or Nielsen Park—they went with a large group and arrived early, around 7.30 am, before the Australians, 'so that if they picked on anyone they'd have to pick on this big group'.

There were, of course, kind Australians. Like Maureen, the only girl to invite Mum to a birthday party in school. Maureen was of Irish background, and later worked with Mother Teresa in India.

'Are you sure I'm invited?' Mum asked Maureen in disbelief when she received the invitation.

'She said, "Yes, come to my party." I went there and I felt like a fish out of water. It was the only birthday party I'd ever been invited to. It was incredible, I couldn't believe it.'

I wanted to understand for myself, in a more visceral way than textbooks can offer, the public debates that were shaping the attitudes of the schoolgirls and train passengers my mother and her family encountered. I read clippings from local and national newspapers, stories and letters to the editor on the subject of Italian immigration in Australia, published in 1957.

I found newspaper columns filled with the insulting sentiments of politicians, religious and other community leaders, anxious about the damage inferior Italians with their Catholic beliefs were doing to the 'traditional British character of the Australian population'. According to the Anglican Archbishop of Sydney, Dr H.W.K. Mowll,

'We do not think disparagingly of these Continental people', whose 'brains' and 'strong arms' were needed to help populate Australia, 'but we are concerned that both our British and Protestant heritage should be maintained and strengthened'. The president of the British–Australia Association, Mr L. Clapperton, said, 'You don't hear of British migrants taking over whole suburbs, as the Italians are doing in places like Woolloomooloo.' Dr Herbert (Doc) Evatt, leader of the federal Labor opposition, said the government needed to try harder to attract more Britons, because they 'knew how to live in a democracy'.[13]

More thoughtful Australians urged tolerance and reason. These counter voices warned of the 'incalculable harm' racial bigotry was doing to Italians already living in Australia, bringing up their families, going to work every day, trying to fit in. Evatt was upbraided by a reader, Mrs Carolyn Berntsen from Cammeray, who observed, 'Democracy is not the prerogative of British countries alone.' The national president of the RSL, Sir George Holland, said 'having invited people from European countries to migrate to Australia . . . it is to a degree insulting that they should learn that they are here, according to some vociferous and unthinking sources, on sufferance, and that "we would, of course, really have preferred Britishers".' Another reader, Jan Novak from Randwick, wrote, 'I fail to see why immigrants from Europe should be treated as second-class human beings.'[14]

For Mum's parents the humiliation took other forms. This included a dependency on their daughters, whose English was better and for whom a grasp of Australian culture and bureaucracy came sooner and more easily. The parents were forced to rely on their children's assistance to conduct adult transactions, like talking to government agencies and solicitors and doctors.

Mum helped her father study for exams to obtain a boiler attendant's certificate in 1968, which he needed for his job at the tobacco factory. She also got him his first bank loan.

The bank kept knocking Alfredo back. After she got her job with the GIO, Mum told her dad she'd have a try. She put the application in at the Commonwealth Bank in the city and walked to St Mary's Cathedral to pray that it came through for her father.

'That's when I said, "God, if I don't get this loan for my dad I'm never going to church for the rest of my life." And would you believe—he got the loan.'

XII

Shame, I found unexpectedly, was a recurring theme in my family's story.

Shame takes many forms. It can be political, cultural, physical. You don't need to have done anything wrong to feel shame.

The shame of the Italian prisoners whose country didn't want to know about their experiences, because they were a reminder of its Fascist past. The shame of being Italian in a country that needed their labour but didn't want its British blood to be diluted by their inferior, southern European kind. The shame of being bullied. The shame of surviving trauma. The shame of disfigurement.

Shame is socially constructed and historically contingent, brought into being because of dominant cultural ideas about physical well-being, honour and civilisation. It is imposed by others, and works to regulate identity, to mark out certain social groups. At its core, shame is about who you are and its power over the individual can be profound. Shame causes you to hide, to cover up, to turn inwards, to make yourself as small as you can possibly be, so as not to be seen. It can cause you to bury your story and repress your suffering.[15]

As I excavated the stories of my grandfather, mother and myself and found, embedded in them, the different shames of my family, I was struck by a question. Was I trying to undo the shame—these shames that should never have been felt?

Why did my grandfather and the other Italian prisoners remain silent about their wartime experiences and the unjust treatment of their suffering on their return, when in fact their resistance against deplorable twentieth-century ideologies was brave and possibly entailed great personal sacrifice?

Why was my mother so determined not to be Italian when she cherished her childhood and the culture she left behind in coming to Australia? When buried inside her was a deep love for the place where she was born and that had shaped her identity—a love that she hadn't been permitted to feel, wouldn't let herself feel?

Why did I let that man at Parliament House on the day of the apology to the Stolen Generations make me feel so ashamed of my injured body? Why do I never go out in public without my prosthetic legs? My scars and missing limbs are a mark of my survival, a survival I fought so hard for, that many believed was impossible. Why be ashamed of that?

I don't want to think too deeply about those who would make us feel ashamed. Such feelings, I am certain, emanate from a sense of threat—a threat, perhaps, to the stories we tell each other about ourselves. Because maybe Fascism was not just an aberration. Because perhaps the idea of a British-based Australian identity is actually a tenuous thing, and white people's claim on this country—with its prior Aboriginal inhabitants and their continuing suffering—is more constructed, mythical, than many want to believe. Because an able body is not a birthright, and bodies lucky to be born perfect and whole can lose their intactness in an instant.

I am more interested in understanding why we who would be shamed let ourselves be shamed. Is it because we don't want to upset these more comfortable, accepted narratives either? Do we bury our stories, repress our suffering, to escape the perception of shame? By not speaking, can we pretend to have a regular life? I had a perfectly standard story, one I was happy to tell, until I survived a cataclysmic event. I responded by hiding away until I was healed enough, had accomplished enough, and once again had an acceptable story to tell. What had I done in not letting myself be seen?

The book *A Woman in Berlin* purports to be the anonymous true account of a German woman, a journalist, raped by occupying Russian forces in Berlin at the end of the Second World War (its authenticity is contested).[16] The woman began a diary on 20 April 1945, which ended shortly after the return of her boyfriend from the front two months later. He left her after learning about her and her neighbours' responses to the rapes. 'You've all turned into a bunch of shameless bitches, every one of you,' the boyfriend told her.[17] He was appalled by their stoicism, their ability to joke about the rapes, by the fact that many women took Russians as protectors to keep others away and save themselves from worse horrors. The women's shamelessness was the unacceptable part—not only for the boyfriend but also, it might be said, for many German readers of *A Woman in Berlin* who were not ready to confront this painful episode in the nation's history when the book was first published in the German language in 1959.[18] The anonymous author was criticised for her 'shameless immorality' and the book went out of print for many decades.[19]

Shame may be thrust upon us; we do not have to accept it.

Was my great-aunt Amelia 'shameless'? Amelia didn't have a regular life. Her life is full of gaps, of details that are impossible to verify; it resists neat explanation. But I know enough to wonder whether the strong appeal her story has for me is just this: she refused to conform, refused to be caged, refused, in fact, to be shamed. Her life weaves in and out of those of my relatives, she appears and disappears, yet she presents such a different reality that it set me off on my investigations into my Italian family. Amelia defied norms, lived a life most women of her time wouldn't have dared, was governed by her heart's desires and love for her family—not by her fears. She pushed the boundaries of that which would confine her: expectations of society and family; rules of the forced labour camp; restrictions of America's post-war immigration laws. She exercised the power of free choice and refused respectability. She stands in opposition to the vision of quiet normality that the rest of my family, including me, have sought.

They say shame can be liberating, a change agent for the self—when one no longer cares about being ashamed. It is too late for my grandfather. My mother is not there yet, and may never be. Nor am I.

XIII

Alfredo had been in Australia just over two years when he found out that Amelia was dying in America.

He was working at the tobacco factory on Amelia Street, a job he couldn't afford to lose. His wife and children, recently arrived immigrants in a country they were still learning to navigate, depended heavily on him. It must have been a heartbreaking realisation for him: knowing he was not in a position to travel to the United States and give comfort to his sister in her final days.

Before coming to Australia, Alfredo had tried to join his sister in the United States. He had applied to migrate there under provisions in American immigration laws for family reunion (Amelia became a US citizen in 1957). Amelia put great faith in her brother's being able to join her in America. But Australia, more open to Italian immigrants at the time, accepted Alfredo's application first. Once his children were settled into schools in Australia, my grandfather didn't pursue the US option further.

Sometime after Amelia's cancer diagnosis, when she knew she did not have long left to live, her trusted friend 'Miss Trieste' contacted her siblings in Italy. At first when I saw Amelia's reference to 'Miss Trieste' in her diary, I thought it might have been a pet name: perhaps the woman was from Trieste, or had some other connection to home. But no. Miss Trieste was an older Italian-born lady and the executor of Amelia's will, and it was in that document I discovered her first name actually *was* Trieste. Miss Trieste implored Amelia's siblings to come to America to see their dying sister before it was too late. Only one family member, Rosina— Amelia's elder sister by four years—made the trip. Rosina arrived in America about a week before Amelia passed away in hospital.

Rosina discovered Amelia's diary while sorting through her possessions in her house. Opening the diary for the first time, she would have been horrified by its contents. Like a precious travelling artefact, the book—a receptacle of unwitnessed suffering—followed our family across the world, from Rosina in America to Alfredo in Australia and on to other relatives in Italy.

Mum, who was a young teenager at the time, remembers her father's anguish and fury as he read about the abuse Amelia endured at the hands of the restaurant owner. She asked her dad if she could read it too, and he let her. Alfredo must have despaired on reading of Amelia's forlorn hope that he would soon arrive to rescue her.

'*Speriamo bene che Alfredo venga al piu presto e cosi sono un po' sollevanta,*' she wrote. 'I hope that Alfredo comes quickly and then I will be a little relieved.'

Amelia probably saw her brother for the last time in about 1950; neither imagined they would not set eyes on the other again. The tragedy of Amelia's final wretched years in America remained with Alfredo through the rest of his life. My dad, in his chats with his father-in-law while building the back fence of our house in the late 1970s, recalled that whenever the conversation moved to Amelia, Alfredo became upset and withdrew.

'That was it, he stopped talking and never said anything else.'

Nobody in Amelia's family had suspected her life in America was anything other than prosperous and happy. In her letters home, she kept up the pretence that it was. My mother recalls the excitement that greeted the arrival in Trieste of her aunt's parcels from America. Inside these packages were brightly coloured clothes for her nieces and nephews, the likes of which did not exist in post-war Italy, and money for her siblings.

'There was always a feast when one arrived,' said Mum.

Amelia's diary was contained in an 'Agenda Italia 1954' that her faithful suitor, Vincenzo, sent from Naples. Writing evidently brought Amelia solace. Amelia was desperately sad and alone and writing was, in her words, her only comfort, though she sometimes wondered who she was writing to. The extracts of Amelia's diary entries that came into my possession in Trieste centred on her work in the Sicilian's restaurant. According to her Alien File, she began this job in 1953 and remained there for more than a year.

What can I tell you about this man, about what he did to Amelia? He had a wife and grown-up children. He was, from a photo I have seen, pudgy with dark, bushy eyebrows that crowded out his face and small eyes. Amelia referred to him as '*il bos*'. He was vulgar, violent, manipulative. He refused to pay her wages, insisted on controlling her appearance and social interactions, threatened to shoot her with his revolver, and pushed her to near physical and emotional collapse. After hurting her, he cared for her, taking her to hospital to get medical treatment. He brought her food when she was too unwell to work and, when she got better, took her to the cinema to watch the Marilyn Monroe and Barbara Stanwyck films that she loved.

Amelia's accounts of her abuse and suffering were graphic and distressing to read.

In one diary entry, she described asking *il bos* for her wages. He refused, telling her there was no money for *her*, then a moment later demanded she take a ride in his son's brand-new, expensive, yellow-and-black car (she called it a '*carro*'). The following day, after she went to work early at the boss's request, he attacked her—using, she wrote, words that would make your hair stand on end. He punched and kicked her, until she couldn't take it anymore. Afterwards, she wrote, '*tutto se chiuso in me*', 'everything is closed inside me'. The next day Amelia complained about her treatment, and her boss beat her again until her head was spinning. He then took her to the hospital, where a doctor—understanding, Amelia wrote, that she was desperate in her soul and body—gave her injections to calm her.

Her boss, Amelia wrote enigmatically, '*vuole divertirsi e a me come schiava*' ('wants to have fun and [keep] me like a slave'). She was not allowed to talk to or interact with other people.

'I don't look at anyone, I must not smile, I must not put lipstick on, I must not even brush my hair, nothing, nothing,' she wrote. 'When will it end? Will I resist?'

Amelia knew she was close to mental collapse. She suffered terrible nightmares, and wondered how long her nerves would hold out. She suspected her boss and his wife were trying to poison her food, and believed God was punishing her for something she had done.

'When will I be free?' she wondered.

Amelia wished she had someone to help and support her, but there was no one—no family, no friends, except for the kind-hearted Miss Trieste.

'It is as if the world has forgotten me,' she wrote.

Perplexingly, despite the horror of her existence in America, in the final extract I read of her diary, on the third anniversary of her leaving Italy, Amelia wrote that it didn't seem real to her that her dream had finally come true. What dream was that? To come to America, to buy a little house *'tutta per me come l'o sognata da sempre fin da piccola'* ('all for me, like the dream that I have always had since I was little').

Reflecting on this puzzling side to Amelia's character, I was reminded of other appealing but flawed female figures of literature and film, driven by desperate or unsatisfactory circumstances to take risks that ultimately did not pay off for them. I thought of Ingrid Bergman's character, Karin, in *Stromboli*. Karin was a displaced person like Amelia—a Lithuanian refugee—living in a camp in Italy (she also had an affair with a German officer during the war). She married an Italian fisherman in order to escape the camp but, once ensconced in his village in the foothills of the island volcano, found herself in a prison far worse than the displaced persons camp.

The house where Amelia lived at the time of her death, in 1960, was not the only real estate she owned. From her probate file, it appears she had a half-share in another. If home ownership really was Amelia's big American dream, the price she paid for this piece of suburban security was appallingly high.

XIV

It is clear that for my grandparents, Alfredo and Anna, their dream of a better future was realised at the cost of huge social and emotional dislocation for their family.

For my mother, emigration meant a treasured promise of completing high school and attending university was taken from her, as was any possibility of feeling that she ever truly belonged in the society in which she lived. Her father erred in not letting her accept the scholarship to St Vincent's and continue her education; her mother admitted as much in later years. For her part, Mum sees that by not finishing school she lost not only the opportunity to realise her potential but also the chance to ever fit in. Mum was no longer Italian and couldn't feel proud of her heritage, but she was never fully Australian either.

My generation is the beneficiary of all that loss—not that I understood any of this growing up.

I carried small reserves of guilt, though, as a daughter.

I remember an incident in primary school. There was an annual Mother's Day stall. Mum volunteered to work on it and came upon a small, dark blue glass bowl with a lid and delicately painted, colourful flowers. She asked if I would buy it for her but I refused, wanting to choose my own present for her. During the course of the day, the lid of the glass bowl broke, and my mother took it home. She got her preferred Mother's Day gift (as well as my unmemorable one; I have forgotten what it was), but it was broken into many pieces which she had to glue back together. Mum put the broken bowl on a mantelpiece where it remained for years.

Sometimes I've felt I have not been the person my mother wanted me to be. I've railed against her for refusing to approve of the person I was. Learning about Mum's story has shown me that, in reality, it wasn't a matter of my not being the person she wanted me to be. Rather, I was not the person she herself wanted to be but never would be.

My mother carries guilt too.

One evening on the telephone, I asked my mother about her father's death. I saw Nonno for the last time at Canterbury Hospital, a day or so before he passed away in July 1993. I knew that revisiting this period would be difficult for Mum, but I pushed ahead anyway.

'How long was Nonno in hospital before he died?' I asked.

Mum paused, then, like she always did, answered my latest painful question.

It all began, Mum said, when she received a frantic telephone call from my grandmother at 6 am. Alfredo couldn't breathe, Nonna told her. Mum drove straight to her parents' house in Campsie, missing work that day. Her father was still conscious when she arrived.

'I've never told you this,' Mum said, her voice quavering as she recalled that morning. 'He said, "Don't let them take me to hospital, I don't want to go to hospital," and I sent him to hospital. An ambulance came and took him up the street. He never spoke to any of us again.'

I was surprised at how Mum described this episode to me—as if she had done something wrong in calling the ambulance.

She was sobbing. 'If I didn't call the ambulance he may have got his breath back.'

'It was the only decision you could have made, Mum,' I told her. 'You made the right decision for your father—the decision to try to save his life.'

'I'm always the one that has to make these awful decisions.'

'What do you mean?'

'I had to make that decision too—those amputations,' she said, and hung up the phone on me.

Even if my mother could not see it, I could. Our stories were all interconnected. It was impossible to separate what happened to any one of us from the effects it had on other family members. We were all shaped by each other's traumas and suffering, just as we were all shaped by each other's love.

XV

In researching this book, I demanded a lot of my mother in asking her to revisit multiple episodes in her life that were traumatic: her father's unspoken POW experiences; her severance from Italy as a child; her early years as a migrant in Australia; my coma after the crash.

It took a friend to point out my mother's sacrifice in giving me permission not only to probe her pain, but also to write publicly about it. Mum didn't have to. She let me do it—she endured the hurt involved and the return of deeply distressing memories, then accepted whatever consequences would flow from having her life exposed in this way—all because I told her that I needed her to, in order to process my own pain.

In the end, by sharing her memories, my mother gave me an invaluable gift. She enabled me to confront what happened to me, but she did more than that. My interest in Mum's story began with a desire to understand myself better. I wanted to test a theory that by pushing me so hard, Mum sparked in me a fighting spirit that helped me to survive my ordeal and conquer it. Ultimately, I learnt more about the forces that shaped my mother, about what she endured for the love of family, than I did about myself.

Every time Mum and I spoke about the period of my coma after the crash, she provided a new detail I hadn't heard before. We had discussed the surgeries many times, the ongoing requests from doctors to remove yet another body part, the anguish this caused my parents. Each conversation was so difficult—she could only tell me so much; I could only listen to so much—that we always had to stop. In one of our final conversations for this book, my mother again revealed something more.

Mum told me that on the night my second leg was taken, she went to the hotel swimming pool and swam a couple of laps 'to see if I could swim not moving my legs'.

'"Can I swim without legs?" I asked myself. See, when the doctors said they took something else from you, Cynthia, I felt as though they were taking it from me. When you were losing a leg, I was losing a leg.'

Mum's high expectations of her children are outweighed by the depth of her willingness to sacrifice for us. Her anguish at my amputations—her preparedness to let me go, rather than make me live a life without limbs—came from a sense of empathy so deep, she couldn't separate herself from me.

Was it empathy, or was it something else? A love without limits, where the boundaries between self and other are blurred? Is this simply what maternal love is?

Mum and I don't argue any less today. But knowing my mother better for the process of writing this book has enabled me to love her more.

7

Crashing

I

IT HAS TAKEN ME CLOSE TO A DECADE to be able to write about the events of 7 March 2007. I did not expect it would take so long.

I read somewhere that the flight number of the plane that crashed that day no longer exists. The airline—even now it pains me to say its name aloud—no longer has a flight leaving at 6 am from Soekarno-Hatta Airport, Jakarta, to Adisucipto Airport, Yogyakarta. Its early-morning flight on that route is called something else today and leaves at a different time. Almost as if it never was.

I have tried to write about the day before.

The first time was on the Indian Pacific, on the way home from Perth, in late August 2007. Michael and I boarded the train in Kalgoorlie after driving seven hours in a hire car from Perth because of an earlier derailment. I felt each bump of the carriage on the tracks in my wounds and skin grafts and traumatised bones. Every loud noise sounded, to my ears, like a jet aircraft. Sitting in the dining car that first evening, looking out on to the red, dusty landscape, my right leg was bent and hung over the end of the narrow wheelchair I'd been given to use for the train journey. This caused my knee, with its tissue paper-thin skin graft, to start bleeding uncontrollably. My physiotherapist, Caroline, was with us and frantically rang the doctors in Perth who, over the phone, helped her to get the bleeding under control.

I tried writing again one day in 2008 when I was home alone in Canberra. At that moment, I wrote, it was the only thing I could do 'to stop me falling into depression, a black abyss, where I just want to end this life that I do not recognise anymore'.

Both times, the words wouldn't come. It was as though they were stuck somewhere deep in my belly, so inaccessible were they to me. The effort to expel them was exhausting and futile.

Typing these introductory words here, somewhat circuitously because even now I am trying to delay arriving at the critical moment, my heart is pounding in my chest. This time, however, it feels like I'm ready, in as much as when it is done, when the impossible words are finally on the page, it will be a relief.

Still, I have felt nervous leading up to this moment, not knowing what unexpected memories the process would recover. In confronting the reminders of the crash that I have avoided before now my travel companions came back into my daily consciousness, sometimes in the most confused way.

For example, I dreamt about the dead pilot of the 2005 Sea King helicopter crash, whom I wrote about as a journalist. In the dream, I passed the man in a street in Canberra near the Australian National University. He was surrounded by his family and had just received an award or a promotion. I smiled and said to Michael, 'Isn't it good to see him doing so well?'

In the dream, I confused the Sea King pilot with one of the Australian Federal Police officers who died on my flight. I mixed up the crashes, and thought he was in mine. Or was I in his?

There is one more thing. In revisiting the crash, I have not tried to reconstruct the event. I have not tried to embellish, to fill in the gaps of my incomplete recollections with what I imagined happened; nor, by and large, have I sought out witnesses who might remember details I cannot. What I give you is what I am able to give: my memories—after ten years, patchy and faded, no doubt altered by the passage of time, but all mine.

II

I organised a wake-up call for 4 am at the hotel, the upmarket Shangri-La in Jakarta, on the Wednesday, my last and busiest day of the trip.

I was supposed to interview the foreign minister on his VIP flight from Yogyakarta back to Australia later in the afternoon. First, I had to get to Yogyakarta.

My last phone call, late the night before, was to Michael. I told him about my lunch with two colleagues, Morgan Mellish from the *Australian Financial Review* and Mark Forbes from *The Age*. They were Jakarta correspondents, both of whom I'd worked with previously in the press gallery in Canberra. In the hotel restaurant, Morgan was chatty. He talked about many things, while Forbes and I mostly just listened. Morgan was easy to like: laid-back, friendly, intelligent, with a wry sense of humour. He had just won a Walkley Award (Australian journalism's highest honour) for his reporting of a tax scandal involving a former Reserve Bank of Australia board member and he happily told us the story behind the story.

The telephone's trilling woke me and I switched on the light. I can still picture the hotel room. The bedhead was along the right wall as you entered the room. The window was to my right as I sat up in bed to lift the handset. The desk where I wrote my final story about the Sea King crash was opposite me. The bathroom, where I had a shower that morning—the last I would have standing up—was to the left of the bed, immediately inside the door of the room. I remember that final shower: I can still see, feel, the running water pouring from the nozzle onto my upright body, running down my legs onto my feet.

I got dressed. To my eternal regret, I selected business attire appropriate for conducting a formal interview with the foreign minister as if we were in his office in Parliament House in Canberra. I put on a black suit with a knee-length skirt (I can't remember which shirt) and a pair of dressy, low-heeled shoes. I have wondered, often and pointlessly, whether things might have turned out differently if I'd been wearing different clothes. Had I worn tough leather work boots, as I did covering ministerial visits in Afghanistan and Iraq, and long pants instead of a skirt, would they have protected me from the fire? Could I have saved one of my feet, one of my legs? Could I have kept two knees instead of one?

When I fly now (in business class to give me space to take off my prostheses because they hurt if I leave them on for long periods) I sometimes look around at the female passengers dressed in corporate wear. They are so serene, so unaware, I think to myself. I observe their high heels, their open-toed shoes, and I want to warn them about their clothing choices. 'Don't you realise the risk?' I want to say.

In the hotel room, I packed a small bag. Most of my clothes, including my running gear (I had jogged on the treadmill in the hotel gym the previous morning), were in a larger bag that was travelling in the minister's VIP plane.

I went downstairs into the cream-and-brown marble foyer. Liz O'Neill from the Australian embassy was waiting for me and we walked through the glass doors, into the early-morning darkness, to get a taxi to the airport.

III

Before writing this chapter, I forced myself to watch television footage of the burning plane.

I read, for the first time, the coverage of the pilot's trial over his role in the crash, his conviction for negligence, then his successful appeal. I pored over the report of the National Transportation Safety Committee investigation into the crash. I tried to understand, from its technical analysis—of wing flaps, runway thresholds, thrust reversers—how a plane of the kind I travelled on normally lands, and what went wrong on my flight.

Reading the report dislodged one memory—just a small one—of fastening and tightening my seatbelt when I first became aware that something wasn't right.

In the midst of reading and writing about the crash, I had to go to Brisbane for a conference at the University of Queensland. I had to get on a plane.

I fly as infrequently as possible these days, but when I do I always board first, before the other passengers. My wheelchair is taken to the door of the aircraft, and I walk the few steps to my seat. A flight attendant comes up to me to give me my own personal safety briefing. I am told where the exits are, how if there is an emergency, somebody will help me. Usually I just listen to them with a blank face, though inside my head a cynical voice says, 'We both know this information will be useless if there really is an emergency.'

This time, curiously, the attendant, a kindly older woman, returned to ask whether I minded that she had given me this briefing. I told her that I didn't, but added that I had been in a plane crash and nobody was there to help me. 'Not that I expected anyone to come to my aid.' I was, after all, engulfed in a raging inferno.

In the crash report, I read that, while the pilots escaped unharmed, one of the five flight attendants died. I don't know her name. She was seated in the business class passenger section. I don't know whether she died in the plane, or from her injuries afterwards, in hospital. It is difficult to find information about the Indonesian victims; there was very little about them in the Australian coverage of the crash.

'You should have told me you were in a crash,' the flight attendant on the Brisbane flight said. 'It would help us, and you.'

She returned again to assure me that, if there was an emergency on her flight, she would not forget me. She asked if I wanted to move from the aisle to the window seat.

'No, thank you,' I replied.

I was in an aisle seat on the flight to Yogyakarta and survived. I never want the window seat now.

Telling every flight attendant who gives me a safety briefing that I have been in a plane crash before does not seem appropriate. If passengers knew that sitting among them was someone who had previously been in a plane crash, would that not be unnerving for them? If the air crew knew I had been in a crash before, what would they do differently? Would the pilots try harder on the landing?

One consequence of having been in the crash is that I cannot tell, now, what a 'normal' landing feels like. Every landing feels, to me, like the plane is crashing. I compulsively tighten my seat-belt, which I never take off, every couple of minutes throughout the entire flight.

'Is the plane going too fast?' I whisper to Michael as we approach the runway to land—not too loud, so as not to disturb the other passengers—and I grip his hand ever more tightly.

He assures me it isn't, but I am doubtful.

'It feels like it's going very fast. Is the plane crashing? I think we are going to crash.'

I expect to crash. Crashing has become my normal.

I do appreciate every kindness the air crews show me, though. Once, on a flight back to Perth for surgery in 2008, a pilot sought me out and congratulated me on my bravery for flying again. It was a lovely thing for him to do.

I can't help but regard all pilots warily now.

IV

We were both too sleepy to talk in the taxi, and soon Liz was checking us in at the airline counter, using her fluent Indonesian, which she spoke with a heavy Australian accent.

Liz had done the same for me two days before, when, booked on an earlier domestic flight from Semarang to Jakarta after arriving in Indonesia on the VIP, I found myself with a ticket, paid for by my office in Australia, but no seat on the plane. Liz—outgoing, confident, persistent, able—took charge. She spent an hour negotiating with airline staff and airport police until, somehow, they found me a seat in the first row of business class, on the left side of the plane. As we stood waiting for the unhelpful airline officials to yield, Liz talked about her eight-month-old baby girl, who was at home in Jakarta. I asked her how she found juggling an overseas posting with a young family, for I hoped one day to be doing something similar as a foreign correspondent.

This was my third visit as a journalist to Indonesia. I'd been to a 'young leaders dialogue' in Bandung and, later, to Bali with the foreign minister on an anniversary of the terrorist bombings of 2002. I was interested in the country not as a tourist, but as a political journalist. Difference and ignorance on each side under-pinned the testy Australia–Indonesia bilateral relationship, which made the journalist's job an especially important one. I was interested enough in the country to have started Indonesian language lessons in Canberra.

After checking in, without any further hassles on this early morning in Jakarta, Liz and I walked off to find coffee. We bumped into Morgan at the newsagency.

The three of us, along with a couple of other Australian and local journalists and another embassy staffer, had shared bar food, drinks and stories in the hotel the night before, after finding ourselves stranded for an extra night in Jakarta. We'd all missed our 7 pm flight to Yogyakarta when the foreign minister's itinerary ran late. Forbes was already in Yogyakarta, having decided to fly up early, leaving me to cover the minister's afternoon in Jakarta.

Because I was travelling home with the minister's entourage, Liz changed my booking for me and got us both business-class seats on the early-morning flight to Yogyakarta. Morgan ended up on the same flight as Liz and me when, unexpectedly, a spare ticket from the embassy became available.

Chatting in the newsagency with Liz and Morgan before the flight, our conversation turned to Indonesia's air crash record. There had been a plane crash two months before, in January, involving a low-cost Indonesian carrier, in which all on board were killed. Liz declared she would never fly with any Indonesian airline other than the national carrier; Morgan said he would fly with any airline and that a bad crash history would not stop him.

Listening to them, I thought to myself how grateful I was not to be flying with a local budget carrier that day.

The three of us wandered off and found the coffee shop. We had juice and coffee, then headed to the departure gate.

As I boarded, I saw the two AFP officers—one of whom, Brice Steele, I had chatted to at the counterterrorism meeting earlier that week—sitting in the front row. Liz said hello to them as she passed. I sat in an aisle seat, maybe three rows back from the front on the right side of the plane. Liz sat next to me, in the window seat. Morgan sat across the aisle and slightly ahead of me on the left side of the plane.

We buckled up. I declined a newspaper. The aircraft took off.

V

The flight from Jakarta to Yogyakarta was meant to last an hour and ten minutes.

A flight attendant offered us breakfast. I recalled the strange meal I was given on the previous flight from Semarang: a sweet bright pink concoction I could not identify. I politely declined.

I did not read—it was too early. I tried to sleep.

The awareness that something was wrong came gradually at first. It was nearing the end of the flight when everyone realised the plane was going too fast to be so low in the sky.

Passengers were commenting on the plane's speed. Liz said something about it; so did I.

The ground was coming into view, I could see it through the window, getting closer at an alarming rate.

I do not recall any warnings over the intercom system. But we put on our seatbelts, very quickly.

Shit, I was thinking. Is this really happening?

Then: Oh God.

I grabbed onto the arm rests. So did Liz.

The situation got more desperate. People started yelling out, 'We are coming in too fast!'

As if the pilot was going to hear, was going to slow down.

I started screaming but, really, the sounds were more like little muffled yelps. Screams were rising in my throat but I was so panicked—also so disbelieving—the full sound would not come out.

Other passengers were yelling and screaming.

In my mind my thoughts were racing and conflicting. 'Okay, God, I am going to die. No, it's going to be okay, something will happen, the pilot will just go around. Shit, actually, this could be it, this could be the end, maybe this is how I am going to die.'

Then the plane hit the tarmac.

This is what I wrote in 2008: 'I remember coming down, I remember the jolts as the plane hit the ground, bang, smack, collision, bouncing up and down, things ramming into me. It all happened so fast.'

I do not know for certain if I lost consciousness. I think I did, momentarily at least. I do not know how much time elapsed after the plane came to a halt but, suddenly, I became aware that we were stationary, and that the seat in front of me was crushed into my body, into my stomach, into my chest.

I do not recall seeing what other passengers were doing, whether they were conscious or not, whether Liz was conscious. I did not look beyond the crumpled seat in front of me. I may have seen smoke; I can't be sure. I was unaware of anything in that moment other than the seat that was rammed into me, and that I was burning.

First, I heard the sound of crackling, the crackling of the fire that was consuming the cabin around me. Then I realised that my left leg was burning—that the fire was consuming me too. My leg was like a plank of wood in a fireplace. The fire was devouring my leg—it was actually both my legs and left arm, but I was only aware of my left leg burning—from the floor up.

I could hear the fire, I could feel it tearing through my limbs, but I could not see it. Nor do I recall any pain in this moment of conscious burning.

I had two thoughts.

One: So this is what it feels like to burn alive.

I imagine, in this instant, that I was recalling the Sea King accident. Some of the dead had evidence of smoke in their lungs, which meant they were still alive after impact. I remembered the devastation of their parents upon learning this.

A second thought: I am not ready to die. I have to try to get out of here.

I was still locked into my seat by my seatbelt. My right arm (the only one of my limbs that didn't burn) was trapped under the compressed seat in front of me. I pulled my arm out from under the crushed airline seat, reached down to my waist, and unlatched the seatbelt.

I cannot explain what happened next. This was the moment to which I owed my life, but how it was possible I will never fully comprehend. Immediately upon undoing the seatbelt I felt myself fall through the bottom of the plane.

VI

According to the National Transportation Safety Committee's crash report, the pilot landed the aircraft too fast, too steep. He ignored fifteen automated warnings and two calls from his co-pilot to go around, when to do so would have prevented the crash.[1]

Twenty-one people died, twenty of them passengers.

I resist calling what happened to the flight an 'accident'. I always thought that word signified some element of an event being beyond one's control, a case of bad luck. *Webster's Dictionary* defines an 'accident' as a 'sudden event or change occurring without intent or volition through carelessness, unawareness, ignorance, or a combination of causes and producing an unfortunate result'. Still, the word seems too generous to me.

A plane's normal airspeed on landing is 134 knots. This plane's speed was 221 knots. The pilot had approached the airport too high, and in trying to reach the runway descended too steeply, causing the airspeed to increase excessively. Because the plane was flying too fast, the co-pilot refused to extend the flaps as instructed by the pilot (which would have helped slow the plane down). The pilot said the co-pilot never informed him he was travelling at excessively high speed. The pilot ignored the co-pilot's pleas to 'go around'. The co-pilot, who had not been trained in what to do in such an emergency, failed at that point to take control of the aircraft from the pilot, as he was supposed to do.

The plane bounced twice and overran the departure end of the runway, crossed a road and hit an embankment, its engines smashing into a concrete gutter. The aircraft stopped in a rice paddy field, whereupon it was 'destroyed by the impact forces and an intense, fuel-fed, post-impact fire'. The engines and landing gear separated from the aircraft, the right wing was severed from the fuselage and swung around the body of the plane, coming to rest on top of the left wing. The cockpit folded back and came to rest inverted on top of the forward passenger cabin, where I was sitting.

I imagine that this, the folding back of the cockpit, at least partly explains how I fell out of the burning plane. (Nobody has confirmed it for me, and it is almost impossible to visualise, but I assume the plane must have broken apart right under my seat, that I must have been suspended over the crack, with my seatbelt the only thing stopping me from dropping through the hole below.)

Making the situation worse, the Yogyakarta airport's rescue and firefighting service vehicles could not reach the aircraft. They were stopped by the airport's perimeter fence and there was no access road. Their spray guns couldn't reach the plane so they deployed hoses which were punctured by rescue vehicles and onlookers' vehicles driving over them. This 'may have resulted in increasing the number of fatalities and injuries'.

It feels surreal to write these clinical sentences, to digest this report as I would if I were writing a news story or feature article on someone else's tragedy or misfortune, when this one was mine.

After the crash, when I was recovering in the rehabilitation hospital at Shenton Park, I declined to receive the Indonesian diplomatic officials who came to visit me on multiple occasions. They left behind flowers and cards that went unread. It was like I blamed the whole country for what had happened to me. Like I experienced the plane crash almost as a betrayal by a nation that I had been prepared to invest myself in.

'To forgive is not always appropriate or virtuous,' I read somewhere, and the words resonated with me.[2] It read to me like a permission of sorts—not that permission was needed—to feel whatever I needed to feel about the plane crash, about those responsible. Forgiveness must be consistent with the dignity of the victim.

I can't say I've forgiven the pilot for what happened, because for years I have refused to think about him.

According to the National Transportation Safety Committee's crash report, the pilot's behaviour is best understood as a condition called 'fixation'.

Fixation: A state of being locked onto one task, or one view of a situation, even as evidence accumulates that attention is necessary elsewhere, or that the particular view is incorrect.

The 'tunnelling' that can occur during stressful situations is an example of fixation, the report explains. The 'stressful situation' was that the pilot found himself too high on approach. The report hypothesises that 'a pilot may be convinced that a high, unstabilised approach to landing is salvageable even when other flight crew members, air traffic control, and cockpit instrument strongly suggest that the approach cannot be completed within acceptable parameters'.

Maybe this happened. Maybe the pilot, who earlier in the flight had been singing in the cockpit, suddenly lost his senses on landing.

I do not hate the men who crashed my plane. I simply choose not to think about them.

VII

I landed in a rice paddy field, in puddles of water.

My body was on fire and I rolled in the water to put out the flames. I was alone, lying next to the plane, which I think was to my left, aware of it but not seeing it.

I stared at my left hand. The skin was melting away like a waxy film, separating from my fingers as I watched. I was startled, momentarily, and amazed. My skin was slipping off my hand like a translucent, waxy glove.

Lying on my stomach (I think), my body no longer on fire, I was terrified, thinking the plane that was so close to me was about to explode and kill me. But I couldn't get up from the watery field.

Something felt very wrong; I suspected then that my back was probably broken. I could still feel my legs, but I couldn't move myself, could not even drag my body away from the burning plane.

Looking up, I saw two Indonesian men watching me from a distance in the field.

'Help me, help me, please!' I screamed out desperately to the men.

My breathing was heavy, furious, and I sobbed between every breath.

The two men, who were slightly built, came to me and awkwardly started carrying me away from the plane, but did not get very far. Whether I was too heavy, or they were scared of the raging fire consuming the plane, I don't know, but they stopped and let go of me. I looked back and saw the burning plane still close by and cried out to them again, pleading with them to take me further away. I was terrified the plane was going to explode.

'Please take me away from the plane, please,' I begged.

After a time—it may have been seconds—they picked me up again and this time carried me up to a barbed-wire fence, where we could go no further. By now I was whimpering, in terrible pain and struggling to breathe. The only way to get out of the rice paddy field was to get over the fence.

Soon after, an ambulance arrived and backed into the other side of the wire fence. The men who were with me—it might have been the same two, though I don't know—began trying to lift me and pass me over the fence. I was terrified, knowing my back was broken, that I should not be moved in this way, and pleaded with them not to throw my body over the fence. The men, who spoke no English, made some reassuring sounds and somehow got my body over the fence. I was placed inside the ambulance and taken to Sardjito Hospital.

These brave men must have saved my life, but I don't know who they were.

Later, when I was in the burns unit in Perth, I was aware that my parents had made contact with a local Indonesian man who lived near the airport in Yogyakarta. I have seen a photograph of him: his light brown eyes look gentle.

According to newspaper reports, it was this man, a farmer and department store worker, and another, a labourer who transported sacks of cement on foot around work sites in the city, who carried me away from the plane.

I don't recall having many conscious thoughts as I lay waiting for the ambulance. I was incredulous at what had just occurred. I was also scared. I knew my injuries were very, very grave and that I was possibly going to die. I was completely at the mercy of people I could not understand, who could not understand me. I didn't know what was going to happen to me, but I desperately wanted to live.

I don't recall thinking much about God. In this desperate, shocking moment I did not feel His presence at all. I just felt abandoned.

VIII

The first thing I remember about Sardjito Hospital was lying face down on a stretcher in a corridor surrounded by other bodies also on stretchers, begging passers-by for water.

I remember an Indonesian man, concerned about my modesty, kindly pulling my skirt down over my legs as I lay on the stretcher. It was a small gesture, but it gave me a modicum of dignity when

I had lost all sense of control over my person. This might have occurred in the corridor, or possibly it was while I lay on the stretcher in the field before I was put into the ambulance.

In the corridor, among the other injured people, I saw doctors and nurses walking by. I was asked my nationality a few times, and managed to get the word out: 'Australian.'

I pleaded, again and again, for some water. My thirst was excruciating. Eventually, somebody held up a bottle, briefly, to my lips.

At some point, probably when I was taken for X-rays, I was turned onto my back.

Eventually my colleague, Mark Forbes, found me on a trolley in the corridor, waiting to be X-rayed. He and his local assistant had been searching for me (the injured passengers were scattered throughout different hospitals in Yogyakarta, making it difficult for embassy staff to locate their nationals).

A year after the crash, I asked Forbes what happened that morning, when he found me.

In an email (because it was too hard for me to talk about it), Forbes told me he'd received a call at his hotel in Yogyakarta at 7.15 am from his driver, who told him there had been a plane crash. Forbes rang his assistant and together they headed out to the airport. On the way, a series of ambulances passed them going in the other direction, and Forbes asked his driver to turn around and follow them. At the first hospital they came to (the air force hospital) he found a DFAT official who told him the Australian embassy didn't have enough people on the ground to cover all of the hospitals; could Forbes help? The official gave him the address of the hospital where the most seriously injured were being taken and Forbes headed out there, calling my editor, Alan Oakley, on the way.

When Forbes arrived at Sardjito Hospital he found a chaotic scene: injured people were arriving in ambulances and others were turning up in private cars. Hospital staff told him there was a Western woman inside, but he couldn't get any more information and was blocked—along with the rest of the local media, who by now were gathering around—from entering the front doors of the hospital. Forbes kept asking about me and eventually a nurse confirmed my name. Hearing this, he and his assistant snuck into the hospital via a side entrance. They asked after me everywhere, running from ward to ward trying to find me.

When Forbes found me, I was 'in a pretty bad way'.

'I don't think I've seen anyone more distressed than you were,' he wrote.

'You were crying. You kept telling me you wanted to die. You said you were paralysed and could not feel your legs.'

My colleague tried to reassure me that it was just the burns and I asked him to call Michael, which he did.

I remember making this request: all I could think of when I saw Forbes was that he had to contact Michael and tell him what had happened to me.

Forbes also called the DFAT official, who soon arrived at Sardjito Hospital (another injured Australian was at the same hospital), and my editor. He urged them to organise a medivac to get me out of Yogyakarta. Forbes stayed with me most of the morning, including as I was moved into the intensive care unit, then he went off to try to locate Morgan.

The rest of the day was a long, agonising wait, first for the Australian doctor, whom I was promised was going to come and see me, and then the medivac. I was scared, crying, in intense pain (I'm told Indonesian doctors were reluctant to give stronger drugs than paracetamol due to fear of addiction). When the Australian doctor arrived, he found me severely dehydrated and barely conscious. The official from the Australian embassy stayed with me from the middle of the day, ensuring that I did not lose my bed, which was threatened at one point, and helped organise my medivac. This was difficult, I'm told, because the airport was closed and I had spinal damage.

The long hours were interspersed with visits from different officials to my room. I managed a smile for Alexander Downer (robot-like, I adopted a professional demeanour when I saw him, as if I were still on the job). When the Sultan of Yogyakarta, whom the Australian foreign minister had planned to meet that day, entered my room though, I remember thinking, For God's sake, leave me alone.

I spoke to Michael and my father.

Australian journalists I knew filtered in, concerned for me (though, even then, I feared becoming somebody else's news story).

Years later, on the internet, I came across news photographs of me taken by a stringer from Reuters. I am lying on a blue stretcher in a blue gown in Sardjito Hospital. My eyes are closed, my hands rest on my stomach, the left one is bandaged, my shoulders are bare and I am surrounded by Indonesian medical staff. One of the medics is holding up a couple of drips, another appears to be adjusting the position of my head. They were taken, these intimate photos of my private devastation, unbeknownst to me, somewhere deep inside an inner ward of the hospital.

Somehow, in that Yogyakarta hospital, I already suspected I was going to lose my legs. By the time I touched down in Perth at 2 am local time—eighteen hours after the crash—I knew in my heart that it was a certainty.

IX

Liz and Morgan died in the plane crash, as did three other Australians who worked in the embassy in Jakarta: Mark Scott and Brice Steele, both AFP officers, and Allison Sudradjat, an AusAID official who headed Australia's aid program in Indonesia.

I did not know Mark or Allison, and had only talked briefly to Brice. Liz I'd only met during the trip to Indonesia; Morgan I'd known longer, though not very well. But the memory of Liz and Morgan, having spent that morning and the previous two days and evening with them, and their proximity to me in the plane, is with me every single day.

I often see Morgan's face in those of strangers on the street. That Liz left behind a baby daughter who is growing up without her mother (in the care of her devoted father) is something I think about all the time.

There is no rational explanation as to why I survived and the others did not. We are all victims of a terrible injustice but they lost so much more than I did. They lost their lives.

I had not thought much about 'survivor guilt' before now. Having spent the last two years writing this book, I can identify with this impulse, though. There are other contributing reasons for my manic busyness since the crash, and I have explored some of them in these pages. But the need to justify my earthly presence is doubtless one of the reasons I have sometimes felt myself spinning in crazed circles, almost fearful of slowing or stopping, as if constant achievement is critical to my continued being. While there is no logical reason why I should feel guilty for not having died when others did, there is, without doubt, an obligation that weighs heavily to make mine a life worthy of surviving.

I have also, in the course of writing, had cause to think about the idea of justice. A concept with no singular meaning, justice can signify different things to different people who have experienced grave wrongdoing. Of course, the injury or crime is so great for some, there can be no possibility of ever obtaining justice.

Great loss and suffering, it is said, can constitute a kind of individual moral authority around the preconditions for one's pursuit of justice.[3] There is truth in this. Losing sight of the victim's right to shape their own path to justice can mean compounding the original wrong done.

The Italian Military Internees, because they were never recognised as forced labourers by Germany or the international courts, have not had justice for what happened to them in the Nazi camps. Some of their descendants are still waiting and still fighting. I think about how Alfredo carried his Alkett pass in his pocket the entire 1000-kilometre journey home, much of it on foot, from the POW camp through the cold of the early European spring, from Berlin to Trieste. Was he thinking about justice? Did he live his life in the hope that one future day he might obtain some sort of acknowledgement for what happened in Germany, and that retaining documentary evidence could be important for when the time came?

My preconditions for justice included a refusal to think about the pilot who took my legs. I never wanted to know anything about the man: his name, why he did what he did, what happened to him at his trial and appeal, whether or not he was allowed to fly again, whether he is flying passenger aeroplanes now. It was a conscious choice: I didn't want to let the crash take from me more than it already had. I knew that if, in the months and years after the crash, I had allowed myself to go down such a path, there was a risk that I would have lost my chance at a 'normal' life.

Spurred on by a deeply ingrained belief that I am the master of my fate, that I hold the power inside to make myself happy, I decided not to let grief and bitterness derail me. I would not live out the rest of my life as a plane crash survivor. In so doing, I gave myself the best chance to achieve happiness in my life—a life that involved Michael, possibly a family, and a new fulfilling career.

Another of my preconditions for justice was the authority to tell my story when I was ready and on my terms. I waited ten years. The crash and my injuries were experiences that altered me, inside and out, and left me feeling permanently cut off from a world in which, after so many years of searching, I had just found a place. I had to look to history to find any parallel to my own traumas. Quite unexpectedly I found a connection in my own family's stories.

The stories of my grandfather and mother were, of themselves, unremarkable ones. They reflected the tragedies and ruptures of the twentieth century, including a world war and post-war mass migration, that uprooted and derailed the lives of millions of other people. Yet, somehow, these stories brought me out of the silence the crash had imposed on me. That I was finally able to give expression to an event that had been indescribable for a decade, that had remained hidden away in cardboard boxes in the garage unable to be processed, was only possible by first uncovering and writing the stories of my family. Their stories allowed me to see a tragic event that has always felt devoid of meaning—one so random and senseless—as having a significance, one to be discovered beyond the incident itself. The years I spent immersed in the hardships of family members from different times and contexts ultimately gave me the perspective I needed to write about mine.

Researching my grandfather's past affected me in surprising ways. His war experiences gave me permission to express feelings I'd had but never articulated and helped me to feel less isolated about my own situation. The commonality I found between his and my stories, despite their differences, gave me a distance and a way of seeing suffering as something that was fundamentally human—and shared.

Our stories are fragmented. I couldn't go back and speak to my grandparents about their experiences; the story of Nonno's imprisonment is permanently fractured and will never be whole. The fragments are both physical and metaphysical. There are missing memories—and there are memories that are very much present, feelings I have even though the physical body parts to which they belong are no longer there. I still feel, occasionally and unexpectedly, the sore toe or itchy arch of a foot or cramped calf that remembers many years of classical ballet classes and the joy of running laps of the Bay Run in Sydney.

The memories of my family, incomplete as they are, created for me a fuller self-understanding; they grounded me and bound me to a shared life that preceded me and will follow mine. I now see what happened ten years ago as part of a more enduring history: my family's, one that begins (at least in my own consciousness) with Alfredo's wartime imprisonment and continues with my mother's uprooting from Europe.

'All time is eternally present and so all time is ours,' Jeanette Winterson wrote.[4]

These pieces of personal history, these broken memories of my family, are a collective history that has been made present for me, and for my son too.

The meaning, then, comes from writing it all down: a family history whose details were previously mostly unknown to me, because, for those who lived them, they were impossible to tell, but also impossible to forget. I have broken the trend in my family of not talking about the past and carrying so much pain and trauma alone. Perhaps I have achieved a modicum of justice for my nonno, who was denied recognition from the courts? For my mother, if nothing else, the research I did on Australia of the 1950s reassured her that the prejudice she felt as a girl, that caused her so much hurt, was not something imagined.

I avoided examining my wounds for so long, thinking if I did it would break me, but, in the end, telling my story came as a kind of liberation.

In a way, this book is my justice.

X

What of Amelia?

Reading the extracts of her diary, I pondered why Amelia decided to document her abuse in America. It was her first diary; she started it three years after emigrating. Why then? Why, knowing she was going to die, did she leave her diary behind to be discovered? Why did she not destroy it?

Amelia was lonely and the diary was her confidante; she shared with it things she could not tell her family, who were oceans away. Amelia also felt an acute sense of injustice at her situation, trapped by a tyrannical boss who was exploiting her. She sought the help of a solicitor, but he apparently sided with her boss and refused to take on her case.

Did Amelia foresee that one day someone would find her diary and understand what she endured? Did she hope to be remembered by the future—this woman who felt as if the world, her present, had forgotten her? A woman who can only be understood in the context of her time, yet who was not of her time.

Amelia cast a shadow over this book and the telling of the stories of her brother, his daughter and me. Her heroic acts to save Alfredo in Germany in the closing years of the Second World War—real or embellished with the retelling over time—provided the original inspiration to write about my family. I got so lost in her story at times I forgot I was writing about myself at all. Searching for Amelia's story was endlessly frustrating and occasionally deeply gratifying. Like an archaeological excavation, the search for Amelia is ongoing and will never be finished. Each find, from the tiniest fossil (her connection, as a young dancer, to the famous comedian Dapporto) to the buried walls of ancient script (her diary extract), came as an unexpected marvel. Who knows what evidence of her life is still out there somewhere, missed in the dig?

I continued to make discoveries about Amelia's life until the final days of writing this book.

Amelia's Alien File was the last personal document I unearthed and it offered further morsels about her life—including details about her 'Istria' connections that were not mentioned in the carefully selected extracts from her diary.

The Alien File arrived in my email inbox stamped with the intimidating imprimatur of the US Justice Department. It contained a series of photographs of Amelia I had never seen before—actually, they were more like old-fashioned photocopies, so stark and bare in detail I wondered if they were an artist's impressions of my great-aunt. The file disclosed other employers Amelia had, including a local fast food chain, and the fact that on her original application for immigration made at Bagnoli, she listed her occupation as 'knitter'. The file revealed that a female 'friend' in the United States unknown to anyone in my family today paid for Amelia's passage to America. There was also the affidavit Amelia swore in front of the US Immigrant Inspector in Naples. He happened to be the same official who approved a visa for the Italian actress Gina Lollobrigida. In a story similar to Amelia's, Lollobrigida was apparently entitled to one as the wife of a Yugoslav refugee (the actress and her doctor husband, in the end, emigrated to Canada).

Amelia's Alien File

From the Alien File I know that Amelia was granted permanent residence in America as a 'Venezia Giulia Refugee'. In a document entitled 'Statement of Facts for Preparation of Petition', Amelia gave her last place of residence as Fiume (just beyond the Istrian peninsula, the city, known as Rijeka today, was an Italian territory before 1947). She claimed to have lived there from 1937 until

1946 (from age 20 to 29), and that she had to leave when Italy lost the city to Yugoslavia. Amelia was indeed (or claimed to be) one of the *esuli*, the exiled ethnic Italians whose homelands were lost after the war—possibly through marriage, like Lollobrigida.

Much of what I know about Amelia's emigration from Italy is supposition. I don't know what prompted her to go to such lengths to emigrate to America as a stateless person. I don't know what her precise personal circumstances were. Could she have lived in Fiume for a time and married a local? How can I rule out this scenario when nobody in my family ever knew she was married to an American, something I only discovered myself through researching archives in the US? It was not uncommon in the years immediately following the close of the war, a time of massive upheaval and desperation, for individuals, displaced persons, to refuse to return home. The Italian government at one point had to forbid its own citizens from moving into the country's displaced persons camps, after it discovered some were marrying refugees in order to become camp residents. Apparently, life on the inside was easier than the impoverished reality of post-war Italy.[5]

Was Amelia fleeing a place—a demoralised Italy, with its deprivation and lack of opportunity? Or her past memories of war? When Amelia wrote in her diary, after describing one of her violent beatings by the cruel restaurant owner, 'My Calvary is not finished', and spoke of having to make amends for what she had done, what was she referring to? Did her guilt relate to her emigration to America? Or to what happened in Germany during the war—whatever it was she had to do to get those packages to her starving brother?

Amelia was in her early thirties and her dancing career would have been coming to an end in 1950 (she entered the camp in Naples in April the following year). My mother points out she 'would have led a very nice life' with her Neapolitan suitor Vincenzo, who was 'short and fat but well-off' and loved her, had she stayed in Italy. Yet she turned her back on marriage and security and, possibly, love. Was she bored? Did she think she could be more? Did she try to outsmart her destiny as a woman with limited opportunities? My great-aunt was a brave woman who suffered greatly because of the choices she made. Despite her independence and many acts of courage, she was unable, in the end, to save herself.

I wrote about Amelia with my desk covered by the many photographs I collected of her at different stages of life: the precocious girl with smoky eyes and pearl earrings; the playful dancer backstage in a theatre in Naples without make-up. The last one that was taken was of a haggard-looking older lady, still smiling as she rested by the car of her friend, Miss Trieste, in a residential street in America.

'*O pianto molto molto—non piango piu,*' she wrote. 'I have cried too much, I will not cry again.'

Amelia's story captivated me to the end, and will go on doing so. I wanted so much to know her but, ultimately, Amelia isn't knowable to me. She is the counterpoint to the 'normal' life my grandfather, my mother and I sought and fought for.

XI

I marked the tenth anniversary of the crash by attending a memorial service for my dead friends, for those people I knew and those I didn't, to whom my fate is forever connected.

In past years, I tried my best to ignore 7 March, and inwardly cheered when I made it to midday without remembering the significance of the date. This year was different. It was partly the passage of time but, more than that, it was this book. Writing it had a lot to do with why I was ready to feel whatever frightening pain connected to the anniversary would come, if I let it. I had processed enough memories and feelings associated with that day and the weeks and months after—not all, some are so confronting I may never revisit them—that I could allow myself to acknowledge the significance of the date, of the hour, and let my mind wander to what happened to me in those awful moments.

I completed a full draft of the manuscript late on the evening of 6 March 2017. The following day, I sat inside the atrium of the R.G. Casey building (DFAT's offices) in Barton, Canberra, with Michael beside me. I thought about Morgan, about Liz, about everything that was lost that day: the people, the parts of me, the life that I had. At the service, I met people I hadn't met, or hadn't remembered meeting, before. They included family members of some of the deceased and the DFAT official who kept a vigil by my hospital bedside in Yogyakarta. His name was Alan, and his face was that of a stranger. We all hugged and cried. For a couple of hours I was surrounded by people who had a direct connection to that day, to that event that had changed my physical and emotional self and reset my life. It was a room of people to whom I didn't need to explain.

I tried to pray.

I don't often pray now, though God isn't completely absent from my life. I took my son to church at Christmas for the first time in 2016. The priest's sermon lacked coherence and the woman sitting next to us fainted from the heat, but just being in God's airless room made my eyes well with tears. I miss my relationship with God.

My mother has found her way back to God. It was a gradual process. She told me she initially blamed God for what happened to me, but eventually realised it was also God who didn't let me die on that plane. She says in Perth she felt abandoned by the Catholic

Church, as we all did. (I still recall the Catholic nun who visited my hospital room at Easter time and refused to give Michael a Holy Communion wafer, because he was Anglican.)

Little by little, back in Sydney, Mum's faith returned, though she never says the 'Our Father' these days. Like Alfredo and Amelia, today when my mother prays, she says the 'Hail Mary'. She prays to Mary, not God, 'because I think she's human'. Also, she cannot bear to utter the words, 'Thy will be done'.

In writing about the historical and contemporary events here, I frequently feared the subject matter was too dark. Between my grandfather's POW experiences, my mother's as a displaced immigrant, Amelia's torment and the plane crash—all of our interrupted, altered lives—I could not see where the lightness would come from.

I look at my life now, at my devoted husband, my beautiful son who astonishes me with his love every day. I have taken them both to Trieste—my mother's city, whose ambivalence allowed such sad events to occur and choices to be made, a city that binds us all still. I have finally written the story that I promised myself I would write, about my nonno and his sister. In doing so, I learnt things I otherwise never would have, not just about them, but about my mother and myself.

Mine is a life reclaimed through the love of Michael, our son and my family. Yes, I lost a lot. But, in the end, what does it matter? In every family, one finds pain or loss or suffering of a kind. My parents fervently believe if only I'd listened to them and stayed a lawyer, I would still have my legs. I look at what happened to me and I am amazed, deeply grateful, that the one limb I retained untouched is my right arm and hand: the hand I write with.

I think of Father's Day, 2015. My son was three. He and I had bought a pair of stripy blue-and-green socks online for Michael. We made a purple train card (my boy's favourite colour and form of transport at the time) and baked a cake. We made up our own song, to the tune of 'Frère Jacques'.

Daddy's sleeping, daddy's sleeping, wake him up, wake him up.
We're going on a picnic, going on a picnic, with some popcorn,
and some cake.

We picnicked at Uriarra Crossing, on the Murrumbidgee River in Canberra. We had eaten our peanut butter sandwiches, our mortadella and fresh-cut pineapple. Michael was walking our anxious black labrador, Watson, down on the riverbank. A few teenagers were swimming in the fast-flowing river, although it was cold, and we wore winter coats and jackets.

My son was perched on my knee; I sat on a green canvas chair. I hugged my little boy close, smelt his blond hair, his neck, felt the softness of his face. I looked out across the moving river to the steep embankment on the other side.

We could be anywhere in the world, I thought.

I smelt the campfire from other families' barbecues nearby and remembered the trekking Michael and I did in the Himalayas in India. Such experiences were beyond me now, as was the freedom of simply walking along the steep, rocky riverbank with my family.

Nevertheless, as I held my boy against my chest, with the remnants of our picnic about us, I told myself this was what I survived for, this was why it mattered that I did, even with my injuries. I felt the pure contentment of being with my husband, our son and our dog.

My son's love grounds me in the present. He gives me experiences and feelings I hadn't known before the crash but hoped that one day I would. In spite of life's cruelty, I am so lucky.

Maybe there was meaning in what happened to me after all. Maybe the lightness in the story that I couldn't always see was love, redeeming love.

ACKNOWLEDGEMENTS

I WOULD LIKE TO THANK MY FIRST READERS OF, and believers in, this book: my husband, Michael, who has read it more times than anybody, my parents, Lori and John, and my siblings, Juliette, Anthony and Sebastian. Thank you for answering all my questions.

Special thanks must go to my mother for the many hours she spent translating different Italian texts for me—and for letting me write her story. The texts she translated included various prisoners' testimonies, songs and books, in Italian and the Trieste dialect, especially Fait's *L'emigrazione giuliana in Australia (1954–1961)* and Poloni's *il no 122038 racconta*.

I thank my aunt, Marie, for her support of my writing about her family's story.

Different friends read early versions of the book, and I would like to thank them for their feedback, especially: Emily Tannock (thanks also to her husband Adriano Tedde, who gave me advice and introductions), Lauren Ritchie and Miranda Forsyth.

I would like to thank my two workplaces, RegNet at the Australian National University, and POLSIS at the University of Queensland, for their forbearance in giving me time before starting new appointments to work on this book. My time at RegNet was especially helpful to the development of some of the more theoretical ideas explored in the book, and I'd like to thank in particular Benjamin

Authers, Michelle Burgis-Kasthala, Lia Kent and her husband Tom Davis for introducing me to writers I would not have known to read otherwise. Thanks also to Julia Wee for looking out for me at RegNet. Through my work at the ANU, I had conversations with different people about particular themes of this book—including the peerless and inspirational Hilary Charlesworth—and I came away with a fresh perspective every time. I'd also like to acknowledge helpful conversations I had with Danielle Celermajer and Kirin Narayan in the early days of writing.

A number of friends and colleagues helped me with translations, research and advice. I had many helpful conversations about forced labour with Christoph Sperfeldt, who also took the first photographs of Alkett for me. My Canadian friends, Natasha Tusikov and Blayne Haggart, found Amelia's grave (I gave them the Sydney Swans). Aureliana Di Rollo helped me to obtain some of Alfredo's military records in Italy. Grazia Micciche helped me to understand Umberto Saba's poetry and educated me in twentieth-century Italian film. Gabrielle Hooton and Marija Taflaga carried out research for me at the National Library of Australia. I'd like to thank Gabrielle, especially, for being there for me since the first day I arrived in the press gallery in 2001; she is still answering my questions about Parliament sixteen years later. My translators included Alessia La Cavera, who translated Avagliano and Palmieri's *Gli Internati Militari Italiani: Diari e Lettere dai Lager Nazisti: 1943–1945*. Dario Di Rosa translated Hammermann's *Gli Internati Militari Italiani in Germania 1943–1945* and some of Alfredo's papers. Mareike Riedel undertook research in Germany and also translated Schlickeiser's *Borsigwalde Einst und Jetzt: Wohen und Industrie*; Schrage's '". . . und man schickte uns in die Baracken": Zwangsarbeit in Berlin-Reinickendorf 1939–1945. Ein verdrängtes Kapitel deutscher Zeitgeschichte'; and Geppert's 'Vom "Verbundeten"

Acknowledgements

zum "Verrater": Die italienischen Militarinternierten 1943 bis 1945'. Milena Selivanov researched displaced persons and other aspects of Amelia's life in Italy, Germany and Switzerland. She also translated Sanfilippo's 'Per una storia dei profughi stranieri dei campi di accoglienza e reclusione nell'Italia del Secondo Dopoguerra'; Fauri's *Storia Economica delle Migrazioni Italiane*; and Miletto's *Istria allo Specchio: Storia e Voci di una Terra di Confine*.

Genealogical and other research was carried out for me by AncestryProGenealogists in the United States; Facts & Files Historical Research Institute Berlin in Germany; and Rene Nilsson and Raquel Mendelow in the United States.

I'd like to thank Paul Angerer, who showed us around Klagenfurt (and to Barrie Cassidy, for the introduction), as well as the men at the Museo Nazionale Dell'Internamento, especially General Maurizio Lenzi, and the staff at the Nazi Forced Labour Documentation Centre in Berlin for explaining the history of the IMIs and the significance of my grandfather's artefacts. Thanks also to Massimo Dapporto.

To my relatives in Italy: thanks to Gloria for allowing me to bring home her collection of photographs of Amelia; to Anna, Gigi, Andrea and Giuliana for sharing their memories of Alfredo and Amelia; to Romana and Rosie for lending me Amelia's diary extract; to Armando for his kindness; and to Vera for her patience and help.

Thanks also to Sue Dale.

There are many medical professionals from Royal Perth Hospital whom I would like to acknowledge, who did so much it is impossible ever to thank them adequately. This seems an appropriate place to try. To Professor Fiona Wood and her team, the doctors, nurses, physiotherapists (especially Dale Edgar who, along with Fiona, answered many questions about my medical treatment for this book), occupational therapists, prosthetists and others from RPH—thank you for everything you did for me. Thanks also to the medical professionals who have continued to look after me in Canberra (and Wollongong), including Dr Chris Katsogiannis and Melissa Parker and all the other doctors, nurses, physiotherapists, OTs and prosthetists. Thanks also to Lanette Gavran.

I would also like to thank my literary agent, Gaby Naher (and Paul Daley for the introduction), and publisher Allen & Unwin, especially Annette Barlow and Angela Handley, for their patience, sensitivity, encouragement and support of this book. Thanks also to Ali Lavau for her thoughtful and careful editing and to Sandy Cull for her wonderful cover design.

I cannot ever know, but I hope that my nonno, Alfredo, and his sister, Amelia, would think that what I have written is okay.

My son was too young to read this book, but he was aware I was writing it, and always called it the 'Love Book'. I hope, when he gets older, he thinks it's okay too.

Lastly, I apologise for any errors, including of translation; the responsibility is mine.

NOTES

PROLOGUE

1 See M. Hirsch, *The Generation of Postmemory: Writing and Visual Culture After the Holocaust*, New York: Columbia University Press, 2012, pp. 11, 34.

CHAPTER 1   THE BOXES

1 C. Delbo, trans. R.C. Lamont, *Auschwitz and After*, 2nd edn, New Haven: Yale University Press, 1995, 2014, p. 239.

2 E. Simpson, in W. Zinsser (ed.), *Inventing the Truth: The Art and Craft of Memoir*, New York: Mariner Books, 1998, p. 98.

3 See E. Hoffman, *After Such Knowledge: A Meditation on the Aftermath of the Holocaust*, London: Vintage, 2004, 2005, p. 41.

4 P. Brickhill, *Reach for the Sky*, New York: Bantam Books, 1954, 1978, p. 334.

5 A. von Plato et al., 'Introduction' in von Plato et al. (eds), *Hitler's Slaves: Life Stories of Forced Labourers in Nazi-Occupied Europe*, New York: Berghahn Books, 2010, p. 8.

6 P. Filipkowski and K. Madoń-Mitzner, '"You can't say it out loud. And you can't forget": Polish experiences of slave and forced labour for the "Third Reich"', in von Plato et al., p. 84.

CHAPTER 2   TRIESTE

1 J. Morris, *Trieste and the Meaning of Nowhere*, London: Faber & Faber, 2001, p. 8.

2 U. Saba, 'Avevo', in U. Saba, trans G. Hochfield and L. Nathan, *Songbook: The Selected Poems of Umberto Saba*, New Haven: Yale University Press, 2008, pp. 468–9.

3   Richard Ellmann (ed.), *Selected Letters of James Joyce*, London, Faber & Faber, 1975, 1992, p. 193; J. McCourt, *The Years of Bloom: James Joyce in Trieste, 1904–1920*, Dublin: Lilliput Press, 2000, pp. 137, 252.

4   McCourt, p. 170.

5   Saba, 'Trieste', pp. 82–3.

6   M. Hametz, *Making Trieste Italian, 1918–1954*, Woodbridge: Boydell Press, 2005, p. 101.

7   G. Sluga, *The Problem of Trieste and the Italo-Yugoslav Border: Difference, Identity, and Sovereignty in Twentieth-Century Europe*, New York: State University of New York Press, 2001, p. 3; K. Pizzi, *A City in Search of an Author: The Literary Identity of Trieste*, London: Sheffield Academic Press, 2001, p. 38.

8   Quoting Silvio Rutteri, in McCourt, p. 27.

9   See P. Ballinger, *History in Exile: Memory and Identity at the Borders of the Balkans*, Princeton: Princeton University Press, 2003, pp. 129–67.

10 Hametz, p. 80.

11 Hametz, pp. 128, 132–3.

12 Sluga, p. 167.

13 M. Wyman, *DPs: Europe's Displaced Persons, 1945–1951*, Ithaca: Cornell University Press, 1989, 1998, p. 195.

14 V.E. Frankl, *Man's Search for Meaning*, London: Rider, 1946, 2004, pp. 9, 110.

15 M. Sanfilippo, 'Per una storia dei profughi stranieri dei campi di accoglienza e reclusione nell'Italia del Secondo Dopoguerra', *Studi Emigrazione*, 2006, vol. XLII, pp. 835–56; Report of a Special Subcommittee of the Committee on Foreign Affairs, *Displaced Persons and the International Refugee Organization*, 80th Congress, First Session, Washington: United States Government Printing Office, 1947, pp. 26, 31.

16 E. Miletto, *Istria allo Specchio: Storia e Voci di una Terra di Confine*, Milano: Franco Angeli, 2007.

17 R. Daniels, *Guarding the Golden Door: American Immigration Policy and Immigrants Since 1882*, New York: Hill and Wang, 2004, p. 110.

CHAPTER 3   SEARCHING

1   P. Levi, 'If this is a man', in P. Levi, trans S. Woolf, *If This is a Man / The Truce*, London: Abacus, 1958, 1987, p. 160.

2   R. Robinson, 'Deaths a test of faith', *Herald Sun*, 10 March 2008, p. 4.

3   N.F.F. Ribeiro et al., 'Burn wounds infected by contaminated water: Case reports, review of the literature and recommendations for treatment', *Burns*, 2010, vol. 36, p. 11.

4   J.P. Reemtsma, trans C. Brown Janeway, *In the Cellar*, New York: Alfred A. Knopf, 1999, p. 223.

5   N. Heller, 'Semi-charmed life', *New Yorker*, 14 January 2013, p. 67.

6   E. Hemingway, *A Farewell to Arms*, London: Arrow Books, 1929, 1994, pp. 291–2.

7   Royal Australian Navy, *Nias Island Sea King Accident Board of Inquiry Report*, Canberra: Department of Defence, 2007.

CHAPTER 4   ALFREDO

1   For the history of IMIs, throughout this chapter I draw on: M. Avagliano and M. Palmieri, *Gli Internati Militari Italiani: Diari e Lettere dai Lager Nazisti: 1943–1945*, Torino: Giulio Einaudi, 2009; G. Hammermann, *Gli Internati Militari Italiani in Germania 1943–1945*, Bologna: Il Mulino, 2004; D. Felsen and V. Frenkel, 'The deportation of the Italians 1943–1945' in von Plato et al., pp. 310–23; C. Pagenstecher, '"We were treated like slaves." Remembering Forced Labor for Nazi Germany', in R. Hörmann and G. Mackenthun (eds), *Human Bondage in the Cultural Contact Zone: Transdisciplinary Perspectives on Slavery and its Discourses*, Münster: Waxmann, 2010, pp. 275–91; Giovanni B____, Alessandro F____ and Claudio S____, 'Interview from the archive "Forced Labor 1939–1945"'.

2   For the history of the Italian armistice, I draw on P. Morgan, *The Fall of Mussolini: Italy, the Italians, and the Second World War*, Oxford: Oxford University Press, 2007; and R. Lamb, *War in Italy: 1943–1945: A Brutal Story*, London: Penguin Books, 1993.

3   Nationalsozialistische Deutsche Arbeiterpartei, *Rundschreiben Nr. 55/43 g.Rs*, 28 September 1943.

4   Felsen and Frenkel, p. 315.

5   A. Speer, *Inside the Third Reich: The Classic Account of Nazi Germany by Hitler's Armaments Minister*, London: Weidenfeld & Nicolson, 1970, 1995, p. 395.

6   K. Schlickeiser, *Borsigwalde—Einst und Jetzt: Wohnen und Industrie*, Berlin: Arbeitsgruppe Borsigwalde einst und jetzt, 1989.

7 P. Chamberlain and H. Doyle, *Encyclopedia of German Tanks of World War Two,* revised edition, London: Arms and Armour Press, 1978, 1993.

8 G.E. Schrage, "'. . . und man schickte uns in die Baracken": Zwangsarbeit in Berlin-Reinickendorf 1939–1945. Ein verdrängtes Kapitel deutscher Zeitgeschichte', *Jahrbuch für die Geschichte Mittel- und Ostdeutschlands,* 2007, vol. 53, pp. 193–284; G. Corallo, 'Memoriale', *Le Belle Pagine.*

9 C. Leitzbach, *Rheinmetall: Vom Reiz, im Rheinland ein großes Werk zu errichten,* vol. 1, Köln: Greven Verlag, 2014, p. 386; C. Leitzbach, '125th anniversary of Rheinmetall—the years 1936 to 1945', *Rheinmetall Group.*

10 G. Guareschi, trans F. Frenaye, *My Secret Diary,* London: Victor Gollancz Ltd, 1958, pp. 35, 62; N. Timofeyeva, 'The experience of citizens of the former Soviet Union as forced labourers in Nazi Germany', in von Plato et al., p. 280.

11 C. Fogu, 'Italiani brava gente: The legacy of Fascist historical culture on Italian politics of memory' in R.N. Lebow et al. (eds), *The Politics of Memory in Postwar Europe,* Durham: Duke University Press, 2006, p. 149; Felsen and Frenkel, p. 315.

12 C. Kidron, 'Toward an Ethnography of Silence', *Current Anthropology,* 2009, vol. 50, no. 1, p. 6.

13 V. Poloni, *il no 122038 racconta,* Biadene: Vittorio Poloni, 1981.

14 G. Saathoff, 'Foreword', in von Plato et al., p. ix.

15 von Plato et al., 'Introduction', pp. 6–9; O. Haller, 'German industry, the Cold War, and the Bundeswehr' in J.S. Corum (ed.), *Rearming Germany,* Leiden: Brill, 2011, pp. 143–76; B.B. Ferencz, *Less than Slaves: Jewish Forced Labor and the Quest for Compensation,* Bloomington: Indiana University Press, 1979, 2002.

16 Alessandro F——, 'Interview from the archive "Forced Labor 1939–1945"'.

17 *Jurisdictional Immunities of the State (Germany v Italy: Greece intervening) (Judgment)* [2012] ICJ Rep 99, pp. 123, 144; F. Francioni, 'Access to justice and its pitfalls', *Journal of International Criminal Justice,* 2016, vol. 14, pp. 629–36.

18 P. Levi, *The Drowned and the Saved,* London: Abacus, 1986, 2013, p. 29.

19 I draw here on the ideas of W.J. Booth in his book *Communities of Memory: On Witness, Identity, and Justice,* Ithaca: Cornell University Press, 2006, p. x.

20 Levi, *The Drowned and the Saved,* p. 84; Delbo, p. 142.

21 R. Kluger, *Landscapes of Memory: A Holocaust Girlhood Remembered*,
    London: Bloomsbury, 2001, 2004, p. 107.

CHAPTER 5 MICHAEL

1 J. Didion, *Blue Nights*, New York: Alfred A. Knopf, 2011, p. 18.
2 See Hoffman, *After Such Knowledge*, p. 41.
3 F. O'Hara, 'Now That I Am in Madrid and Can Think', in D. Allen (ed.),
   The Collected Poems of Frank O'Hara, Berkeley: University of California
   Press, 1971, 1995, p. 356.
4 V. Woolf, *On Being Ill*, Ashfield: Paris Press, 1930, 2012, p. 8.

CHAPTER 6 LOREDANA

1 See Hirsch, p. 22.
2 M. Nussbaum, *Upheavals of Thought: The Intelligence of Emotions*,
   New York: Cambridge University Press, 2001, pp. 2, 175.
3 F. Fait, *L'emigrazione giuliana in Australia (1954–1961)*, Udine: ERMI,
   1999, p. 61.
4 G. Cresciani, *Trieste Goes to Australia*, Lindfield: Gianfranco Cresciani,
   2011, pp. 3, 62.
5 J. Damousi, *Memory and Migration in the Shadow of War: Australia's Greek
   Immigrants after World War II and the Greek Civil War*, Cambridge:
   Cambridge University Press, 2015, p. 47.
6 Cresciani, pp. xv, 29, 54.
7 C. Keating, *Greta: A History of the Army Camp and Migrant Camp at Greta,
   New South Wales, 1939–1960*, Burwood: Uri Windt, 1997, pp. 7, 75.
8 Commonwealth of Australia, *Parliamentary Debates*, House of
   Representatives, 2 October 1957, 1 (Daniel Curtin).
9 J. Wilton and R. Bosworth, *Old Worlds and New Australia: The Post-war
   Migrant Experience*, Ringwood: Penguin Books, 1984, pp. 3, 5, 15, 20.
10 Wilton and Bosworth, p. 11; A. Jordens, *Alien to Citizen: Settling Migrants
   in Australia, 1945–75*, Sydney: Allen & Unwin, 1997, pp. 53–5.
11 Wilton and Bosworth, p. 18; Cresciani, pp. 65–6.
12 Editorial, 'Jobs and migrants', *Sydney Morning Herald*, 27 August 1957,
   p. 2.
13 'Harmful migrant policy alleged', *Sydney Morning Herald*, 5 July 1957,
   p. 5; also 'UK migrant increase "necessary"', 1 October 1957; 'Official
   figures on UK migration denied, Govt.'s policy criticised', 11 December

1957, p. 21; 'Menzies, Evatt in sharp conflict on migrant policy',
22 January 1958, p. 10.

14 'Views on migrants "harmful"', *Newcastle Morning Herald and Miners'
Advocate*, 29 August 1957, p. 6; C. Berntsen, 'Australia should welcome
all', Letter to the Editor, *Sydney Morning Herald*, 25 January 1958, p. 2;
also 'Attitude towards non-British migrants deplored', *Sydney Morning
Herald*, 29 August 1957, p. 6; J. Novak, 'National feelings on
immigration', Letter to the Editor, *Sydney Morning Herald*, 3 September
1957, p. 2.

15 See S. Munt, *Queer Attachments*, Abingdon: Ashgate, 2012.

16 Anonymous, trans P. Boehm, *A Woman in Berlin*, London: Virago Press,
1954, 2011.

17 Anonymous, p. 305.

18 J. Halley, 'Rape in Berlin: Reconsidering the criminalisation of rape in the
international law of armed conflict', *Melbourne Journal of International
Law*, 2008, vol. 9, no. 1, pp. 78–124.

19 H. Enzensberger, 'Afterword by the German Editor', in Anonymous,
p. 310.

CHAPTER 7   CRASHING

1 National Transportation Safety Committee, *Aircraft Accident Investigation
Report KNKT/07.06/07.02.35*, Republic of Indonesia: NTSC, Ministry of
Transportation, 2007.

2 R.I. Rotberg, 'Truth commissions and the provision of truth, justice, and
reconciliation', in R.I. Rotberg and D. Thompson (eds), *Truth v. Justice:
The Morality of Truth Commissions*, Princeton: Princeton University Press,
2000, p. 9.

3 K.M. Clarke, *Fictions of Justice: The International Criminal Court and the
Challenge of Legal Pluralism in Sub-Saharan Africa*, New York: Cambridge
University Press, 2009, p. 21.

4 J. Winterson, *The Passion*, London: Vintage Books, 1987, 2001, p. 62.

5 Wyman, p. 169.

BIBLIOGRAPHY

BOOKS AND JOURNAL ARTICLES

Anonymous, trans P. Boehm, *A Woman in Berlin*, London: Virago Press, 1954, 2011

Avagliano, M. and M. Palmieri, *Gli Internati Militari Italiani: Diari e Lettere dai Lager Nazisti: 1943–1945*, Torino: Giulio Einaudi, 2009

Ballinger, P., *History in Exile: Memory and Identity at the Borders of the Balkans*, Princeton: Princeton University Press, 2003

Berendt, J., *Midnight in the Garden of Good and Evil*, New York: Random House, 1994

Booth, W.J., *Communities of Memory: On Witness, Identity, and Justice*, Ithaca: Cornell University Press: 2006

Brickhill, P., *Reach for the Sky*, New York: Bantam Books, 1954, 1978

Cassidy, B., *Private Bill: In Love and War*, Melbourne: Melbourne University Press, 2014

Chamberlain, P. and H. Doyle, *Encyclopedia of German Tanks of World War Two*, revised edition, London: Arms and Armour Press, 1978, 1993

Clarke, K.M., *Fictions of Justice: The International Criminal Court and the Challenge of Legal Pluralism in Sub-Saharan Africa*, New York: Cambridge University Press, 2009

Cresciani, G., *Trieste Goes to Australia*, Lindfield: Gianfranco Cresciani, 2011

Damousi, J., *Memory and Migration in the Shadow of War: Australia's Greek Immigrants after World War II and the Greek Civil War*, Cambridge: Cambridge University Press, 2015

Daniels, R., *Guarding the Golden Door: American Immigration Policy and Immigrants Since 1882*, New York: Hill and Wang, 2004

Dapporto, C., *Il Maliardo: Mito-Personaggio-Vita*, Milano: Rusconi, 1977

Delbo, C., trans R.C. Lamont, *Auschwitz and After*, 2nd edn, New Haven: Yale University Press, 1995, 2014

Didion, J., *Blue Nights*, New York: Alfred A. Knopf, 2011

Ellmann, R. (ed.), *Selected Letters of James Joyce*, London: Faber & Faber, 1975, 1992

Fait, F., *L'emigrazione giuliana in Australia (1954–1961)*, Udine: ERMI, 1999

Fauri, F., *Storia Economica delle Migrazioni Italiane*, Bologna: Il Mulino, 2015

Felsen, D. and V. Frenkel, 'The deportation of the Italians 1943–1945' in A. von Plato, A. Leh and C. Thonfeld (eds), *Hitler's Slaves: Life Stories of Forced Labourers in Nazi-Occupied Europe*, New York: Berghahn Books, 2010, pp. 310–23

Ferencz, B.B., *Less than Slaves: Jewish Forced Labor and the Quest for Compensation*, Bloomington: Indiana University Press, 1979, 2002

Filipkowski, P. and K. Madon-Mitzner, '"You can't say it out loud. And you can't forget": Polish experiences of slave and forced labour for the "Third Reich"' in A. von Plato, A. Leh and C. Thonfeld (eds), *Hitler's Slaves: Life Stories of Forced Labourers in Nazi-Occupied Europe*, New York: Berghahn Books, 2010, pp. 71–85

Fogu, C., 'Italiani brava gente: The legacy of Fascist historical culture on Italian politics of memory' in R.N. Lebow, W. Kansteiner and C. Fogu (eds), *The Politics of Memory in Postwar Europe*, Durham: Duke University Press, 2006, pp. 147–76

Francioni, F., 'Access to justice and its pitfalls', *Journal of International Criminal Justice*, 2016, vol. 14, pp. 629–36

Frankl, V.E., *Man's Search for Meaning*, London: Rider, 1946, 2004

Genizi, H., *America's Fair Share: The Admission and Resettlement of Displaced Persons, 1945–1952*, Detroit: Wayne State University Press, 1993

Guareschi, G., trans F. Frenaye, *My Secret Diary*, London: Victor Gollancz Ltd, 1958

Haller, O., 'German industry, the Cold War, and the Bundeswehr' in J.S. Corum (ed.), *Rearming Germany*, Leiden: Brill, 2011, pp. 143–76

Halley, J., 'Rape in Berlin: Reconsidering the criminalisation of rape in the international law of armed conflict', *Melbourne Journal of International Law*, 2008, vol. 9, no. 1, pp. 78–124

Hametz, M., *Making Trieste Italian, 1918–1954*, Woodbridge: Boydell Press, 2005

Bibliography

Hammermann, G., *Gli Internati Militari Italiani in Germania 1943–1945*, Bologna: Il Mulino, 2004

Hemingway, E., *A Farewell to Arms*, London: Arrow Books, 1929, 1994

Hirsch, M., *The Generation of Postmemory: Writing and Visual Culture After the Holocaust*, New York: Columbia University Press, 2012

Hoffman, E., *Lost in Translation*, London: Vintage, 1989, 1998

Hoffman, E., *After Such Knowledge: A Meditation on the Aftermath of the Holocaust*, London: Vintage, 2004, 2005

Jordens, A., *Alien to Citizen: Settling Migrants in Australia, 1945–75*, Sydney: Allen & Unwin, 1997

Keating, C., *Greta: A History of the Army Camp and Migrant Camp at Greta, New South Wales, 1939–1960*, Burwood: Uri Windt, 1997

Kidron, C., 'Toward an ethnography of silence,' *Current Anthropology*, 2009, vol. 50, no. 1, pp. 5–27

Kluger, R., *Landscapes of Memory: A Holocaust Girlhood Remembered*, London: Bloomsbury, 2001, 2004

Knittel, S.C., 'Borderline memory disorder: Trieste and the staging of Italian national identity' in B. Sion (ed.), *Death Tourism: Disaster Sites as Recreational Landscape*, London: Seagull Books, 2014, pp. 247–66

Lamb, R., *War in Italy: 1943–1945: A Brutal Story*, London: Penguin Books, 1993

Lebow, R.N., W. Kansteiner and C. Fogu (eds), *The Politics of Memory in Postwar Europe*, Durham: Duke University Press, 2006

Leitzbach, C., *Rheinmetall: Vom Reiz, im Rheinland ein großes Werk zu errichten*, vol. 1, Köln: Greven Verlag, 2014

Levi, P., 'If this is a man', in P. Levi, trans S. Woolf, *If This is a Man / The Truce*, London: Abacus, 1958, 1987, pp. 9–193

Levi, P., *The Drowned and the Saved*, London: Abacus, 1986, 2013

McCourt, J., *The Years of Bloom: James Joyce in Trieste, 1904–1920*, Dublin: Lilliput Press, 2000

Miletto, E., *Istria allo Specchio: Storia e Voci di una Terra di Confine*, Milano: Franco Angeli, 2007

Morgan, P., *The Fall of Mussolini: Italy, the Italians, and the Second World War*, Oxford: Oxford University Press, 2007

Morris, J., *Trieste and the Meaning of Nowhere*, London: Faber & Faber, 2001

Morris, S.J., *Price of Fame: The Honourable Clare Boothe Luce*, New York: Random House, 2014

Munt, S., *Queer Attachments*, Abingdon: Ashgate, 2012

Nussbaum, M., *Upheavals of Thought: The Intelligence of Emotions*, New York: Cambridge University Press, 2001

O'Hara, F., 'Now That I Am in Madrid and Can Think', in D. Allen (ed.), *The Collected Poems of Frank O'Hara*, Berkeley: University of California Press, 1971, 1995

Pagenstecher, C., '"We were treated like slaves." Remembering Forced Labor for Nazi Germany,' in R. Hörmann and G. Mackenthun (eds), *Human Bondage in the Cultural Contact Zone: Transdisciplinary Perspectives on Slavery and its Discourses*, Münster: Waxmann, 2010, pp. 275–91

Pizzi, K., *A City in Search of an Author: The Literary Identity of Trieste*, London: Sheffield Academic Press, 2001

Poloni, V., *il no 122038 racconta*, Biadene: Vittorio Poloni, 1981

Reemtsma, J.P., trans C. Brown Janeway, *In the Cellar*, New York: Alfred A. Knopf, 1999

Ribeiro, N.F.F., C.H. Heath, J. Kierath, S. Rea, M. Duncan-Smith and F.M. Wood, 'Burn wounds infected by contaminated water: Case reports, review of the literature and recommendations for treatment,' *Burns*, 2010, vol. 36, pp. 9–22

Rotberg, R.I., 'Truth commissions and the provision of truth, justice, and reconciliation', in R.I. Rotberg and D. Thompson (eds), *Truth v Justice: The Morality of Truth Commissions*, Princeton: Princeton University Press, 2000

Saathoff, G., 'Foreword' in A. von Plato, A. Leh and C. Thonfeld (eds), *Hitler's Slaves: Life Stories of Forced Labourers in Nazi-Occupied Europe*, New York: Berghahn Books, 2010, pp. ix–xii

Saba, U., trans G. Hochfield and L. Nathan, *Songbook: The Selected Poems of Umberto Saba*, New Haven: Yale University Press, 2008

Sanfilippo, M., 'Per una storia dei profughi stranieri dei campi di accoglienza e reclusione nell'Italia del Secondo Dopoguerra', *Studi Emigrazione*, 2006, vol. XLII, pp. 835–56

Scarry, E., *The Body in Pain: The Making and Unmaking of the World*, New York: Oxford University Press, 1985

Schlickeiser, K., *Borsigwalde—Einst und Jetzt: Wohnen und Industrie*, Berlin: Arbeitsgruppe Borsigwalde einst und jetzt, 1989

Schrage, G.E., '". . . und man schickte uns in die Baracken": Zwangsarbeit in Berlin-Reinickendorf 1939–1945. Ein verdrängtes Kapitel deutscher

Bibliography

Zeitgeschichte', *Jahrbuch für die Geschichte Mittel- und Ostdeutschlands*, 2007, vol. 53, pp. 193–284

Simpson, E., 'Poets in my youth' in W. Zinsser (ed.), *Inventing the Truth: The Art and Craft of Memoir*, New York: Mariner Books, 1998, pp. 83–100

Sluga, G., *The Problem of Trieste and the Italo-Yugoslav Border: Difference, Identity, and Sovereignty in Twentieth-Century Europe*, New York: State University of New York Press, 2001

Speer, A., *Inside the Third Reich: The Classic Account of Nazi Germany by Hitler's Armaments Minister*, London: Weidenfeld & Nicolson, 1970, 1995

Timofeyeva, N., 'The experience of citizens of the former Soviet Union as forced labourers in Nazi Germany', in A. von Plato, A. Leh and C. Thonfeld (eds), *Hitler's Slaves: Life Stories of Forced Labourers in Nazi-Occupied Europe*, New York: Berghahn Books, 2010, pp. 276–85

Travirka, A., *Pula: History-Culture-Art Heritage*, Zadar: Zivko Sokota, 2006

von Plato, A., A. Leh and C. Thonfeld (eds), *Hitler's Slaves: Life Stories of Forced Labourers in Nazi-Occupied Europe*, New York: Berghahn Books, 2010

Wilton, J. and R. Bosworth, *Old Worlds and New Australia: The Post-war Migrant Experience*, Ringwood: Penguin Books, 1984

Winterson, J., *The Passion*, London: Vintage Books, 1987, 2001

Woolf, V., *On Being Ill*, Ashfield: Paris Press, 1930, 2012

Wyman, M., *DPs: Europe's Displaced Persons, 1945–1951*, Ithaca: Cornell University Press, 1989, 1998

OTHER

'Attitude towards non-British migrants deplored', *Sydney Morning Herald*, 29 August 1957, p. 6

B____, Giovanni, 'Interview from the archive "Forced Labor 1939–1945"', Archive ID za119, video, <https://zwangsarbeit-archiv.de/archiv/en>, 2005, accessed 18 August 2017

Berntsen, C., 'Australia should welcome all', Letter to the Editor, *Sydney Morning Herald*, 25 January 1958, p. 2

Commonwealth of Australia, *Parliamentary Debates*, House of Representatives, 2 October 1957, 1 (Daniel Curtin)

Corallo, G. 'Memoriale', *Le Belle Pagine*, <www.lebellepagine.it/res/site51630/res631078_memoriale-rivisto.pdf> 2010, accessed 18 August 2017

Displaced Persons Commission, *Memo to America: The DP Story: The Final Report of the United States Displaced Persons Commission*, Washington: United States Government Printing Office, 1952

Editorial, 'Jobs and migrants', *Sydney Morning Herald*, 27 August 1957, p. 2

F____, Alessandro, 'Interview from the archive "Forced Labor 1939–1945"', Archive ID za121, video, <https://zwangsarbeit-archiv.de/archiv/en> 2005, accessed 18 August 2017

Geppert, D., 'Vom "Verbündeten" zum "Verräter": Die italienischen Militärinternierten 1943 bis 1945', *Lernen aus der Geschichte* <http://lernen-aus-der-geschichte.de/Lernen-und-Lehren/content/11496> 2016, accessed 17 August 2017

'Harmful migrant policy alleged', *Sydney Morning Herald*, 5 July 1957, p. 5

Heller, N., 'Semi-charmed life', *New Yorker*, 14 January 2013, pp. 66–71

Hersey, J., 'Hiroshima', *New Yorker*, 31 August 1946

Hoffman, C., 'Fred A. Kemmeries once okayed visa for Gina', *Tucson Daily Citizen*, 28 December 1957, p. 31

International Tracing Service (ITS), 'Documentation of the Path of Persecution', <www.its-arolsen.org/en/information/documentation-of-the-path-of-persecution/> 2017, accessed 17 August 2017

Leitzbach, C., '125th anniversary of Rheinmetall—the years 1936 to 1945', *Rheinmetall Group*, < www.rheinmetall.com/en/rheinmetall_ag/group/corporate_history/125_jahre_rheinmetall_1/jahre_1936_bis_1/index.php>, 2014, accessed 18 August 2017

'Menzies, Evatt in sharp conflict on migrant policy', *Sydney Morning Herald*, 22 January 1958, p. 10

Nationalsozialistische Deutsche Arbeiterpartei, *Rundschreiben Nr. 55/43 g.Rs*, 28 September 1943

National Transportation Safety Committee (NTSC), *Aircraft Accident Investigation Report KNKT/07.06/07.02.35*, Republic of Indonesia: NTSC, Ministry of Transportation, 2007

Novak, J., 'National feelings on immigration', Letter to the Editor, *Sydney Morning Herald*, 3 September 1957, p. 2

'Official figures on UK migration denied, Govt.'s policy criticised', *Sydney Morning Herald*, 11 December 1957, p. 21

Report of a Special Subcommittee of the Committee on Foreign Affairs, *Displaced Persons and the International Refugee Organization*,

80th Congress, First Session, Washington: United States Government Printing Office, 1947

Robinson, R., 'Deaths a test of faith', *Herald Sun*, 10 March 2008, p. 4

Royal Australian Navy, *Nias Island Sea King Accident Board of Inquiry Report*, Canberra: Department of Defence, 2007

S____, Claudio, 'Interview from the archive "Forced Labor 1939–1945"', Archive ID za126, video, <https://zwangsarbeit-archiv.de/archiv/en>, 2005, 2006, accessed 18 August 2017

Schmidle, N., 'Ten Borders', *New Yorker*, 26 October 2015

'UK migrant increase "necessary"', *Sydney Morning Herald*, 1 October 1957

'Views on migrants "harmful"', *Newcastle Morning Herald and Miners' Advocate*, 29 August 1957, p. 6

Zanolla, V., 'Una leggenda da sfatare: 1943: le Lescano a Genova', <www.trio-lescano.it/Una_leggenda_da_sfatare.pdf>, 2013 accessed 17 August 2017